W9-DAQ-631

Living
THE
Truth

Selected Titles from the Moral Traditions Series

JAMES F. KEENAN, SJ, *series editor*

Living
THE
Truth

A THEORY OF ACTION

KLAUS DEMMER

Translated by Brian McNeil

Georgetown University Press/Washington, D.C.

Original publication, Klaus Demmer, *Die Wahrheit leben. Theorie des Handelns* © Verlag Herder Freiburg im Breisgau 1991.

Library of Congress Cataloging-in-Publication Data

Demmer, Klaus, 1931–
  [Wahrheit leben. English]
  Living the truth : a theory of action / by Klaus Demmer ; translated by Brian McNeil.
      p.   cm. — (Moral traditions series)
  Includes bibliographical references and index.
  ISBN 978-1-58901-697-2 (pbk. : alk. paper)
  1. Christian ethics—Catholic authors.   I. Title.
 BJ1249.D4413   2010
241′.042—dc22

                                                              2010001531

15 14 13 12 11 10   9 8 7 6 5 4 3 2
First printing

Printed in the United States of America

CONTENTS

FOREWORD

To UNDERSTAND THE SIGNIFICANCE of Klaus Demmer's legacy and in particular this newly translated work, we need to go back in time. Klaus Demmer's mentor, Father Josef Fuchs, SJ (1912–2005), taught at the Pontifical Gregorian University in Rome for nearly thirty years. In 1955 Fuchs published his internationally famous book on natural law, *Lex Naturae*. It was published in English in 1965. In 1963, Fuchs was appointed to the Pontifical Commission on Population, Family, and Birth, popularly known as the Birth Control Commission, and remained on it until its conclusion in 1966. Fuchs was nominated to the commission by conservative American Jesuit John Ford, who wanted Fuchs to counterbalance the more liberal views of Redemptorist Father Berhard Häring.[1] As a member of the commission, Fuchs was deeply affected by the testimonies of married witnesses and commission members who spoke about their experiences with decision making regarding contraception and responsible parenthood. Their testimonies eventually prompted him to experience an intellectual conversion.

In his earlier work Fuchs thought of moral objectivity as conformity with already formulated moral norms. After his conversion he became aware of the competency of the moral agent and argued that moral objectivity was accomplished through personal moral judgments. Moral objectivity could only be achieved when persons, knowing already formulated moral norms, brought in deeply relevant circumstances to see where actual moral truth was. His claim that moral truth could only be found in the judgment of the moral agent eventually led him to become a twentieth-century champion for the Christian conscience.

Later the fruits of his conversion appeared in English in five volumes of essays, the last four published by Georgetown University Press.[2] Fuchs treated about ten different themes in these works, including the effect of Vatican II, moral norms, goodness and rightness, moral absolutes and intrinsic evil, conscience, sin, and the specificity of Christian ethics. His legacy was examined in Mark Graham's thoughtful *Josef Fuchs on Natural Law*.[3]

Precisely while Fuchs was reexamining the entire foundation of his understanding of moral decision making, he was directing two young priests who were writing their doctoral dissertations. They would take Fuchs's new position on the competency of the moral agent in two very different directions.

Bruno Schüller (1925–2007), a Jesuit, finished his dissertation on the Lordship of Christ and secular law in 1963. Schüller would teach from 1961 to 1991 in German universities, most especially at the University of Münster. His moral theology was dependent on the philosophy of linguistic analysis articulated by British scholars. He found in their writings ways of articulating more exactly the nature of moral objectivity. Along the way he would become known for clear distinctions between goodness and rightness, the genesis and validity of norms, and direct and indirect acting. He greatly influenced the American Jesuit casuist Richard McCormick, who often wrote about Schüller's latest contributions. On McCormick's suggestion, Georgetown University Press published a number of Schüller's essays.[4]

Klaus Demmer (b. 1931), a Missionary of the Sacred Heart, finished his dissertation titled *Law of Charity: On the Christological Foundation of an Augustinian Natural Law* in 1961. Demmer taught for several years in Paderborn, but in 1970 he became professor of moral theology at the Gregorian University. To date he has published more than twenty-five books on moral theology and is considered the foremost European moral theologian of his generation. He received an honorary doctorate from the University of Fribourg in 1999, and he is a member of the European Academy of Arts and Sciences.

Demmer's work on the relationship between hermeneutics and moral truth has influenced many in the field who seek to bring the moral tradition into the twenty-first century. Rather than making clear distinctions, he constantly engages presuppositions, understands contexts, and works out differences through a dialect of mutual defining concepts.

While Schüller and Demmer are considered two of Fuchs's greatest students, they represent two ends of the spectrum of twentieth-century fundamental moral theology. One loves distinctions, the other loves context. One emphasizes the distinctiveness of language games; the other studies how inevitably all issues are related. One emulates Kant, the other Augustine. If Schüller's work looks linear, Demmer's is like a spiral. The broad differences between them became especially evident when they addressed the same topic. Consider the issue of the genesis and validity of a norm. Schüller emphasizes that the two are very different. Schüller considers the case of a child mistaking a simple arithmetic computation. Was the answer right? Obviously not, but this pertains to the validity of the answer. Why the child got the answer wrong—that is, the genesis of the child's mistake—is another matter.

According to Schüller the origin of a norm does not bear on its validity. This separation not only dehistoricized norms, it also de-Christianized them. A norm's origin deriving from a faith community, for instance, is not cause for its contemporary validity. Validity is a categorically singular issue. Moreover, in this context, faith does not add to our knowledge in the moral sphere. The norm might derive from the Gospels, but its validity today is independent of them.

For those norms in the hermeneutical context, the validity of a moral norm is precisely derived from its genesis. Every generation articulates new norms, and the need to articulate a new norm at some point in time animates the meaning of the norm as well as its legitimacy. Thus, we can ask about the norm that calls us to worship on Sunday as a community of faith. The genesis of that norm comes from eleventh-century concerns that serfs were not free to participate in Christian worship. The law requiring participation in the Sunday liturgy meant that serfs were freed one day a week to become more intimately connected to the community of faith. Does the genesis of the norm for dominical observance validate our being called to worship today? According to Demmer, it definitely does.

When Demmer looks to the relationship between norms founded on faith and contemporary norms, he takes seriously the immediacy of God's presence, building on the Augustinian insight that God is closer to us than we are to ourselves and he aims to draw the ethical implications of faith.[5] Specifically, he opposes the dichotomy that Schüller proposes.

In the United States, Schüller has always been the better known of the two. Although I was mentored by Fuchs, I studied with Demmer, as did my classmate, Thomas Kopfensteiner. When Kopfensteiner and I returned to the United States, we worked to make Demmer's name and legacy better known and appreciated here. We coauthored an essay for *Theological Studies* on recent European works in moral theology, featuring especially the contributions of Klaus Demmer.[6] In 2000 Roberto Dell'Oro translated from the Italian Demmer's *Introduction to Moral Theology*. I edited the translation and Kopfensteiner penned the foreword.[7] The introductory nature of the text prompted scholars to ask for a thicker understanding of Demmer's hermenutical methodology. I selected Demmer's most important work on method from among his twenty-five books: *Die Wahrheit leben. Theorie des Handelns* (Herder, 1991). That work is now in your hands.

Forty-five years ago Fuchs decided that he needed to rethink how it is that we know moral truth. Later his student Demmer would suggest that the context out of which norms derive needs to be recognized in the norms themselves. Those presuppositions that animate our norms very much reveal not only how we should act but also what type of people we should become. In understanding Demmer better, we may also better understand ourselves and our horizons.

James F. Keenan, SJ
Founders Professor in Theology
Boston College

Notes

1. Genilo, *John Cuthbert Ford, SJ*.
2. The Georgetown University Press volumes are *Christian Morality: The Word Becomes Flesh* (1981); *Personal Responsibility and Christian Morality* (1983); *Christian Ethics in a Secular Arena* (1984); and *Moral Demands and Personal Obligations* (1993).

3. Graham, *Josef Fuchs on Natural Law.*
4. Schüller, *Wholly Human.*
5. Augustine, *Confessions*, III 6, 11.
6. Keenan and Kopfensteiner, "Moral Theology out of Western Europe."
7. Dell'Oro, *Shaping the Moral Life.*

INTRODUCTION

H ISTORICAL EPOCHS are accompanied by intellectual challenges that issue an appeal to everyone who is willing to accept intellectual responsibility and then translate this into action. This applies to moral theology too: moral theology bears the unmistakable signature of its own period, and this was vividly exemplified in the lively debate that we all still remember from the period immediately after the Second Vatican Council. This, however, must not be allowed to remain a matter of historical memory, for new questions arise, matters that were not settled in the past. Problems connected with the justification of norms have had a widespread influence on the style of moral-theological work, and these debates were often a response to concrete situations within the Church. To cast doubt on the correctness of this development would be to display a profound ignorance of the "state of emergency" in the Church at that period. It was necessary to make a constructive criticism of modes of ethical argumentation that had lost their rational plausibility. This, however, was not without its price. It is indeed true that after the convincing quality of the solution to individual questions had been scrutinized more closely, it was no longer possible to conceal the shakiness of many traditional "proofs"; the academic neutrality that dominated ethical thinking led to only a tepid interest in the addressee of ethical obligation. In future, it will be necessary to pay more attention to the addressee of ethical obligation.

Ethical questions are existential questions, and their solutions demand not only an acute understanding of the matters at issue but also a knowledge of life that is generated by the experience of proving oneself in life, which in turn brings forth wisdom. Moral theologians are far too little aware that ethical norms are the result of life histories on which people have reflected, and that the root of these histories is experience.[1] These stories have found acknowledgment within a fellowship of communication, and they are valid until the opposite is unambiguously demonstrated. There is, however, a measure of unclarity in their formulation, and this is why they require exegesis. The obvious place to look for such an exegesis is the existential world of their addressee, and as soon as normative claims appear to admit a variety of interpretations, recourse is had precisely to this existential world.

Ethical norms are surrounded by an unspoken interpretative framework, like the halo around the moon. This framework comes from the self-understanding of the human person, which is constructed from ideas about the goal of a successful and meaningful life. Ethical norms do not abandon their grip on us; we cannot distance ourselves from them. No matter what one does, one's own life is always at stake. Everyone shrinks spontaneously from the nightmare of a life that has missed its goal. And this must summon the moral theologian to an ever-renewed reflection because the moral theologian has the intellectual responsibility for human success. Is he at risk of thinking in such a way that he bypasses his own self? His own very personal truthfulness is under examination, and he must repeatedly resist the temptation to flee into an unassailable and exalted moralism that employs resounding imperatives that drive people either into resignation or (still worse) into cynicism. A person may be seduced by the idea of squandering his intellectual energy on the solution of individual questions, for in this way, life presents itself in segments, and a lofty intellectual ethos is developed that has nothing to fear from comparisons on the level of universal communication. In most cases, however, this does not get under the skin. It does not awaken his concern, nor does it cause any pain. The strengthening of the position of the ethics of virtue is one important indicator of a highly problematic situation.

Ethical praxis is not exclusively a matter of carrying out individual obligations. The human person is not an epiphenomenon of a closed ethical system that demands that norms be fulfilled but has no interested in the acting person. Rather, everyone pursues existential goals to the best of his ability—this is true of all those who see their lives in terms of a commission, or even a vocation, that they have received. They live and act in a generous commitment of their spirit and their freedom.

Before we ask what we must do, there is a more fundamental question: "What can I be?" This question is prompted by a self-understanding that perceives ethical truth as a promise of existential possibilities. Morality is no oppressive burden but an empowerment to act, which leads to ever-greater freedom. This is all the more so, in response to a world that has an expanding store of coercions by means of which it seeks to paralyze the ethical élan—indeed, to undermine it completely. The best norms are of no avail if they bracket off the success of life—a success that is far removed from pragmatic or eudemonistic reductionisms. It is therefore only right and proper for moral theology to keep a watchful eye on the ensemble of anthropological premises that accompanies the normative discourse like a shadow. Nor do we forget the boundaries of freedom here. High-flown reflection can obscure the fact that many people live on the edge of their strength, or even on a knife-edge, so to speak. They may indeed act consistently, but this consistency is very much under attack: one little prod and the painstakingly erected construction of their self-certainty collapses in ruins. This should not only make us pensive—it should wake us up! It is no doubt possible to demand too little, in ethical terms: morality can decay into a bourgeois respectability that ultimately conceals nothing other than a conscience in conformity with the system, so that it is no longer possible to speak of great achievements or of the commitment of one's life in testimony.[2] Usually, however, we encounter the opposite phenomenon, and we have the impression that excessive ethical demands are being made. This is due to a verbal radicalism in the field of ethics that can no longer gauge what is meaningfully possible and beneficial here and now. This is perfect hypocrisy. The intellectual construction of one's own system presents itself in immaculate consistency, and there is no point at which it is exposed to attack by theoretical reason . . . but it cannot in fact be lived.

I hope that these remarks will suffice to indicate the principal concern of my reflections in this book. A moral theologian cannot be content to examine whether norms of ethical conduct are justified. Such a task is of course essential, since moral theology cannot wander off into vague appeals, handing human beings over to the dictatorship of slogans. At the same time, however, the ability to educate is neces-sary. The goal is the building up of an ethical personality. The competence in matters of ethical insight must correspond to an ability to engage in conflicts that allow a person to survive the drama of his own life history. Each individual is confronted with a tremendous variety of expectations about the role he should play. In the segmented world in which we live, divergent and mutually contradic-tory criteria of correct conduct apply. This can overwhelm the individual who feels that he is put on the defensive. In the last analysis, no one wants to lose his identity. But no one is simply *given* his identity: this is the fruit of a lifelong and often painful endeavor that requires self-consciousness and self-respect.

Obviously, there is considerable human distress on this point. Many people have only fragments, sometimes nothing more than shreds, of normative contents running through their heads, remnants of a moral education that concentrated on commandments and prohibitions and that in many cases was like the training we give a horse or a dog. However, this education misunderstood the essence of moral-ity. We can live up to ethical claims only when they are put forward in a framework that provides a sapiential orientation. A fundamental self-certainty is required, born of the indestructible insight into the meaningfulness of a person's own life history. He must understand how to associate his life with a commission that transcends all the individual achievements and binds these definitively together. This is the decisive point. Philosophical ethics and moral theology are sapiential teachings that come from the reflective ponderings of many generations who accepted the challenge of the struggle for a fulfilled life and paid the price for this. This gives a long-term perspective to today's generation too. Many individual questions remain unsolved; but this has always been the case, and only a small experience of life is needed to recognize this and accept it courageously. It is much more decisively important to have a goal for one's life that will bear one through all the doubts that arise; the success or failure of one's own involvement depends on the power of this goal to supply conviction. This is not the place for slogans. Only silence and humility give success.

This poses a question to faith. We have been told again and again in recent years that the contents of revelation cannot be translated directly in theoretical norms because the justification of ethical norms belongs in a new context. However, this new context is relevant to ethical norms since it is impossible to think of any justifications that would not be consequent upon discovery and insight—without this they would be meaningless.[3] Where justifications diverge, however, we are compelled to ask about the content of that which is justified. A person can of course offer different justifications for the same contents, but this fact does not make the question improper. Do the justifications perhaps point to discoveries that would have been wholly unthinkable in other contexts? And this is the decisive point: the ethical behavior of the Christian is not inspired by an impersonal law but is the response to the intellectual implications of an historical event. It is generated by a self-understanding born of reflection on God's intervention in history. When we speak of God's action, we are speaking of the place where the human person is completely "at home" in himself, that is, in his insight and in his freedom. Goals for conduct are discovered, and it is worth committing all one's strength to the achievement of the goals thus envisaged, for it is here that one's strength finds its ontological basis. A moral-theological theory about action cannot prescind from this. It must agree to ask whether and to what extent the responsorial character of Christian morals invites one to a new way of behavior that can be explained only with reference to the inspiring power of the Christian image of the human person. We are not thinking here primarily of concrete individual actions; we are interested in the fundamental existential attitudes that prompt these actions. Essentially, all our reflections in this book are concerned with the believer as an ethically competent personality.

This shows us the horizon of our reflections. On their own, evaluations based on ethical norms will always fall short. They must be supported by perspectives from the theory of action. This is because ethical decisions cannot be reduced to the fulfillment of norms. They are generated by a fundamental self-consciousness that is always antecedent to the norms and that makes it possible to fulfill them. The abiding task of moral-theological reflection is to carry out self-reflection from the perspective of its relevance to action, and so that the moral theologian is an existential thinker in the purest meaning of this term. He reflects lovingly on how God is active in his life history and on how a person can grasp, experience, and elucidate intellectually God's action vis-à-vis the human person. This demands that the moral theologian bring his own biography into the general discourse, not by absolutizing it but by employing it as a salutary corrective. Such a procedure compels a person to be truthful; above all, it makes him perceptive. The appeal to the obligating will of God is free from hypocrisy only when it refuses to evade the challenge of being anchored in the history of one's own life. This appeal must be made concrete, for it is an invitation—it does not bring death! Moral theology leads to disappointments wherever people have the impression that the moral theologian is speaking of morality in the same way that the atheist speaks of God. Naturally, a healthy distance is required, respecting vulnerable feelings and giving each person the space that he needs for his own free development. There is a kind of existential compulsion that suffocates other people, and this is why the objectivity of ethical norms is necessary. This objectivity exposes itself to an unconditional investigation. At the same time, however, it shows the path that leads into the profound dimension that is accessible only to experience, since that is where this objectivity itself has its origin. And this is an instruction to which we must listen.

Notes

1. Schwemmer, "Die Bildung der Vernunft"; and Mieth, *Moraltheologie und Erfahrung*.

2. Schockenhoff, *Das umstrittene Gewissen*, 15–20, illustrates the leveling coercions of societies with a democratic constitution.

3. For an overview, see Thönissen, *Das Geschenk der Freiheit*.

CHAPTER ONE

The Existential–Historical Form of Thought

The Experience of the Resolution of Conflict

A N ETHICAL ACTION resembles a symbolic event. It is generated by a life history upon which the individual has reflected, and it issues an invitation to further reflection. It possesses an invisible background, which it attempts to make visible; and we are not meant just to stop short at its manifestation, since it refers back to the world of ideas of the person who acts.[1] But what are the thoughts that move a person, leaving him no peace? The conflictuality of his own existence, with the suffering this has generated, moves into the foreground and cannot be overlooked. He can easily become confused about his own identity when he considers the variety of social roles in marriage, family, professional work, and politics, each of which brings its own ethical challenges.

Considerable intellectual effort is required if a person is to establish a dialogue between all these strata and carry on this dialogue in a responsible manner. But conflicts are also inevitably generated by the limitations inherent in being a creature, and by the fact that human life is inextricably woven into time and space. Every act of evaluation of individual goods in the endeavor to discover unambiguous rules about what one should prefer, and every reflection on the possibilities of action, reminds us that the process of becoming an ethical personality can be highly dramatic. Every individual grows into his own form by overcoming boundaries. A life project takes shape, and this requires an impetus from outside. And finally we must remember all those boundaries that have their origin in the history of guilt (one's own and that of others). These boundaries have been given the name "structures of sin"; they are a leaden weight that oppresses the élan of freedom, and they propel us from one life crisis to another. They generate an a priori propensity that inevitably leads to failure. Thus we are fenced in by a sadness that makes it more and more difficult to break out into freedom.

Conflicts also have their positive aspect because they keep one's reflection on the move. If the process of ethical insight is to continue, it is probably necessary that I be confronted with the limits of my strength. Are the claims addressed to me justified, and what are the intellectual propositions that lie hidden behind these claims? The more painful the conflict that I experience, the more urgent is my demand for an unambiguous explanation, for what is at stake is nothing less than the comprehensive "success" of my own life. If I make an unconditional commitment that may perhaps entail the loss of fundamental human goods, or perhaps even the breakdown of the plans I have made for my life, I will certainly want to know whether such a risk is justified. Is it compatible with the idea of a meaningful and fulfilled life, a life worth living?

Is this kind of question an attempt to employ the pretext of thinking in order to wriggle out from lofty demands? Not in the least, and it would be easy to see through such a self-deception. Rather, this kind of question is a gnawing, terrible doubt that will not let reflection rest: Am I leading a life that actually passes me by? Is my whole life a lie? This is surely the most dreadful idea of all, and at this point a fundamental truthfulness is required: only a person who possesses the necessary certainty that he is living for a cause about which all doubt is excluded can confront high expectations, for it is only then that his life will be something other than a continuous flight from the claims made on him by these expectations. On this level, truthfulness means the ability to bear the burdens he has in fact shouldered. An accord with one's own self is necessary if he is to confront the truth of individual moral claims based on an ultimately unwavering simple attitude devoid of any lurking ambiguity.

Let us pursue this idea a little further. It may seem a commonplace of moral theology to assert that ethical norms for conduct derive from reflection on one's experience of life and that they are never only the fruit of an abstract speculation that follows the logic of a system and lacks the necessary concreteness. But what does "concreteness" actually mean here? It is certainly not enough to limit this concept to empirical objectivity because that would fail to do justice to the specific character of ethical truth. The term "experience of life" already indicates the necessary amplification: a person gathers experience through lived situations, especially those in which it is necessary to resolve an incipient conflict. In this way models of a solution are generated, and these must be repeatedly tested to see whether they can be applied to comparable situations. However, this act of comparing is a highly complex proceeding that presupposes the gift of discernment. A clear distinction must be made between the agreements and the divergences so that the unique element can emerge unambiguously in each instance. In this sense, models never claim anything more than an asymptotic value. This, however, does not reduce in any way the absolute claim made by an appropriately formulated norm; all that is affected is the understanding of how to deal with norms.[2]

This act of comparing does not stop short at the objectively describable phenomenon. It also looks at the invisible presuppositions. What do the guiding ideas about the goal of a completely successful life look like in specific situations of conflict? Are self-respect and a meaningful quality of life still guaranteed? This already implies the question of what can reasonably be expected. Exaggerated ethical demands offend against the dignity of the person because they cheat him of his happiness. And this brings us to the test case of ethical judgment. Here he needs to be able to discern the boundary that runs between the limits and the possibilities of his own freedom, and this requires a high degree of honesty vis-à-vis his own self. The temptation to flight tends to occur when decisions are not subject to public control, especially when they remain in the intimacy of the world of his own thoughts. Here, however, a second point must be made.

There certainly does exist an immediately lived experience of his own ability and inability. But experiences also remain open to a variety of interpretations. They need to be explained if they are to be understood, and their capacity for expressing the truth depends on the plausibility of the arguments that are employed. It is possible to talk with each other about our experiences—which naturally include experiences of life—although absolute mutual comprehension is not possible because there ultimately remains an incommunicable element. It is here that the proposition *individuum est ineffabile* ("that which is individual cannot be put into words") finds impressive confirmation. Nevertheless, enough material remains to establish a consensus that in turn forms the basis for norms of conduct. A consensus is more than objectified experience, since the act of objectifying also means reflecting. Experiences pass through the filter of convictions. It is only when we reflect on them that they become exempt from the charge of uncontrollable arbitrariness.[3]

This insight supplies us with an important key to understanding. The convictions that we hold give form to our experience of ability and inability. The definition of acceptable and unacceptable demands derives from an antecedent horizon of understanding, which is applied to our experiences. Identical experiences can be interpreted in various ways; by means of this interpretation, they actually become different. The definition of a person's own strength is no exception to this rule. In the last analysis, it depends on a position that has been adopted a priori, and that is essentially distinct from empirical circumstances.

In today's moral-theological reflection, recourse is made everywhere to the constitutive role of practical reason. The ethical claim is made by the *ordinatio rationis* with which it is (so to speak) identical. When the Scholastic tradition speaks in this way, it presupposes the idea of participation: through reason, the human person acquires participation in the eternal divine law. In the act of insight, he reaches out to the fullness of God's Being, and this empowers him to lay down a law for himself.[4] However, this anthropological affirmation in theo-ontological categories must not be allowed to vanish into a mere formal incantation that allows a person to neglect the necessary act of establishing a link between the affirmation and the concrete insights; for if this affirmation is to play an effective role in the moral-theological discourse, it must have a substantial component that is plausible. In the case of the problems we are studying, there are perspectives here that invite us to pursue our reflections.

There can be no doubt that an objective knowledge of human nature exists and that it is indispensable for ethical judgments. Nor should anyone attempt at this point to level the charge of a naturalistic fallacy, for the objectivity of the act of knowing remains within a horizon of metaphysical anthropology, which entails specific values. This may suffice for reflection on the theory of norms but not for reflection on the theory of conduct. Here we need to refer back to a lived relationship to God that is open to the transcendental analysis of conduct, a relationship that draws both on objective and on supraobjective experience. What is possible for freedom? The decision is taken here, in this intimate sphere. Freedom discovers its own ability—and it is on this competence that the practical significance of all the essential concepts depends.

Here, however, a clarification is necessary. Reflections such as these move on the level of a metaphysics of knowledge and of freedom. Objectivity and the subjectivity that are inherently related to transcendence coincide. Besides this—and completely in keeping with the tradition of Saint Thomas—these reflections are guided by an understanding of metaphysics where Being is understood as the undifferentiated fullness of all its attributes. Under this presupposition, there is no problem in speaking about a transcendental content that does not remain in the realm of pure theory but is also disclosed to practical reason. A fundamental mediation is going on here, therefore, and this in turn finds expression in a synthetic form of thought. As soon as we speak of a metaphysics of the person, we must be aware of these presuppositions, for otherwise we shall be engaging in a dialogue of the deaf. "Person" means a proleptic reaching out to the supergenerality of Being: this is how the ontological foundations are laid for the supplying of content to general concepts.[5]

Metaphysics and Norms of Conduct

This sheds light on the ontological status of norms of conduct. At the basis lies a metaphysics that cannot be measured with the parameters of a reductionist objectivism and essentialism. The history of ideas led Scholastic philosophy (which had a decisive influence on the handbooks of moral theology) to narrow down its perspectives, but we must look further back and inquire into the valid concerns of Thomas himself. Metaphysical definitions are indispensable for the moral theologian, but they must be kept free from overinterpretations. Precisely because there is a proleptic reaching out to Being, as the fullness of all definitions, one may take a critical view (in the name of metaphysics) of exaggerated affirmations about contents. Rather, the objects of metaphysical statements are those indispensable basic conditions that establish the horizon for a wider and as yet incomplete story of discovery. They are comparable to prior indications that mark off the terrain but in such a way that, while showing a direction to the *quodammodo omnia* of the human spirit, they do not rush too quickly to prejudice the results. From this perspective we may well say that moral theology can never be "sufficiently" metaphysical.

Norms of conduct embody the same understanding of metaphysics. They claim to record a particular stage of insight that has been reached in the course of history and acquired through conflicts but not to prescribe this stage of insight for all future times. A person who formulates norms thinks always of the consequences; he knows that there is no behavior that would not also generate consequences. Actions without consequences are an abstraction that forgets history. At most, such actions seek to insulate themselves against attack in a sphere of ideal validity, thus categorically exempting themselves from anyone who might claim to revise them. Object and consequences form an inseparable unity, which is why intellectual responsibility applies to both of these.[6] This has nothing to do with either relativism or pragmatism. Under the conditions of history, the decisive power of the object can be grasped only via the consequences. There is no need to demonstrate in detail that the consequences themselves are subordinate to an evaluative authority that belongs integrally to the understanding of metaphysics that I have sketched here. In short, norms assume the status of reflexive principles. We should assume that they are valid until their invalidity is clearly demonstrated. This is true in two senses. First, we must bear in mind the possibility that the external circumstances of conduct will change. We must examine the ethical relevance of this fact if we wish to avoid the risk of compromising the realization of human goods. Second, however, we must face up to the risk that when unreasonable demands are made of freedom, these demands cannot be met in the long term, and that standards of active involvement disintegrate. Norms protect us from relapses on both levels; their validity stands and falls with their presumed protective function. In every instance, their invalidity is something that must be proved.

This means that a large measure of honesty is required not only of the moral theologian but of everyone. The only aim of this protective function is to wrest tolerable existential possibilities from the manifold potential for conflict in human existence, and to reduce the conflicts that break out, where it is impossible to resolve them in a constructive manner. The all-decisive question here is how this is to be achieved. That is why we need goals; the function of norms is to help attain goals. Reflection on the forms taken by successful living is critical of norms. It generates an antecedent knowledge that has an effect both on the formulation and on the interpretation of norms. This impact not only employs inferential thinking; rather, it takes the form of a critically stimulating inspiration that initially contains an element of falsification. Concrete solutions are examined to see whether they are compatible with the accepted goals. This is made possible by an antecedent positive insight that reacts to the intellectual challenges by demanding an increased clarity. This process is liberating—all the more so, the purer the idea of transcendence becomes. For if ethical truth is to be done for its own sake, this necessarily means the purification of everything that is regarded as human fulfillment and happiness. Where eudaemonism accepts this challenge, evading neither conflict nor suffering, it does not in any way contradict authentic morality.[7] On the contrary, the dignity of an anthropology and of its concomitant understanding of morality is seen in the ability to deal in such a way with conflicts that there is no reduction of the consistency of ideas about ethical value, while at the same time the price to be paid—whether in suffering or in the loss of fundamental human goods—does not go beyond one's own strength. Seen in this way, moral theology is the mediation born of conflict between the two levels. And this is why it necessarily demands an action of testimony that goes beyond the merely intellectual management of conflicts.

This also implies a pedagogical responsibility. A moral doctrine cannot be content with the normative presentation of directives for conduct, no matter how well founded these may be. It must also show that the appeal to human generosity and dedication does not deprive the human being of his basic right to a fulfilled life: renunciations must be justified. If this is to succeed, convincing examples are required. All moral theology is tried and tested on life itself. Practical experience has demonstrated that, where it is reasonable, it leads to a higher freedom even if the road goes through the valley of tears. This is why there is a duty to stand up and be counted. No one who teaches or preaches moral theology can exonerate himself from this responsibility. He is not allowed to withdraw into the sphere of unassailability and to abandon to their fate those to whom he addresses his admonitions. But a person who accepts this challenge need have no anxiety about undertaking revisions. He need not fear that this puts his authority at risk. No moral theology ever foundered yet because of honesty.

The Theological–Anthropological Form of Thought

God's Inner Dimension

It is impossible to speak of human action if God's action vis-à-vis the human person represents only one additional interest on the part of the theologian. That would be a travesty of the self-understanding of the believer, since God is more intimate to the believer than the believer is to herself.[8] When the success of a person's life is at stake, no one thinks on two distinct levels, that of faith and that of the earthly realities. It is indeed possible to distinguish these levels conceptually, but they are united in the concrete living of one's life.

In intellectual terms, this gives the believer no peace. If she takes her faith seriously, she will reflect on the place that the question of God occupies in the story of her life: how is God experienced as God? A person who dispensed herself from asking this question would expose herself to the justified accusation of being untruthful. For she is summoned to ask this question, and when she replies, she gives an account of the ultimate motivation for her conduct.[9] This is also true vis-à-vis her own self. On this point, no one can live with evasions—at least not in the long term—for this question has a significant bearing on the respect that one owes oneself. One day, with inexorable consistency, my biography will uncover this sin of omission, and it may be too late then to change course: I am overtaken by the course of events. Inevitably, burdensome situations will arise that demand an unreserved self-revelation that reaches into the uttermost depths of the person.

If this self-revelation is refused, failure is unavoidable (perhaps only in the sense that one's basic attitude to life is noncommittal). I may parry the blows for a long time, securing compensatory advantages from every loss; but this cannot ward off the catastrophe that waits in the wings of my life story. The task of moral-theological reflection is to protect people from this catastrophe.

This intellectual program is not, however, without its difficulties, which are intimately linked to the intellectual form that is chosen here. Everyone thinks spontaneously in the categories of objectivity, even when one affirms the opposite. A person needs contents that are capable of being objectified. In relation to these, she assures herself of her own identity (of which at most she has developed a nonthematic consciousness). Description is the most natural of activities, and she learns only laboriously that a higher intellectual discipline is required if she is to think of nonvisual personal actions using instruments borrowed from the realm of the visual.

This difficulty reaches its peak when we think about God. Quite spontaneously, although they have no wish to eliminate the analogy of Being that links God and the human person, moral theologians will recall here the concern that generated "negative theology," since it is always the reductionist ideas about God that make our theological argumentation look questionable. God as the highest lawgiver, as the unmoved mover of a natural order that exists a priori, as the Lord of history—all these phrases cry out for interpretation if they are not to give rise to permanent misunderstandings or to theological short circuits. And in that case, moral crises are inevitable, since it is impossible to live based on erroneous theological ideas. It is no wonder that the flight into untheological thinking is so tempting: one is content with theories of the natural law that reduce the relationship to God to formal formulae empty of content. Naturally, there is no lack of a clear analysis of phenomena in such theories, and the system itself is free of immanent contradictions; nor is the influence of faith on ethical reason always denied. But the attempt at an intellectual investigation of this influence seldom gets beyond the first few steps. We hear of a Christian context of intentionality and reference is made to the anthropological implications of the faith where these claim the status of contents accessible even to nonbelievers. However, such considerations offer little help in the construction of a theory of action; further work is necessary.[10]

The Interplay between Faith and Reason

I have said that God is more intimate to the human person than this person is to himself. This sheds light on the theological structure of thought, in view of the principle drawn from the theory of science that a methodology must follow the Being of its object. It is indeed true that the Christian context of intentionality and the anthropological implications establish what we might call the indispensable boundary conditions for ethical conduct, and ethical reason has the task of filling out the contents of the horizon that is thus delineated; but a statement like this could prompt incorrect ideas about the underlying understanding of autonomy. We must not give the impression that the criterion of a natural-law thinking directed toward objects is being tacitly applied here (as was common in many of the Neo-Scholastic manuals). This is only one aspect and certainly not the decisive point. Much more importantly, such knowledge of an object never discloses more than a part of the intellectual program. Rather, the center consists of the natural knowledge of God, no matter how distorted and fragmentary this knowledge may appear. The human person is by nature a religious being, and faith is more immediate and more natural for him than reason. In faith the human person is completely at home with himself. No greater intensity of reality can be imagined.

The rationality of the argument takes on a derived status that is less original than this reality, but this does not make it any less significant. Indeed, it remains essential. The demand for argumentative plausibility is made above all when it is necessary to preserve the freedom to give assent. Besides this, a point of contact is needed when a person seeks to engage in an ethical dialogue with the nonbeliever. The ethical relevance of faith can be demonstrated. The argument based on the natural law resists the tendency to a vagueness that withdraws into unassailable niches. Responsibility for the world is assumed publicly in a manner both open to investigation and unafraid of confrontation. This includes those concrete decisions that are often highly conflictual. Additionally, we must criticize the theological short-circuit solutions that attempt to wriggle out from under the beneficial necessity of genuinely thinking through all the details of a question—while at the same time lacking all intellectual modesty. Here it is essential for the theologian to be truthful.

If it nevertheless proves impossible to extirpate all unease, this is because of the fragmentary nature of reason. The autonomy of reason does not mean that a person makes no demands of himself. Rather, faith inspires the indissoluble mutual compenetration of insight and reflection; it is not synonymous with heteronomy in the Enlightenment sense of this word.[11] The elimination of this interconnection would open the door to a reductionist view of the human person since a person would not then take into due account the fact that faith shapes reason through and through in its innermost core. Faith is not in the least something added on externally to reason since reason has an antecedent disposition for faith. The process of shaping through and through necessarily entails that meanings change. Reason operates in a context of meaning that it itself has not posited; rather, this context derives from the insight of faith. The polyvalence of reason receives an ultimately binding interpretative principle that itself cannot be called into question; only thus is it able to carry out its own task. Faith does not make reason superfluous, nor does it relieve reason of the risks inherent in history. But it does provide foundations for reason—namely, basic elements of a theological anthropology—and it thus indicates the direction in which reason must put its questions.

Epistemological–Anthropological Consequences

These reflections point to an underlying epistemological–anthropological conception. The reality that is relevant to action owes its existence to an interpretation
that is based on an insight into meaning. The surrounding world of objects can
indeed be opened up by reason, and it is equally certain that there exists reason
that perceives reality. But if misunderstandings are to be avoided, we must look
more closely. And here we must distinguish different levels of perception, although
these remain united in the concrete act of knowing.

In the act of perception, reason stands over against the empirical world of
objects. The axiom of epistemological realism applies here: *nihil in intellectu quod
non prius fuerit in sensu*. In terms of ontological priority, however, this is preceded
by a perception of meaning as the ultimate "why" of human existence. In both
cases (although in different senses), this is not something under our control. The
world of objects supplies indications that we cannot do without, and in this sense
the world of objects is not under our own control; but the world of objects is formed
through and through, and interpreted, by reason that perceives meaning. This must
be borne in mind when we reflect on the relationship between faith and ethical
reason. The attitude of skeptical resistance vis-à-vis an overinterpretation of the
truths of revelation may be justified, but it must not lead to a tacit abandoning of
the relationship between faith and ethical reason—for this relationship contains
an intellectual problem. Moral theologians will be fighting on the wrong front if
they are content to note ethical agreements between the believer and the nonbeliever, and to explain these in terms of natural law. They are doubtless correct to
be interested in universal communication, and they seek to establish a shared basis
for action in common. But they must not forget that faith enjoys a theoretical
precedence that influences the historical form taken by ethical reason. The primary
task of the moral theologian is the intellectual elucidation of this precedence; it
is only at a secondary level that he must discover whether and to what extent in
individual instances this precedence differs from other ethical systems or agrees
with them. The openness to consensus is thus linked with the courage for dissent,
not because the moral theologian wants to make a name for himself but because
he is conscious of his own identity, which is linked to the anthropological implications of faith. There is an inherent connection between the self-consciousness of
the believer and the concrete modes of his action. On the level of the phenomenon
of action, a person may be doing the same thing, but it is something different—
because he has become another person. The meaning establishes the reality: in
the act of interpretation, the *ordinatio rationis* reaches its high point.[12]

A considerable measure of personal truthfulness is required of a person who
reflects on these issues; it is absolutely necessary to examine one's own self. It is a
commonplace of moral theology that no ethical truths may be inferred from truths
of the faith since these two are moving on distinct epistemological and logical
levels; but this principle does not in the least exclude the synthesizing achievement
of the insight that establishes communication between the two levels. It is through

this synthesis that the lived identity of the believer is constituted. The moral theologian's task is the analysis of this process, in order to forestall erroneous simplifications.

The theological–anthropological form of thinking that is present here includes a number of different aspects that complement one another in an analogous manner. Personal identity is understood initially as a relational reality: it refers to the lived relationship to God. However, it also refers to the existing substance; from this perspective, it is understood as an empirically existing objective reality. Obviously, the theologian is primarily interested in the first aspect. Basic elements of a theological anthropology are identified, which establish a horizon and supply indicators of potential problems in the continuing work of concretization. They show the direction that should be taken by the definition of the contents of ethical action.[13]

This observation gives us the decisive catchword. The theologian cannot be content with formulating frameworks of this kind while leaving it to autonomous reason (in a second epistemological move) to do the work of filling in the contents. Rather, he must demonstrate the rationality of faith by elucidating it intellectually as that which makes action possible. What positive surplus—understood in the sense of an empowering—does faith contribute to history? Clearly, this means the rejection of a systematic thinking that would aim primarily to eliminate contradictions, for when it is a question of taking responsibility for concrete behavior, this kind of thinking can offer nothing more than the knowledge of how to apply principles. The theologian, however, understands the anthropological implications of faith as data that inspire his reflection. For the theologian, the guiding category is newness.

The Critical Potential of Negative Theology

How is it possible to deal with "newness" in an intellectually responsible way? There can be no doubt that the negative theology that I have mentioned is genuinely at home in our own tradition. All human speaking about God is made possible by the analogy of Being, which endures even in the realm of faith; but this speaking finds a critical boundary in negative theology. When we speak about God, we can more readily say what he is not rather than what he is. There is a striking intellectual affinity to mysticism here, and this offers us a significant perspective for handling the anthropological implications of faith. These implications are indicators of problems, and they are meant to intensify our perception. The tendency to a selective reception of reality must be counteracted and corrected so that there may be no loophole for immunization by means of an unquestioned self-reassurance—for intellectual dishonesty on the part of the theologian consists in the art of evasion. One argues either on the level of faith or on the level of reason, and takes refuge in whichever direction promises unassailability.

Negative theology thwarts this temptation. It attempts to transform the reservation in this temptation into something constructive by protecting it from the creeping aggression of positive inferences. The knowledge of what God is not means that statements about the human person take the same form. When we know what the human person is not, a kind of mirror-image shows us positive contents. And knowledge of this kind contains an element of hope. It shows the human person what he may hope for, and this gives a new impetus to intellectual honesty, as respect for the freedom of the person he is addressing: freedom will be best respected where there are alternatives for action, and these alternatives cannot in the least be seen as a limitation, still less as coercion.

Negative theology finds consistent articulation in one form of conviction ethics that establishes a critically constructive relationship to history. Such an affirmation makes sense only if God is the first to be known in one's own life; this affirmation in turn must be understood correctly. It must not be tacitly suspected of ontologism, as always happens when categories of the knowledge of objects are applied directly to the knowledge of God. It is indeed true that God is not the first to be known *in ordine generationis*, that is, on the level of the genesis of knowledge. But he is the first to be known *in ordine perfectionis*, that is, on the level of ontological perfection. This does not in any way exclude the necessary mediatory function of the knowledge of objects. All knowledge has its genetic origin in the empirical realm, and the knowledge of God is no exception to this fundamental law of epistemology (which itself is based on epistemological–anthropological presuppositions).

This is the perspective in which we must understand the word "conviction," which denotes the hermeneutical locus that sometimes appears as a Christian horizon of meaning or context of intentionality. It is here that the anthropological implications of faith are rooted. Ontological and gnoseological questions are interconnected in their very origins. Ethical knowledge—which establishes the practical correspondences to these implications—does not stop short at general affirmations but takes soundings in concrete praxis. What must be done here and now because it is beneficial and liberating? Philosophical theories of knowledge prove inadequate in the face of this question. We need epistemological–theological reflections that translate the concern of negative theology into the moral-theological context.

One example is the theological–anthropological interpretation of death in which the Christian self-understanding reaches its highest intensity; every other fundamental element of theological anthropology is based on this. We may say without fear of contradiction that all these are accessible (in varying degrees of purity and perfection) even outside the sphere of faith, but this cannot be said of the Christian understanding of death. There is an inevitable parting of the ways when people seek to interpret and cope with death. Because death dominates life and holds all the threads of history in its hand, there can be no situation in life that would not be subject to interpretation by death. Living means making sense of death—and this affects all that we do in shaping our world.

This is why all ideas about order and all goals in life must pass through this critical filter. It is here that negative theology is summoned to offer guidance for our actions. Just as God in Jesus Christ expropriated himself into the world, so the Christian, in his life and his conduct, expropriates himself into his death. He reaches out proleptically beyond his death; and he can do this because the resurrection guarantees knowledge of perfection, knowledge that outlives history. The bliss of seeing God face to face provides a convincing point of reference for a person's conduct, and this point of reference cannot be gainsaid by any experience within history, since it grants an unwavering certainty. This is the starting point of Christian conviction ethics. A world of ideas is generated, casting a veil of hope over all the superficial clarity of innerworldly goals. In his conduct, the believer is a visionary who has the courage to pursue utopias, and who thereby gives proof of his truthfulness. To behave ethically is to bear witness.

God's Action and Human Action

Experiencing God as God

The affirmation that the ethical praxis of the Christian is a response to God's prevenient salvific action is considered a theological commonplace. The theologian utters this as though it were the most natural thing in the world—like one of those verbal clichés that permeate theological discourse and (when examined more closely) rob it of its credibility. Is there anything in lived reality that actually corresponds to this affirmation? If we are to answer this question, we must enter the world of ideas in which the believer lives and inform ourselves about the ideas that actually move the believer as well as the questions that his intellect seeks to penetrate.

If the believer takes his faith seriously and makes the existential commitment that is required, there can be only two questions that move him: How do I experience God in my life? Where can I glimpse correspondences between the intellectual demands faith makes of me on the one hand and the story of my own life on the other? The questioning begins with the believer's own self and thus bears witness to his intellectual honesty.[14] For everyone, whether believer or nonbeliever, reflects on the course of events, the many twists and turns of life, and what these have led to.[15] The believer who reflects attains a relationship to himself as soon as he looks at his past. How and why has he become the person he now is? An absolute truthfulness is needed if he is to stand the test of the claims that confront as well as the claims he chooses to face, and if he is to protect his life from catastrophes. This always involves the dismantling of illusions, uncovering any ambiguity or half-heartedness, and establishing communication between the ideal and the real "I," to see whether he is in fact fleeing from himself.

Such ideas are prompted by the first-hand experience of the fragility of everything that belongs to the temporal sphere. The goals that the believer had set for his life turn out to be utopias, situations of happiness disintegrate, and people on whom he had relied turn their backs, take other paths, or even let him down. The believer who begins to ponder will be discouraged by the pointlessness of making such a high commitment, and he will be reluctant to take decisions. A miasma of tragedy cloaks the believer's life. The course of events seems persistently to thwart his expectations. This puts the purity of his interior dispositions to the test, and the only way to survive this is to cling to what is truly enduring—even (or especially) when this is not strikingly obvious—but can be perceived only in stillness. The human person is spiritualized to the highest degree when he discovers, despite all outward appearances, a basis that can give support to his actions, a basis that still continues to promise fulfillment even when all his plans, wishes, and expectations founder. We owe it to our own self-respect to ascertain where such a basis can be found.

Theology of Providence

The Christian places his life and his conduct under God's kindly providence. God is present to him in all the turns and twists of his biography, and there can be no situation that is exempt from this claim. This makes high demands of his ability to understand—for he does not take on the role of a neutral observer here, where his unique life is at stake both in understanding and in acting. He must develop a theology of history that can stand up to the course of events, especially when he must not only endure borderline situations but must also cope with these in a constructive manner. Accordingly, the hearer who has experience of life may be shocked to hear a Christian speak simplistically of God's lordship over history. He will feel that his struggle for an honest intellectual investigation is no longer being taken seriously.

But what is the hearer actually doing here? What is it that moves him to protest? He endeavors to sharpen his perception; he is instinctively aware of the danger of a selective view of reality that tends to take over as soon as he operates with all too familiar intellectual clichés. What is needed is hard thinking that penetrates through the course of his own biography into the unique significance of the self. Events are prompters to thought, building up a world of ideas that must be considered the most original existential milieu. When he thinks, the human person is completely at home in himself; the experience of his historicity helps him to achieve this, since there is no such thing as "coincidence" for the person who reflects. At the very least, he senses dimly that everything that happens to him (despite what may seem at first sight to be the case) is appropriate to him, or at least can become appropriate to him. His biography becomes his teacher, and his own profile is delineated before his inner eye. Possibilities and boundaries can be discerned, and realism and an increasing modesty occupy more and more of his life.

A fundamental self-understanding comes about. Dominant concerns, to which it is worth committing all one's strength, are examined to see how they can be put into practice. This is already a high ethical achievement, and only the truthful person succeeds here, since it demands the willingness to be led out of bottlenecks and to discover that level of conduct that brings erupting conflicts to a constructive reconciliation. In this way one learns from history in a way that is liberating, provided that one understands freedom here to mean the power to extend one's own possibilities of action. The person who learns is empowered to recognize and anticipate better alternatives, thereby constructively resolving situations of conflict and apparently unbridgeable antitheses in such a way that the dynamic identity of the self is further developed (although this may take the form of springs and U-turns). The price to be paid is the unreserved examination of the available strength. This sometimes entails the revision of accepted criteria, once their provisional character has been recognized.[16]

All this intensifies the urgency of the theological question. How are we to think of God's providence in the biography of the believer? Do we perhaps need to subject customary ideas to a critical evaluation? The reflections we have presented on the form of thinking make it possible to deal impartially with the truth of the faith on which we have touched here. The affirmation that God does not miraculously interrupt chains of causality within history may safely be regarded as a theological commonplace. His action is linked to secondary causes; but this is not a limitation on his freedom because he himself called these secondary causes into being. Besides this, there is no other way in which his activity could be perceived because the human person—himself a secondary cause—lacks the direct knowledge of God.

The problem can be resolved only when we abandon the unspoken remnants of a deterministic worldview and of an insufficiently thought-through epistemological realism that has decayed into an objectivism that is understood in a material sense. Only an existential-personalistic form of thinking can lead us out of the dilemma. If we take seriously the insight that God is more intimate to the human person than this person is to his own self, and that this intimacy contains the highest concentration of personal reality, it follows that God's activity in history binds itself to history. This deep dimension is the hermeneutical locus where God allows himself to be experienced. It is here that God becomes visible to the human person, uncovering himself to the eyes of the human spirit. This is knowledge *in actu*, and (as I have said earlier) we cannot apply to this knowledge the criteria of the knowledge of objects. The knowledge of objects limits the act of knowing, but knowledge *in actu* removes all limitations on this act. It seems perfectly appropriate to equate this removal of limitations with liberation. The human person possesses a prereflexive awareness of this process, which is essentially different in kind from the thematic reflexiveness of the knowledge of objects. Here one does not know as one knows vis-à-vis but indirectly, as in a concave mirror.[17]

Obviously, the next step here is to refer to Thomas' doctrine of the *reditio completa* of the human spirit. Scholarly discussion has emphasized the systematic element in this doctrine, its provenance in the teaching of Plotinus. How is this relevant to the present problem? God's activity in history begins at the point where history takes its origin, that is, in the intimate relationship between knowledge and freedom. Moral theology speaks of the Christian context of intentionality, which lays down the basic conditions for this procedure. The ability to interpret events is developed in the intentionality of the one who acts, so that he possesses a hermeneutical key that shows reality in a new light. Behind this proposition lies the epistemological premise that objectivity comes about through interpretation. In short, God intervenes in history via knowledge and freedom: this is how he binds himself to secondary causes. But this does not in the least abolish the directness of his action.

God's Providence in the Jesus Event

God's providence over history reaches its high point in the Jesus event. All subsequent events must be understood and interpreted in the light of this event, and this means that when the Christian speaks of God's intervention, she will always bear this unalterable criterion in mind. This has consequences for her theology of ethical conduct; and indeed, these consequences have already found expression in the christological foundations of her work.

Naturally, no moral theologian would claim that ethical norms of conduct can be straightforwardly inferred from the Jesus event. But this does not in any way diminish its relevance to ethical norms—a relevance that can be grasped in the various New Testament christologies. This a topic to which moral theology repeatedly returns. A dialogue must be instituted between christological reflection and anthropological reflection. The unique achievement of the Christian theology of revelation consists in welcoming the antecedent religious understanding that is one element in all anthropologies and then purifying and perfecting this by linking it to a concrete event. God's active presence in history is revealed in a historically tangible person, which lends a new mark of distinction to the history of every single human being. In this history, God's eternity is immediately present.[18]

It is impossible for the basic self-understanding of the believer to remain untouched by this insight. She believes that the perfection of all that is human consists in the eternal vision of God face to face, and all the goals within history toward which her longing is directed are the outcome of an interpretation that seeks to look ahead and find a balance between the present and the future. This means that a purely normative ethics will not serve because it holds fast (even if only in an asymptotic manner) to essential and generally communicable results of this process. Here, however, we must employ a mode of evaluation that cannot be grasped by means of the usual ideas about an evaluation of goods. It is not a question of establishing a hierarchy of goods and discovering supratemporal criteria of evaluation, since that on its own would not do justice to the premises of a theology of history. Rather, the present and the future are coordinated with one another—something that can be done only in hope. It is hope that constitutes the evaluation, and all the rules of preference that have been elaborated in normative ethics must submit to this.[19]

The way in which God's providence becomes effective over history depends ultimately on the moral competence of the Christian. Her personality determines the criteria of a prospective evaluation. This means that she must reflect on the conditions of discipleship. A thoughtful personality is not content with well-tried criteria and intellectual clichés but tackles the issue at once, pondering on how, in the many conflicts of history and in view of the many boundaries, the ethical message of Christianity can become an attractive, inviting, and consoling potential for action. The christologies lay down the framework, which must be filled out by means of an experience of life that has been understood and interpreted. Here one will bear unceasingly in mind the story of Jesus's life, since it is here that we see what is meant by the ethical implications of the Gospel, which are expressed above all in the antitheses of the Sermon on the Mount. All evaluations of goods must pass through this critical filter. Ultimately, it is here that the theology of grace, which is relevant to action, is spelled out and takes concrete form.

Here we must formulate our own question more precisely. The word "newness" must be employed in a way that is theologically defensible and "covered" by one's life story. In recent years, reflection on the foundations of moral theology has emphatically shown that the Christian faith did not generate any new norms, in the sense of norms that had not yet been known. Rather, what is new is the governing perspective. Here we are entitled to speak of a paradigm shift, but how is this to be understood more specifically? Most scholars refer here to the secondary antitheses in the Sermon on the Mount and the criticism of the Law that they contain, together with all the ethical implications of this criticism. These logia aim to establish the new competence of the disciple of Jesus by shattering the compulsions and entanglements of a conflictual history in a way that brings healing. In the freedom to which a person is empowered, the miracle of divine activity becomes a reality experienced in his own life.[20]

But the paradigm shift goes further than this: it sheds light on the ontological status of the ethical truth itself, on the essential form of imperatives. Christian morality consists essentially, not in a crushing demand but in a liberating mercy. The Christian is characterized not by fear but by trust. The object of her thinking is not the better norms but the better possibilities of freedom. It is in this sense that we speak of a new thinking, and indeed of a new spirit. For the Christian, God is no empty word: in Jesus of Nazareth, God has become visible. This newness disconcerts the observer. It is unexpected, something no one reckons on; it turns the customary evaluations of goods upside down. In the context of faith, norms are characterized by this "surplus." They give expression to a new ability, and this is why they lead out of the disastrous past history of freedom. The governing perspective for dealing with norms is the expropriation of God in Jesus of Nazareth, which supplies the ultimately binding interpretative key that the Christian employs in relation to the fact of the universal prior understanding in the field of ethics. This implies a radical transformation of the form of thinking. The newness of the spirit opens up the new reality. It is here that the truthfulness of the Christian finds its starting point.

The Intellectual Demands Addressed to Moral Theology

This indicates the task for moral theology. For this discipline, systematic reflection means facing the intellectual challenges posed by the death and resurrection of Jesus Christ. It is impossible to think more radically than this of the conflictual history of humanity. But the key to the solution already exists, namely in the conditions of discipleship. A person could of course be content with a sentence like this, and go on to elaborate a philosophical ethics of norms that no longer bore any traces of the theological intellectual presuppositions, but that would be the height of theological untruthfulness because reality would already be falsified on ground level. This is why systematic reflection too needs a change of ideas. At the center of its endeavors stands not a closed system but the fresh start toward better possibilities. Here, however, we must be modest. A person who does her thinking in a situation of ultimate contestation weighs her words and does not allow herself to be thrown off course by the seductive power of resounding imperatives. Modesty aims at intellectual clarity, which is not a mere matter of precise definitions and logical consistency but extends to the uttermost boundary of human strength, that is, to that point where all that exists is a grateful act of receiving and the enduring ambiguity of every human achievement is unmasked (so to speak) and can be seen plainly. Here we grasp the truth about the human person, the truth that contains the challenge for theological thinking. This is why the moral theologian is primarily one who thinks about existence, rather than primarily one who engages in systematic thinking. What then does this mean?

At stake here is the interest that guides one's thinking. This does not seek to identify normative contents where there is a difference between the Christian and the non-Christian, for on this point (as the moral-theological discussion of autonomous morality has correctly emphasized) there exists no exclusively Christian ethos. In principle, the ethical contents of the Christian are accessible to all persons of good will. In the course of the centuries, however, under the influence of faith on ethical reason, differences have been elaborated based on the perfect form of the *humanum*, since Christian morality claims to be the perfectly human morality.

This is where the problem begins. It would be misleading—indeed, it would fail to do justice to the essence of Christian morality—if one were to understand the history of this influence as the imposition of heavy burdens, for that would prompt the suspicion of an ethical rigorism. The opposite is true. The perfecting of human existence begins with the admission of one's own weakness. The ethical claim meets the Christian where she is thrown back on her own resources and suffers under the limitations on what she can do.[21] Here she is completely true because every escape route is blocked. This means that ethical thinking that is at the service of the truth must discover and formulate imperatives that anticipate, capture, and redeem the weakness and the contestation of human freedom. Ethical reason demonstrates its inventive power by assuming this intellectual responsibility to the full. It is not a question of outdoing the non-Christian by heightening the demands that are made. Such a tendency can end only in hypocrisy because it constructs a façade that can be torn down by the commonest experiences of our lives; this is a symptom of a deep-rooted thoughtlessness that fails to do justice to the essence of Christianity. A person who reflects on God's prevenient action in Jesus of Nazareth will have other priorities: her aim will be to construct an intellectual world of mercy, which then reflects ethical teaching both in form and in content. Only under these presuppositions is ethical action in truth made possible. It may indeed happen that higher standards of commitment are proclaimed, but not in the manner of a normative demand. Rather, these higher standards are the outflow of the spontaneous realization that no other kind of conduct is possible. The courage to draw this distinction comes from the fascinating power of the New Testament experience of God.

A moral-theological reflection that disregards these perspectives falls short and fails to do justice to the fullness of reality; it is content with a reduced anthropology. Nor does it grapple with the intellectual problems that face the theologian. On the contrary, it tacitly promotes the trivialization of its own work. It is indeed true that revelation does not bring about any direct increase in knowledge with regard to the shaping of the innerworldly spheres of life; from this point of view, revelation does not contain any categorical directives for behavior. However, we must add at once that to put the question in this way is to get the very point of Christian morality completely wrong, for the relationship to transcendence is a constitutive influence on every innerworldly sphere of life—all the spheres of life are ontologically constituted by this relationship. Either the normative correctness of behavior is affected by this relationship or else what passes for normative correctness does justice only to one segment of reality. Nor does it suffice to assert that faith involves only the motivational structure of behavior while leaving untouched the objective substantial correctness of one's conduct, for the responsibility vis-à-vis one's motivation includes the task of discovering the substantial structures that correspond to this motivation. This is why we need an intellectual structure that mediates between these various realities, a structure that does justice to the Christian understanding of reality.

Similar reservations arise when we are told that faith does not bring about any specific change to human nature, with the consequence that (once again, on the level of the innerworldly structure given to life) it would be impossible to speak of a specifically Christian morality. Such an idea bears the traces of essentialist-objectivistic speculations about the natural law, and it tacitly assumes that the ethical natural law is the same thing as the law of Christ. In what sense could faith bring about a specific change, since all it can do is to perfect an historical mode of existence? We must be careful not to overload the metaphysical categories here. The decisive point is the practical interpretation that can be seen in priorities, strategies, and the demands that are made. We must also remember that the equation of the ethical natural law with the law of Christ derives from an anti-Reformation polemic and has nothing to do with today's intellectual-cultural situation. Besides this, it remains stuck in a formal assertion; it does not tell us how this equation is to be understood in terms of content.

Finally, we must not give the impression of a surreptitious fideistic understanding of revelation. When faith lays down substantial rules for the faculty of ethical judgment via the basic elements of a theological anthropology (as I have said earlier), faith is acting in accordance with reason—despite its abiding character of mystery. Faith provides reason with food for thought by empowering it to interpret and evaluate the earthly realities in the light of eternal perfection. This is where theological reflection is needed. Theological thinking means making the present, which we experience directly, transparent to eternity. What does it mean to live and to act *sub specie aeternitatis*? Appeal has often been made to the Christian horizon of meaning. What does it mean to translate this into an intellectual existential world that lays the foundations of a behavior that corresponds to this specific meaning? It is not the theologian's task to hunt down possible ethical agreements between the Christian and the non-Christian; at most, this is a by-product of his work. Rather, the theologian's problem is how to discover those ethical contents that come from the *adhaerere Deo* of the spirit and to pass them through the filter of normative reflection, for therein lies the perfecting of reason. This makes the Christian's time a fulfilled time. An ethical personality is constructed on the basis of such ideas. Inspired by the anthropological data supplied by faith, an ethical personality seeks to open up the enduring tension between eternal bliss and temporal happiness so that it is possible to act in the present. And this requirement brings to the ultimate point of decision every evaluation of goods that becomes necessary in the context of normative ethics.

Notes

1. See Cassirer, *Freiheit und Form*; and Cassirer, *Philosophie der symbolischen Formen*.

2. Mieth, *Moraltheologie und Erfahrung*, operates consistently with the concept of model.

3. For details, see Demmer, "Erwägungen zum 'intrinsice malum'," 58–61.

4. Anzenbacher, *Was ist Ethik?* 38–43.

5. Riesenhuber, *Die Transzendenz*.

6. Furger, *Was Ethik bedeutet*, 40–48.

7. Engelhardt, ed. *Glück und geglücktes Leben*.

8. Augustine, *Confessions* 3.6.11 (PL 32: 683); and Augustine, *Soliloquies* 1.2.7 (PL 32: 872).

9. Türk, "Gottesglaube und autonome Vernunft, 395.

10. For an overview, see Gillen, *Wie Christen ethisch handeln und denken.*

11. Sala, "Immanuel Kants Kritik"; and Feil, "Autonomie und Heteronomie nach Kant."

12. See Arens, "Zur Struktur theologischer Wahrheit."

13. I have in mind here the indestructible dignity of the person, the fundamental equality among human beings, the meaningfulness of every situation in life, and the overcoming of death in the "here and now" of all its anticipations.

14. Muschalek, *Gott als Gott erfahren*, 159–72.

15. Dunkel, *Christlicher Glaube und historische Vernunft.*

16. For a comprehensive presentation, see Römelt, *Personales Gottesverständnis*; see also Schaeffler, "Wahrheitssuche und Reinigung des Herzens."

17. Schulte, "Wie ist Gottes Wirken."

18. Demmer, *Deuten und handeln*, 78–86.

19. In the course of a lifelong journey of discovery, the evaluations of goods are converted into an equilibrium between time and eternity. God is not so much the motive as the very substance of what one does.

20. For a comprehensive presentation, see Schnackenburg, *Die sittliche Botschaft*, 98–124.

21. Ethical knowledge tends to make progress in border situations.

CHAPTER TWO

Person and Personality

Nature and Person in the Fullness of Being

THE MORAL THEOLOGIAN finds it natural to think in the categories of personalism since this approach is appropriate both to his philosophical and to his theological reflection. This leads to the reception of insights that have their origin in the sphere of contemporary philosophy. What is true in general of the history of this discipline proves true today too: moral theology is a child of its time and can be compared to an open system that develops in a living exchange by letting its own concepts be challenged by the questions posed by new insights and needs.[1]

It would be presumptuous if this fact were to lead us to forget elements of the tradition that are unquestionably present, although perhaps only in embryonic form, still awaiting a full elaboration. It may well be that there was no need in the past to set them out fully; today, however, it may be necessary to emphasize something that was taken for granted in the past, something that no one had occasion to mention. This is certainly true of the thinking of Saint Thomas, but it also applies to parts of Neo-Scholasticism. There are more than enough impulses here that we ought to develop today.[2] It is unsurprising that documents of the Church's magisterium display the same tendency (although this is a relatively recent phenomenon) since the theology of the magisterium, at least in part, is a faithful reflection of the theology of the age in which it is produced. The concept of the nature of the person endowed with intellect, which is virtually a commonplace in the language of the magisterium and of theological science, attempts to unite personalistic thinking with thinking in terms of objects. The goal at which personal thinking aims is the effective power to shape history, and this would be thwarted if it were to get lost in a formal nonobjectivity; it would degenerate into an improvisation devoid of criteria and would thus lay itself open to the hackneyed charge of subjectivism. It is therefore logical that texts of the magisterium insist on the essential unity between nature and person, which must not be torn asunder by a subliminal anthropological dualism that would lead either to spiritualism or to naturalism. Nor is it surprising that the same texts appeal to the human person's unity as body and soul. Biological integrity is at the service of personal identity because it is via the body that one touches the soul. (I remark only in passing that this integrity is to be understood functionally: in other words, it is subject to the competence of judgments based on experience.[3])

These observations indicate the parameters of our discussion and the interests that are at stake. The approach to the understanding of "person" lies in our own Scholastic and Neo-Scholastic inheritance. Thomas defines a "person" as *esse subsistens in natura rationali* (being subsisting in a rational nature).[4] It is obvious that the governing idea in this definition is a descriptive way of thinking in terms of objects. The definition also remains highly abstract so that it seems at first sight rather unhelpful, especially from the perspective of the moral theologian. Nevertheless, it is open to development, and modern personalistic thinking can offer inspiration here. Both subsistence and the rational nature are subject, each in its own manner and rhythm, to elaboration in natural history and the history of ideas, and social factors play a decisive role here. Nevertheless, the person is never an object at the mere disposal of such factors. The person is always antecedent to the historical sphere of his or her relationships, since the person is the ontological basis that makes these relationships possible. This a priori contains a "surplus" that firmly resists every attempt to reduce the person to relationship or to sensitivity.

This idea is indispensable but it does not do full justice to the demands of the contemporary metaphysics of the person. The metaphysics of substance that this idea contains must be complemented by a metaphysics of the subject. The person is the proleptic outreach of the act of knowing and willing toward Being as the fullness of all its individual aspects. In this proleptic outreach lies the transcendental basis that makes categorial identity possible. This is a genuinely Thomistic element in our tradition. It must be developed, since it supplies a basis for a differentiated moral theological understanding of the essential unity of nature and person as the ultimate point of reference for ethical evaluation. Our first reflection concerns the convergence between the metaphysical and the historical levels of thinking: the immanent dynamic of the human spirit raises temporality to the level of historicity, and history means the progressive grasping of the absolute in the medium of time. The metaphysics of the person is characterized by this kind of processuality. If history is to be thought of in personalistic categories, we must accept the temporal unfolding of this dynamic. (I mention only briefly that since this is linked to freedom, it can go wrong; this is a result of the freedom of the act of knowing.) In this context, the underlying concept of Being seems more important. This is genuinely Thomistic and completely avoids the idea of a formalized empty concept that came to play a central role in Suarez's thinking. Thomas should not be read with Suarez's glasses! This makes it possible to think in profound dimensions in an act of knowing that accepts the analogy of Being and links the metaphysics of knowledge with the metaphysics of the person. "Person" is openness to Being. It is here, in this transcendental quality, that the source of its history lies.

This has direct consequences for the relationship between nature and person. These consequences are linked to the metaphysics of knowledge that is presupposed here. There is a nonthematic, preconceptual act of knowing in which the fullness of all individual aspects is grasped in a confused manner; this corresponds to the proleptic outreach toward Being. Precision grows in the course of the necessary thematization so that the existent is then known more and more clearly. This process is driven by the interplay between intuition and reflection. These differing intellectual activities complement each other, and one cannot play the one off against the other because that would not take account of the immanent historicity of this process, and ethical knowledge would relapse to the level of an objectivistic essentialism.

On these premises, we can now grasp what autonomy means. It designates the ability to open up the fullness of Being in relation to the limitations of the existent. This tension is reflected in the relationship between person and nature. When we speak of the nature of the person, we are not speaking of a material reality that presents itself to the descriptive reason but of a process of intellectual mediation between the supramaterial quality of Being and the material quality of the existent. The former makes it possible to understand the latter, but both belong inextricably together. This unity cannot be understood by means of a static-mechanic model. It is open to an ever increasing deepening and differentiation.

In this light, the materially empirical nature constitutes only one partial element of the nature of the person. It is insufficiently specific on its own. It performs the function of an indicator (a function that is of course indispensable). Normativity comes from definition by reason, which—far from any reductionist decisionism—stands in the fullness of Being. Criteria are applied to the empirical-material nature, which cannot be inferred from this nature alone. These criteria do not impose a dualistic rupture upon the essential unity between nature and person; rather, they establish this unity on a more differentiated basis. The affirmation (with reference to Thomas Aquinas) that the ethical claim is constituted by the *ordinatio rationis* is meant not only in a formal sense but also in the sense of the mediation described here. The transcendental and the categorial contents form a unity *in actu*, which the person takes hold of in the course of his or her history, thereby becoming a personality.

A Project that Aims at the Ultimate Goal

Moral theology must subject its tradition to a critical reappraisal. In Thomistic thinking, *finis ultimus* was a moral principle that could be put into practice, but this teaching was formalized largely in the moral-theological handbooks. It became merely a sign outside the brackets without affecting what was inside the brackets.

With regard to the genesis of the ethical personality, there is still a great deal of catching up to be done on this point, since the Christian makes her life history a project aiming at the vision of God. In other words, her life story has theophanic traits. One specific key is used to understand all events and happenings so that the ultimate goal may emerge with greater clarity. This is accompanied by the progressive clarification of the goals that a person has set for her life. No one lives *only* based on the claims made by norms. On a much more original level, there is the power of fascination generated by ideas and causes, a power that demands the unreserved commitment of one's life. Norms are certainly not superfluous: they record and transmit a consensus and make action easier. One who trusts spontaneity makes excessive demands of his intelligence and freedom. We cannot do without the parameters and boundaries that norms provide; by giving orientation, they also give security. But norms are not everything. They point to a "surplus" that derives from the intense experience of being "gripped" by God. Ultimately, the Christian is dependent on her conscience, which is shaped by faith. In the silence of this sanctuary, she stands alone before God and takes responsibility for her life.[5]

The first way in which she does so is by reflecting on her faith. A world of ideas is created, a world that makes high demands. This original existential world is the basis upon which all decisions are made. The believer must feel at ease in this interior space; she must feel at home, so to speak, because here she finds the happiness that consists in spiritual joy, delight in God, and a consolation that carries her through every tribulation. And here it is above all the idea of God's eternity that captivates the believer and gives her an unshakable security of spirit, no matter how much she may experience human fragility. The idea of God's eternity transforms from within all the goals we set for our lives so that they acquire an existential significance for us when we act. They are not merely relativized, nor is it merely a question of recognizing their preliminary character, for that would be too little—in the end, faith would decay into a sapiential doctrine of resignation. Rather, from the perspective of eternal perfection, the knowledge of temporal limitation is profoundly liberating because it removes the pressure exerted by the expectation that fulfillment must at all costs come within history. It generates a serenity of mind that bestows sovereignty over history. This results in a clarity of spirit that courageously summons a person to take up such goals for life and to pursue them with all her strength; these are goals that deserve such a commitment, not goals that cheat one of the uniqueness of one's own history.

In reflection on the bases of moral theology, there is a consensus that while revelation does not bring about any immediate growth in knowledge on the normative level, it does establish a new context for the foundations of normative ethics. This comes about through the anthropological implications of faith, which I have already mentioned. These function like indicators of problems, offering inspiration to the inventive power of ethical reason. To introduce the word "paradigm" at this point may give rise to misunderstandings because its meaning is disputed by philosophers of science. Nevertheless, "paradigm" seems helpful in describing the impact made by faith on ethical reason. As this term is usually understood, a paradigm opens up the parameters of a problem and at the same time indicates possible solutions. One cannot put too much weight on this definition, epistemologically speaking; its strength lies precisely in its self-limitation.[6]

If we apply what has just been said to the relationship between faith and ethical reason, a typical inference would be that faith, by means of its anthropological implications, establishes paradigms that offer food for thought to ethical reason and indicate the direction in which questions should be posed. The final goal is rendered transparent by these paradigms, although this takes place via a multiplicity of attempts at thinking, and the price to be paid is an entire life story. In this process, falsification may sound the dominant note, but the priority always belongs (even if in a nonthematic manner) to a positive insight of faith, which gains clearer outlines as it progresses and thus almost imperceptibly fashions the religious and ethical profile of the person who possesses the insight. Step by step, a person's life is reinterpreted and all the events and happenings invite her to enter intellectually into this profound dimension and to decode the guiding concerns of the anthropological implications of faith in the context of her own life story.

This is the real existential achievement of the believer. As an ethical personality, she knows how to discover goals for her life under the powerful inspiration of faith, and to translate these goals into concrete situations. This ability gives proof of her discernment. Doubtless, she also needs exact argumentation, clear concepts that are applied consistently, and the analysis of a situation that takes in all of the ethically significant details and perspectives—this is what normative ethics always does. But this intellectual activity takes the believer onto a secondary level. Creative insight is antecedent to all this and cannot be replaced by even the most careful reflection. Naturally, no one is capable of sounding the intellectual depths of the entire breadth and depth of faith, and of unfolding the ethical consequences; our eye sees only fragments, and the trigger here is our own life story. But in the confrontation with all those areas known only to the individual, where one must prove one's worth, completely unique insights emerge, like crash barriers that guide a person's life history onto the appropriate track, thus permitting a distinctive ethical physiognomy to come into being.

The Courage to Seize Spiritual Happiness

An ethical personality can come into being only where unwavering truthfulness exists. Lies about one's life—lies that may be woven in very fine thread—must be uncovered. The basic elements of theological anthropology, which acquire the status of open meanings, offer a kind of network that safeguards the process of discovering the truth. This is not a question of truths about things: the instrumental reason would be responsible for grasping these. Rather, what we need here are existential truths that make a successful life possible. And this makes truthfulness something that must be achieved throughout one's whole life. This task ends only at death.

This is the decisive point. A successful life is lived in the face of death. The interpretative coping with death is the key to the dignity of a life project, and all the individual anthropological elements are oriented toward this ultimate point of reference. All the events of a person's life story must be integrated in such a way that they clarify this inevitable challenge and help him to come through it successfully. Only thus does wisdom come: it is given to the person who is not a hopeless prisoner of the time that is inexorably measured out to him.

In view of this experience, the paschal event of the death and resurrection of Jesus Christ leads us into the very heart of the Christian message of salvation. If Jesus Christ is the perfect human person, and in him the human person is revealed to the human person, it follows that the history of the human person is recapitulated in him: he is the genuine locus of human self-realization.[7] In his death and resurrection, the truth and the promise of every single life story are disclosed. Death does indeed retain its terror because death is more than just the dying of the body; it includes all the sufferings, persecutions, and sacrifices that are courageously assumed for the sake of one's own ethical and religious consistency. But death is not an experience of being distant from God—an experience that would kill one because it is meaningless. Death is a passage to immortality, transparent to the light of indestructible happiness in the eternal vision of God from face to face. A person who has been taken hold of by God wishes (like Saint Paul) to be "dissolved" and to be with Christ. He has banished all paralyzing fear from his heart. The one who truly believes finds his satisfaction in God, and this fills his mind. Truthfulness is possible where one has the experience of being "at home." When existential lies are decoded, they always turn out to be a flight from death. But now they become superfluous.

Here lies the whole point of Christian morality. Successful life begins where a person succeeds in interpreting all the events of life in terms of this end. Happiness consists in the joy that the Spirit gives and in the consolation of a good conscience. The affirmation that the human person is a self-transcending being takes shape in the structure of hope that is supplied by faith.[8] The preferential context for this experience is the silence of prayer. Not only is the person who prays touched by the breath of eternity, it is only when he endures the silence that he becomes self-transcendent and is capable of the selfless commitment that is borne of overflowing love. This demonstrates whether he has the truthfulness needed to remain faithful to a life project that has the open horizon of eternity. Then he can confidently accept the perspective of the Gospel, as this is expressed in the conditions of discipleship, in the unrestricted commandment to love, and in the primary and secondary antitheses of the Sermon on the Mount.

A person needs the courage to seize spiritual happiness if he is to be an ethical personality. To choose ethical consistency at the cost of his own happiness is a false alternative. Even to consider such an alternative would be a sign of an inhumanity with dire consequences in the short or long term, which would lead to ambiguous compromises and to an inevitable hypocrisy. The formation of the personality requires a realistic judgment. Everyone feels the spontaneous drive to realize himself and to have a good time (in a manner completely above suspicion). Faced with the claims made by morality, everyone wants to be completely himself.

This is the most fundamental human right imaginable, and every individual ethical truth must protect this right. Its ontological basis is the dignity of the person, and self-respect is the basic attitude in life that corresponds to this. A Christian cannot be content with a naïve eudemonism. He is guided by ideas about the good life that have passed through the critical filter of faith, a filter that preserves them from being narrowed down and impoverished.

This entails an intellectual and existential challenge for the Christian. Self-respect must be united to self-sufficiency, and ethical conduct presupposes an independence of action that must be acquired through lifelong intellectual training. This is related to one's own life project. The absolute obligation of ethical truth is linked in its origins to the uniqueness of a life story. Here, we leap over Lessing's celebrated "ditch" between truth and history. As a sign of his autonomy, the person commits himself to a project and grows into a personality through faithfulness to this project. He must carry this project through, for otherwise he would lose his life; this requires him to commit all his strength to the task, beginning with the continuous endeavor to cultivate an intellectual world in which it is possible to live. The higher the commitment, the stricter is the self-examination: the Christian must reject everything that is not the best, and must think in such a way that generates an attitude to life that gives support. There is nothing unrealistic about locating the beginning of responsibility for a favorable environment in the inner sphere of one's thoughts and imagination: one day thoughts will be translated into action, even if they have to follow tangled paths. When we think, we are training ourselves in particular modes of conduct.[9]

This kind of prophylaxis is not dictated by a timorous defense mechanism. It has the positive aim of building up, and it issues a challenge to the constructive imagination of ethical reason. Disciplined thought is capable not only of discovering ideals for one's life but also of gradually penetrating into the full substance of these ideals. Every circumstance in life offers material for reflection, and it is possible that although the ideals remain constant, they can open up new perspectives in the various periods of one's life through which one reaches maturity. And this is not all. The person who follows an ideal goes through his life with open eyes. He thus perceives more clearly the situations of crisis and distress that he encounters—and that his ideal urges him to resolve. Accordingly, it is not too much to say that these situations embrace the whole of his life, tasks to which it is worth committing all his energy. These tasks focus and absorb his thoughts and protect him from unnecessary disappointments. The disinterested dedication to tasks brings self-certainty that is not lost even in the face of failure. And this self-certainty protects his heart from bitterness.

The Mastery of Time

An ethical personality has mastery over the period allotted to his life. When the human person experiences time, he becomes conscious on the most basic level of his freedom. He is neither tied fast to his past nor imprisoned in it: he is capable of alternatives that are open to the future. The dedication to an ideal gives him the staying power that he needs if he is to come through his life story without yielding to compromises.

The first requirement for gaining mastery over time is the ability to wait, but not in the sense of a passivity that allows the reins to slacken and thus runs headlong into situations of inevitable failure. Rather, the mastery of time gives a person the prudence to organize the situations of his life in such a way that he grows into the tasks that are set before him. There are of course spurts of growth that are triggered by new challenges, but there is nothing arbitrary about these. The challenges are prepared long beforehand, and his own thoughts have made him receptive to them. A strategy of action is at work that is not limited to the short-term organization of concrete situations. A person who has his life story in his own hands thinks in overarching contexts; he consciously and courageously thinks out beyond his own death because he is certain that his good will will get the chance to prove itself (even if this chance is different from what he expected). He is guided by an infallible moral instinct that recognizes in the concrete challenges the power of his own freedom, and he resolutely seizes it. This makes life livable.

Ethical conduct is genuinely related to knowing how to live. It makes possible a realistic relationship to a person's own self and to all those who cross her path and who may perhaps share very intensively in her life. Irrespective of the conditions in which a person lives, autonomy and self-consciousness are absolutely necessary if she is not to be crushed by the sheer weight of the dominant constellations. An ethical personality is not a burden on her neighbor. An ethical personality does not make others dependent on her; a fortiori, she does not employ the guise of a selfless dedication to create such a dependency in others, for dependencies drive people inevitably onto the defensive and may even result in an open rejection. Nor does an ethical personality feel driven to compel others to like her.

On the contrary: a pure inner disposition brings freedom. No thinking person is ever completely immune to self-doubts, but when these arise, she lays them confidently in the merciful hand of God. The art of pruning back her self-importance and arriving at a realistic self-assessment is bestowed only on the person whose grasp of the greatness of her goals progressively increases. Sometimes she will have the impression that her generosity is seen as mere good nature, and that it is being abused; but that is no catastrophe. She does indeed have a right to self-defense. This is demanded by the self-respect without which no one can live. But realism will not degenerate into a methodological skepticism. An ethical personality resists this temptation, because she knows all too well how much an inner reserve imposes a burden on human relationships (indeed, this attitude may well prevent human relationships from coming into existence in the first place). Great existential achievements, which require a sober naivety, are nipped in the bud, so to speak.

People grow gradually into ethical personalities. Often, the individual is not at all aware of this growth. It is only in retrospect that she sees that she has become someone else. Drastic events or demands serve to bring this insight to light. Here, more than anywhere else, it is true to say that everything takes time; and this means that we must be modest. The more intensive our experience of temporal transience, the happier will we be to realize that we have grown. A whole number of perspectives accompany this process. Let me mention a few of these here. We must emphasize at the very outset that there is a temporal correspondence between the height of the goal and the length of the path that leads to it. Before a person finds her definitive form, she must start out on many roads. The whole palette of qualities that she possesses makes the task of self-assessment more difficult. Nevertheless, the time she spends on learning this is never in vain. Even if only a small amount of the potential alternatives remains at the end, every insight and experience that a person gains contributes its own nuance to the rich profile that she acquires. One could speak in this context of the principle of superabundance: the period a person spends on learning is prodigal with its gifts, and this benefits the end product.

We have already said that a person must have an intellectual existential relationship to her own history. Events and happenings prompt reflection on her own self. This entails a change of perspective vis-à-vis the claim that norm-ethical reflection makes to exclusivity. Norms begin by assuming the normal case, and their basic competence is to regulate the normal case in a way that is capable of attracting a consensus. Unexpected situations, where the established norms appear not to offer sufficient help, are subject to the intellectual virtue of *epikeia*, which must contribute perspectives that take our reflection further and thus offer a constructive development of our understanding of the norms. In the period of learning, our thinking functions differently, because *epikeia* has the leading position here; the norms move on a derivative level. It is the extreme situation that is assumed a priori. Boundary situations and extreme cases are already included in one's calculations (though perhaps only in the background of conscious thought). This also includes the burdens that will arise, and this is why *epikeia* is always accompanied by magnanimity. A suspicion of rigorism here would be tantamount to saying that norm-ethical categories are sufficient for the understanding and regulation of a life history.

A spontaneous emotion is at work here, and the demands inevitably increase. One who sets out on such a learning process will be afraid lest she fails to grasp all the possibilities that exist: she is terrified, not by the thought of excessive challenges but by the thought that the challenges may not be great enough. It is here that truthfulness is put to the test. Nothing is harder than the evaluation of a person's own powers, and this is why the virtue of *epikeia* comes close to the intellectual honesty of the scientist who proposes a theory and submits it to the rigorous filter of experiments. Prejudices must be eliminated. An ethos of neutral objectivity must dominate, and this requires a sober self-evaluation.[10]

The Ability to Engage in Conflicts

In Thomas's thinking, *epikeia* serves to improve the law. This can succeed only if a person encounters friction at the boundaries of the law, but where his own mediocrity no longer perceives the boundaries that do in fact exist, this is the beginning of a decline. His life sinks down into an existence without tensions; he no longer dares to do anything new; timidity rules, rather than courage; the necessary ability to engage in conflicts is lacking. This is connected with the way in which interpersonal relationships take form, and a variety of constellations are possible here. For example, there is a kind of intolerance that has unrealistic expectations of those around us; in other words, our neighbor is required to be as we would like him to be. This attitude is based on a presumptuousness that is the unconfessed reason why we become less and less interested in our neighbor. Intolerance is a camouflaged flight, a capitulation before the claim that the otherness of the other person makes on us. It is all too easy to forget that every person who crosses the path of our lives is a gift, a chance for us to grow. The tendency to a self-sufficient isolation, which is always present, becomes stronger and makes us incapable of an encounter that would enrich us. We assiduously suppress the fact that our neighbor is a salutary lesson, prompting us to examine our conscience. We are unwilling to accept that we tend to meet precisely the kind of people we need—because the encounter with them brings to light our own unadmitted faults.

Accordingly, the ability to engage in conflicts means having the courage to make this admission. This does not in the least mean abandoning our own autonomy; modesty, or indeed humility, is perfectly compatible with autonomy. It then becomes a matter of course to grant our neighbor the freedom that he needs. We rejoice in the good that he does, and we take our share in this. But a weak personality pushes himself forward, curries favor and dispenses favors to compel others to give him the gratitude and devotion that he needs. In this way, he preempts all potential criticism: by bestowing favors, he brings his neighbor to silence. But reducing his neighbor to dependence is a sign of his own dependence. The predominant feeling is that he is under threat. This would in fact offer a good occasion to pose self-critical questions. With what good things in life is this experience connected? What are we in fact clinging to? Is it not also possible to grow through renunciation? Are those modes of self-realization that appear to be under threat truly indispensable for our own lives? Or are there alternatives that might even be better—alternatives that we have not yet had the courage to seize?

We demonstrate our ability to engage in conflicts when it is a matter of defending inalienable rights. The critical question is, what must be regarded as indispensable? It should certainly not be doubted that such rights exist; their definition is subject to objective standards of evaluation. To yield ground on this point would mean abandoning not only one's own dignity and self-respect but also the inalienable right to a truly humane life. Alongside such rights, however, there exists a wide freedom where the individual must exercise his own judgment. It is the task of *epikeia* to transform the act of judgment into an honest assessment of the possibilities of his own freedom. This cannot succeed where self-realization has tacitly been corrupted into the enforcement of one's own views at all costs. The ability to engage in conflicts is thus accompanied by the ability to accept suffering. It is only through suffering that one learns the potential of one's powers of resistance. Renunciations are no longer perceived as such, especially when they are undertaken in the service of an effective reconciliation.

This has nothing to do with being afraid to stand up and be counted. The person who stretches out his hand in reconciliation is not running away from the burden and the risk of resistance in order to surreptitiously acquire a good conscience at the thought of all he has renounced. Rather, a sober self-assessment and his knowledge of life have taught him that conflicts that are fought to the bitter end impose a tremendous burden on human relationships. He knows that we are all inclined to engage in an exaggerated polemic, and that we run the risk of unworthy motivations. We want to see our advantages confirmed and to consolidate them through our own actions. But even if a person is in fact in the right, he is entitled to be skeptical about attendant circumstances like these because they all too readily harden people's hearts instead of achieving reconciliation. Nor is a person really certain of the purity of his own attitude. This is why we should prefer to renounce the recourse to law; the obligation of proof lies on those who would argue the opposite. At the same time, our reflections look at our neighbor. How far is he able to sustain burdens? Does he possess the moral strength to work through a conflict that is now over, or will he be driven irresistibly into bitterness? An ethical personality is one who takes this into account. He must also see clearly through his own motives. Is he refraining from putting up the resistance that is required because he does not want to forfeit the sympathy of his adversary? This is a test of his own humility and of his readiness to admit his own share in the guilt that attaches to situations of conflict. The consciousness that he must render account before the judgment seat of God gives him the courage both to put up resistance and to do so with moderation.

The Ability to Integrate

An ethical personality is characterized by the ability to integrate. She knows instinctively that every act of erecting barriers in self-protection entails the dangers of impoverishment and of exhaustion. From this perspective too, every life history is a history of learning. We need the strength to expose ourselves to risks and to open ourselves to things that are unknown and may appear unsettling at first sight (here I have in mind not the quantity of things unknown but the intensity). What would I have become without the Other, without the permanent thorn in the flesh that his otherness represents? A considerable measure of intellectual honesty is required before a person can pose this question, especially where it involves the discussion of her own competence to make ethical judgments. Those who cross the path of her life, or accompany this path for lengthy periods, not only draw her attention to her human deficits, they convict her of moral fragility and point out wounds that she does not dare to admit even to herself. All this must be integrated, and she must react constructively—an attitude of resigned acceptance is inadequate. The ability to integrate means that she is capable of further development. Mere resignation does not give the power needed to get through the whole of her life; it leads ultimately to either apathy or hypocrisy. She must endure the tension between the "ideal self" and the "real self." The greater her commitment and involvement, the greater and the more painful will this discrepancy be. Without abandoning the ideals she once embraced, she must learn to accept courageously her limited possibilities. This dichotomy will endure, but she must not allow it to wear her down utterly, for then the story of her life could never be anything other than a catastrophe punctuated by rash explosions.

It follows that she must possess an *ars vivendi*, which gives her the courage to be self-critical, reducing an exaggerated view of herself and realistically acknowledging her own limitations. This is a necessary step, but it does not go far enough because it concerns only the external manner in which she lives her commitment; it does not inquire into the purity of the underlying attitude, which is essential for a successful formation of the personality. This is why the ability to integrate means that she must purify her motivation—otherwise she will despair, for it will be impossible to keep her own death in view and yet live confidently. Where do those false attitudes lie hidden—attitudes that never appear openly but insidiously and utterly poison all that she does, thus generating a life that remains unreconciled, no matter how much others may admire my achievements? This reflection may be prompted not so much by those around her as by the way in which she reacts to influences from those around her: the key lies in her own self. It is impossible to elude this test. Crises in the course of her life are particularly apt to uncover mercilessly the secret ways in which she has deceived herself or kept herself immune from risk. And such crises always cut off her potential escape routes.

The ability to integrate also allows her to practice the art of small steps. This is a kind of existential casuistry that resolutely does what is possible here and now in the hope that possibilities for further growth will present themselves in the future. When she accepts the present, she prepares the future. At this point, we may confidently refer back to the moral systems and the reflexive principles.[11] Reflection on one traditional theme led to the formulation *in dubio pro libertate*, but this cannot be simply transposed to a way of thinking that employs categories drawn from the life story of human persons because the underlying concept of "freedom" has a different meaning. It is not a question of freedom from legal stipulations that enjoy the presumption of authority but of freedom as a positive possibility of action. In cases of doubt, the presumption is on the side of a recognized competence (which in turn derives from the intensity of an emotion that both knows and thinks).

From this perspective, light is shed on a problem that is usually discussed under the heading of "incommensurable goods." In the context of the unavoidable evaluation of goods, obvious situations of checkmate can arise. This is always the case where incommensurable goods conflict with one another, and the only way to resolve the dilemma is to sacrifice one of them. This must however be looked at more closely. When conflicts of this kind occur, our thinking usually remains on a high level of abstraction: an irreconcilable antithesis is posited between life and freedom, or between success and friendship, and we cannot achieve the one at the cost of the other, unless we are willing to end up in a hopeless confusion of precisely those distinctions that must be respected if human living is not to collapse. All the various individual spheres possess their own autonomy, which must be protected—not leveled down. Where this respect is lacking, the human person is impoverished, and it is impossible for an ethical personality to come into being. To speak of incommensurable goods is thus a sign of a high culture of ethical thinking, where all our intellectual endeavor seeks to develop and maintain distinctions, rather than to break them down.

This, however, is only one aspect of the question. The ultimate aim that we pursue when we make all these distinctions is to discover a balance that is intellectually defensible—but also livable. In individual instances, therefore, we must define precisely what we understand the specific goods to mean: they have an inevitable abstraction that must be made concrete in life stories. This is because all the goods converge upon one single person and upon his or her basic self-understanding, that is, upon the conviction about what constitutes a comprehensively successful and humane life. We need to understand the various goods and relate them to one another without leveling them down. It must be possible for all who are involved, not only for one single party, to accept this solution. Conflict may indeed be unavoidable, but we must discover alternative forms of conduct that at least make it bearable. We must endeavor to transform the sacrifice of goods into a postponement of goods. This brings us to the core of the problem. Whenever we discern a constellation of incommensurable goods, we must look for alternative forms of conduct that point the way to a future resolution of the conflict. This is our basic responsibility, and we must ask what objective sacrifices and subjective commitment can be demanded to achieve this goal.[12]

The Indispensability of Normative Ethics

This underlines once more the urgency of reflection on ethical norms, and no moral theologian would seriously call this into question. Norms establish a safe structure. Only an intellectual arrogance would attempt to do without them—and the result would be an intolerable burden, especially in situations of conflict. We all need relief from burdens of this kind; no one is capable of thinking through every aspect of every conceivable constellation. A clear canalization of thought protects it from squandering its potential on insubstantial matters. Norms also compel us to be modest. They offer protection from the aggressive dictatorship of the big words to which we always have recourse when we cannot offer any convincing arguments to support our assertions. We know what is meant when ethical imperatives are formulated, and this is in fact the only way to speak responsibly in this field.

However, this is not the whole story. We certainly need to know exactly what it is we are communicating to one another, and the meaning of concepts must be clarified. We must resist the temptation of an intellectual flight—a person can employ concepts to establish wholly arbitrary connections, sparing herself the job of thought and making herself immune to any claims that might be made of her. This is linked to the protection of personal spontaneity; but this is possible only where she has a comprehensive overview. Norms concern segments of our varied lives, and they make orientation a realistic possibility. At the same time, they create a freedom that must be respected—but that brings about a "surplus" that goes beyond what can be foreseen by norms.

In this context, we must rethink the traditional distinction between commandments and counsels. Although this does offer protection against a lack of orientation, it also entails the danger of a normative rigorism that makes its appearance whenever we employ a univocal concept of norms. Even when a person follows a counsel, normative considerations are involved; but they cannot be generalized because the existential presuppositions are lacking. The distinction between commandment and counsel lies in the respective potential for generalization. When the inadequacy of norm-ethical reflection is criticized in the name of virtue ethics, the critic presupposes (without admitting to herself what she is doing) a concept of "norm" that cannot be justified in the light of her own tradition. In fact, the concept of norm is employed here in an analogous sense. This is why we must not press the word "freedom" too hard: there is nothing arbitrary about this freedom. The individual always remains under obligation, but this takes place in the form of a wholly personal imperative. To be an ethical personality means that one accepts this emotional commitment without reservations. One does not evade the burden by a recourse to general ethical norms.

Nevertheless, this analogous relationship is not static: work is in progress, so to speak. Norms do more than just define the substantial correctness of concrete behavior; and we must ask what this word "correctness" means. There is an obvious temptation to operate with a reduced idea that is borrowed from subpersonal reality. In that case, an ethos of substantial correctness would mean detaching the ethical judgment from all the subjective conditions of the one to whom it is addressed, including the prejudices and the limitation of freedom that have always occurred. To think in this way does not do justice to the full reality of morality because its starting point is a reduced metaphysics of ethical behavior that begins its reflection with empirically objective phenomena and presupposes the immanent rationality of reality. The consequence is that the acts of knowing and willing move over to the side of the psychology of ethical behavior so that an object–subject pattern is established that corresponds exactly to the distinction between metaphysics and psychology. This makes it impossible to construct an inherently coherent metaphysics of conduct that embraces equally the inner and the outer spheres, the intention and the performance of the action. The one sphere communicates with the other; the person who acts differently is also doing something different, although it is difficult to perceive this. But norms do not stop short at the external phenomena; they claim to regulate the action as a unity, as a complex totality.

At this point we should note a perspective that concerns the relationship between person and norm. Persons accept existing norms and make them their own; at the same time, they keep these norms in motion. A person who grows into an ethical personality in the course of his life history brings with him a "surplus" of insight and freedom that leaves its traces upon the customary understanding of norms. This is done with respect and tolerance, for what is born of higher insight and freedom can in turn lead only to higher insight and freedom. It becomes easier for the members of a fellowship of ethical communication to act. The conditions under which they act are not a law of nature but have been tested in human history. When norms are viewed as isolated propositions, they never yield full information about their meaning for praxis: they need to be complemented by approved praxis. Often it is only in retrospect that one recognizes the existence of an influence of this kind.

Standing Firm in the Truth

The Analogy of the Truth

The use of personalistic categories brings us back to the question of the truth. It is not legitimate to speak of "person" and "ethical personality" as long as the relationship to the truth remains unclarified. If we thought of "person" without any reference to the truth, this would necessarily end in an epistemological-anthropological torso. This becomes particularly significant when the practical dealings with the truth become a problem, for it is here above all that one must prove one's moral worth. It is in the lived and responsible relationship to the truth that we see the most genuine and vivid reflection of the ethical personality's relationship to his or her own self. It is thus not surprising that the moral theologian senses that this issue concerns him. If his reflections pass it by, he will be making a detour around a central question of his own academic discipline and a crucial point of successful human existence.

We are therefore entitled to be astonished at the small amount of intellectual energy that the moral theological tradition has devoted to this area. There is of course no doubt that the tradition has endeavored to find viable solutions to particular cases, but it has not pursued an intellectual project in the form of the speculative elaboration of an ethos of truthfulness. Lost ground must be made up here; we must regain credibility. Clearly, we lack a fundamental reflection on truth and truthfulness, the cornerstone on which the construction of an ethical personality is based.[13] In comparison, all the other problems of moral theology remain on the periphery. The guiding ideas of a comprehensively successful life, of personal dignity and self-respect, and of what constitutes a wholly personal happiness cannot be detached from the truth; there is no human fulfillment that passes by the truth. These remarks indicate the perspective that will govern the following discussions. We shall attempt to consistently continue the approach that has been developed up to this point and to present the basic elements of a personal metaphysics that can be harmoniously combined with the metaphysics of knowledge and the theory of the truth.

The truth lies outside our control. It always lies ahead of the act whereby we seek to take hold of it and know it, and no human being has power over it, since it is always greater than he is.[14] These words may appear so obvious that they are virtually a platitude, but a further differentiation is required, for in this form they offer little that is relevant to the moral theologian. First we must speak of the analogy of the truth. Various classes of truth encounter the act of human knowing and challenge it in distinctive ways. For example, there are factual truths that sometimes have the status of objective truths and sometimes that of historical truths. Our relationship to these truths is receptive, although it must be admitted that there is an unavoidable element of interpretation in historical truths. The clearer the relationship to the existential human world, the more strongly does the accompanying interpretation move into the foreground, and passive reception mingles with an active shaping—although the latter cannot be accused of attempting to "control" the truth. Rather, it is in the act of knowing that one makes one's own contribution to factual truths by locating them within a previously existing epistemological framework, even if this framework does not always find an unambiguous verbal formulation.

In addition to this, there are truths of meaning that have their place in the fundamental affirmations of a metaphysical anthropology. Through these (unlike the factual truths) a new element is introduced. It is unquestionable that "meaning" is open to insight. There is no risk of misunderstanding if we speak of "intuition" on this level because the intuition meant here remains open to further development in reflection and exposes itself to public control through an argument that is generally comprehensible. The intellectual endeavor penetrates the full meaning of truths of meaning in a permanent exchange and a mutual corrective. Definitions must be made. Concepts must be mapped out precisely if communication is not to be squandered on inessential issues. The result is a reciprocal process of growth that can be described as the paradigm of an intense movement. This process is inconceivable without the knowledge of facts because it is in the medium of facts that meaning is recognized.

This makes interpretation all the more significant: facts exist in a context of interpretation that both encompasses them and transcends them. What now appears to be a factual truth is the outcome of an interpretation: indeed, it is *constituted* by interpretation. This, however, implies openness to the process of interpretation since facts per se remain underdefined. This deficit is made good by an interpretation based on an insight into meaning. Unsurprisingly, this structure can be seen most clearly in a truth of faith: the truth about God and what he does in relation to the human person can be attained only in the medium of human self-understanding. Salvation is indeed tied to facts, but the truth that these facts contain is the fruit of interpretation. The community of believers is originally a community of interpretation. A meaning is ascribed to facts, and therein lies the reality of the facts. When a transformation of reality takes place, this is a work of interpretation. One who thinks in physical-objective categories can never comprehend this event.[15]

The Specific Character of Ethical Truth

In this context, ethical truth deserves special consideration. One who adopts a cognitivist standpoint will find a warm welcome among moral theologians. Ethical truth is not the product of an arbitrary decision that would be exempt from control by the intellect. A consistent decisionism would be completely incompatible with our own moral theological tradition.[16] However, this does not suffice to clarify the epistemic status of ethical truth. What precisely is meant here by comprehensibility and communicability?

First we must emphasize that the specific object of ethical reason is the good. However, the convergence of the true and the good—which is typical of ethical truth—presupposes the Scholastic doctrine of transcendentals.[17] It seems worth mentioning this specifically because in this context the good is thought of on the level of metaphysics. The claim made by ethical truth is absolute and exempt from control by the human person because it is based on Being. Criticism of this position presupposes a superficial concept of Being, and thus a reductionist understanding of metaphysics. Being is tacitly reduced to the existent, and transcendence degenerates into an abstraction that is technically devoid of content. As I have already said, the metaphysics of the ethical good is transformed surreptitiously into a psychology.[18]

It is not surprising that such a proceeding poses problems with regard to communication. At most, one can achieve a consensus about what is ethically correct and about the contents of norms, but the subjective sensitivity of the human person is consistently ignored. There is of course no doubt that this development has its good aspects. It followed models from the natural sciences and jurisprudence, but (whatever first impressions might suggest) this did not lead to naturalism or juridicism. Rather, this development accepted the legitimate concern to have certainty about whether one's actions were right or wrong and endeavored to provide this certainty, but it could not solve all the problems because it necessarily overlooked the fact that communication is more than handing on information about clearly defined and verifiable contents. Communication also includes the existential world of the partners and allows the other to share in this world. Communication means uncovering all the presuppositions in the subject that are relevant to the success of the communication: not only anthropological options (including the guiding ideas of a meaningfully successful life) but also the possibilities of freedom (under-stood as the competence for self-determination and self-possession). Only an ethical personality is capable of facing the challenges of ethical communication.

The ethically good is linked immediately and originally to the good that consists in a fulfilled life; this allows us to see what is meant by the "ethically good." There is a radical unity here that does not in the least signify a merging (and still less a leveling down) of the differences. This unity develops into the consistent realiza-tion of individual human goods in a twofold sense. In terms of correctness, the criterion is the good of a fulfilled life; conversely, the goodness takes effect via the various ideas about ethical value. This is the presupposition that makes normative propositions possible at all, and the normative propositions make this procedure communicable. Communication begins with norms, but it is not limited to the presentation and reception of norms; rather, it invites us to reflect further on these norms. This reflection begins with that evaluation of goods that is available in coagulated form, so to speak, in the norms. To accuse this evaluation of goods of relativism would be to misunderstand the specific character of the procedure. The intellectual reference back to the underlying fundamental good is not abrogated; on the contrary, it is confirmed again and again. Accordingly, the human person does not exercise control over the fundamental good since it is laid down in advance and the instrumental reason is unable to seize the good and bend it to its own plans.[19]

We must not overlook the fact that this reference back to the fundamental goods also contains an element of relativization, but this means something quite different from what is commonly supposed. If the individual good is to avoid an inappropriate absolutization, it must demonstrate its character of service vis-à-vis the fundamental good. The aim of the evaluation of goods is to grasp in a more appropriate manner the absoluteness of the ethical, avoiding the mistake of an absolutization of individual aspects. Only then can we see the true significance of the individual human good. Such a procedure would be unimaginable without an accompanying interpretation. The reference back to the fundamental goods finds expression in the significance that is attributed to the individual goods. Evaluation is possible only thanks to interpretation—and this is precisely what we mean when we speak of the evaluation of goods. In short, the accusation of relativism is unfounded. Rather, the reference back to the fundamental good of a comprehen-sively successful good life offers a sure guarantee that every individual human good can throw his or her own full weight onto the scales. Here, relativization means completion, and the criteria of the evaluation are differentiated in the course of this process.

Intellectual fairness requires increasing precision in view of the danger of mak-ing excessive demands of human freedom. Here we must respond to the accusation of a technicist thinking. It is indeed true that moral theology has been influenced by academic ideals that are foreign to this discipline, but this has not had a purely negative effect on moral theology—on the contrary, the result is a more acute discernment. The more precise a normative statement, the greater is the respect for the freedom of the one to whom it is addressed, provided that this general increase in precision combines the sympathetic assessment of the individual good with an exact analysis of the situation.

I have already mentioned the relationship between intuition and reflection, and we must now return to this topic in the context of ethical truth. The ethical good, the contents of which are classified by means of various ideas about value, is first the object of intuition, since the human person necessarily encounters it as something already in existence. However, we must resist an inappropriate exaltation of intuition that fails to do justice to the reality of the act of knowing in history since this opens the door to disastrous false inferences in the field of gnoseology—and these inevitably end in an uncontrollable dogmatism. We need a reflection that penetrates the significance of ideas about value while at the same time making the link to the guiding ideas about a successful life, and to pre-ethical (but ethically relevant) human goods. This is the only viable path to communication and a responsible consensus.

But what kind of reflection is meant here? There can be no doubt that inferential thinking plays a major role here since, despite all its dynamism, the coherence of the system must always be ensured. But a decisive role is also played by the effort to define and uncover the truth, an endeavor that goes hand in hand with experience, with knowledge of life, and indeed with wisdom. Thoughtfulness is required because the truth discloses itself only to the one who is patient. This is presupposed by those norms of ethical conduct that give expression to a consensus. These store a potential for insight and experience that has proved its worth over the course of time. It would be quite wrong to see these norms only as directives for correct behavior since we would then be constructing the normative discourse programmatically on the conceptual *distinction* between goodness and correctness—and that would be too little. It is of course indisputable that norms are primarily concerned to ensure the appropriateness and correctness of conduct, not only because we need a general certainty about our actions but also (as I have said earlier) out of respect for the freedom of the individual. At the same time, however, norms presuppose a *convergence* between goodness and correctness; neither of these is livable without the other. No matter how good a person's intention may be, he can err in individual instances, but the assumption is that he will not in fact err. Where goodness holds sway, he acquires a fundamental correctness in general terms, at least within the context of his own knowledge. This idea is significant for the construction of a consensus because it contains a potential for freedom, a power to do what he has recognized to be good—a power that is presupposed and is genuinely present. In this sense norms also protect the goodness of the one to whom they are addressed. They cannot be separated from the good will.

It is therefore wrong to accuse reflections on ethical norms of an obsession with feasibility. This accusation is in fact completely inappropriate, especially when it is accompanied by an exaltation of virtue ethics.[20] Naturally, norms cannot dispense with the virtues, nor do they seek to do so. But norms are characterized by a healthy realism. The realistic theory of knowledge, which is indispensable, generates a realistic theory of freedom. The norm ethicist is not only concerned with the appropriateness of action but also with what is conducive to freedom. He seeks to avoid making excessive demands of human beings. This has nothing to do with minimalism, and still less with legalism. Rather, in each specific situation, the foundation stone for a higher commitment is to be laid. Accordingly, norms can be equated with frameworks that open up a free space for further existential evaluations. But this too remains in principle within the framework of normative reflections; the concept of "norm" is misunderstood whenever it is guided by a mechanical principle of generalization. One fails to perceive that there are wholly personal norms that cannot be generalized without any further differentiations because the presuppositions with regard to freedom are not present.

The ethical personality must exercise discernment here, a discernment that takes the form of the gift of discernment of spirits with which we are familiar from spiritual theology. This allows us to decide what demands we can and may make of ourselves, and what existential goods must be sacrificed if we are to lead consistently the life that we want to lead, but without thereby abandoning spiritually mature ideas about happiness. The discernment of spirits has the task of identifying the *bonum conveniens* that matches the measure of a person's own religious and ethical commitment; this *bonum conveniens* is the certain guarantee that the individual is doing the good for its own sake. The individual will have a good conscience when he lives in accordance with a freedom that is understood in this manner. This is the supreme illustration of the fact that ethical truth is of its very nature a free truth.

We must avoid giving the impression that the individual acts on his own here. On the contrary, as I have indicated, the whole panorama of ethical norms is engaged in an unending dialogue between the various arguments and existential testimonies. Consensus keeps norms in movement; it is more than a mere record of a past that is over and done with. Let me give some examples. The discernment of an ethical personality is not exercised only in assuming the existential responsibility for ethical progress by means of an analysis of standards of freedom since the outcome could all too easily be an intolerable rigorism. If we wish to improve norms, therefore, we must take into account the totality of their existential presuppositions. I have written that ethical reflection includes an element of sapiential consideration; it is not merely the elucidation of clever proofs. This observation is connected to a perspective that usually receives short shrift, that is, that ethical progress makes action easier. It becomes easier for the spontaneous "surplus" of freedom to act, and the intellectual horizon is widened. This daily phenomenon in the life story of the individual has a corresponding reality in the community of ethical communication. Ways of making life easier are discovered in the course of a person's life history, and he learns how to dismantle intellectual obsessions so that he is no longer a prisoner in the self-created dungeon of the soul. Reflection on these existential experiences encourages us to move onto new, liberating levels and to distance ourselves from sore points. It is virtually impossible to heal the wounds that life brings by tackling these directly; all this does is to make the situation worse. Rather, he must acquire certainties that promise well for the future, thus sparing himself unnecessary disappointments and altering his fundamental attitude to life. The same thing happens in the framework of the ethical communication between human beings and in the institutions of society. Ethical elites have a perceptible influence: models of a fulfilled life that are lived out by others, and that have been thought through on the intellectual level, give one's contemporaries food for thought, inviting them and empowering them to dare to change their own lives to attain the promises.

Theories of Truth and Ethical Pluralism

These considerations require us to ask, on what theory of truth is ethical truth based?[21] Moral theology generally assumes the Aristotelian theory of exact correspondence: *veritas est adaequatio intellectus et rei*. In other words, truth consists in the exact agreement between the act of knowing and the object of this act. Truth is a formal relationship. There can be no doubt of the validity of this theory on which all our further reflections are based. Nor can there be any doubt that ethical truth contains an a priori element that is not at the disposal of the human person— otherwise it would be impossible for ethical truth to impose absolute obligations. There are thus good reasons for emphasizing that the act of ethical *knowing* is also an act of *accepting*.

However, we cannot be content with this kind of reference to traditional positions since we cannot exclude the risk of intellectual reductionisms. We must go into greater detail. Theories about truth and theories about knowledge interlock: each points to the other. Our first question must be, in what sense (if any) may we say that the act of ethical knowing posits something? Are we in fact faced with two complementary aspects here, each of which involves one particular problem? In our discussion of the concept of person, we have already seen one central concept of the scholastic metaphysics of knowledge, namely the proleptic outreach of the spirit to Being as the true and the good. Here accepting and positing merge into one another. The act of knowing is in accordance with the transcendental definitions of Being.[22]

When this is granted, we can move on to look at the present problem. To begin with, there is an act of positing with regard to the empirically existing world of objects. The *intellectus agens* opens this world up so that it can be discerned. This, however, gives us only one building brick of ethical knowledge, and certainly not the decisive one. The point lies in the ability of ethical reason to define the underdefined nature of the person. Any suspicion of decisionism here proves unfounded because it is existence in the fullness of Being that empowers ethical reason to undertake this task. The competence of the spirit lies precisely in the act of definition. Order is imposed upon an existing reality, order is read into it. This is what Saint Thomas calls the *ordinatio rationis*.[23]

However, this idea too is inadequate. Indeed, it is highly unsatisfactory since it does not do justice to the specific character of ethical truth. Empirical experience cannot be limited to the objective phenomenon of human nature since it also includes an existential dimension of action, and this is essential to the act of ethical knowing. Here too, there is something "underdefined," but the meaning of this term is completely different: it is the opposite concept to freedom, understood as the existing and intellectually ordered power to do the good. Defining means creating free spaces for action. A project of freedom is applied to the underdefined nature. It is only on this presupposition that freedom can be called normative. Seen in this light, freedom is the transcendental precondition of truth. If we combine all these perspectives, they permit us to operate in a less harmful manner with the positing character of the act of ethical knowing.

Once again, the community of consensus has an influence here: in the act of positing the truth, understood in this way, a community of ethical communication asserts itself.[24] A community makes discourse possible, by virtue of the fact that all its members can make contact with one another. Ethical personalities are the driving force here because they possess the necessary intellectual breadth and lack of prejudice—in short, because they are willing to learn and do not regard as dangerous the possibility that new points of view may emerge. This is comparable to the pieces of a mosaic, which only gradually grow together to form a recognizable picture. In such a procedure, the formation of hypotheses is inevitable. Such hypotheses reflect the fragmentary nature of our knowledge; and ethical reason cannot dispense with assumptions and reservations. But we must not forget the reverse side of the medal, the necessary limitation on the discourse: if there is no limitation on questions, the consensus that has been achieved will be dissolved into insubstantiality. The individual must learn to live with this! Conversely, this fact does not in the least dispense him from responsibility for a constructive promotion of the discourse. He may indeed know that the achievement of a consensus removes a burden from his freedom, and that only such a consensus makes relaxed and spontaneous decisions possible; nevertheless, he is oppressed by the fear that such a consensus might no longer do justice to the changed demands of a new situation and to the greater differentiation of thinking, so that the consensus would have a fatal impact on the individual and on the community. Usually this work of revision takes place in the realm of concrete issues since it is always specific unanswered questions, and situations of conflict under which we suffer, that compel us to engage in further reflection.

This means that a community of communication cannot avoid enforcing specific evaluations. Its own self-respect depends on its ability to do so. If a community were to be content only with statements indicating a general framework, it would collapse before the onslaught of the counterforce. This would lead to the self-dissolution of the community. Concrete stipulations can of course change in the course of history, but this fact does not make them any less necessary.

All this poses a question vis-à-vis the obvious phenomenon of ethical pluralism. The thoughtful observer notices a great variety of forms. There is certainly a broad palette of anthropological approaches. These various approaches need not in every case generate ethical differences, but it is very easy for them to do so in situations of conflict. We must also bear in mind that there is a correspondence between anthropological premises and ethical positions, although we cannot speak of necessary inferences from the one to the other. We can therefore certainly envisage a case where, despite different premises, the opposite occurs—that is, a shared ethical position on very specific questions. Finally, we must not forget the (at least relational) autonomy of ethical reason. In any case, we cannot avoid the question of the dignity and relevance of these premises since the critical comparison of ethical positions involves their premises: are there qualitative differences between them, and what criteria can be employed to measure these?

This is where the natural law reflection begins, and we can see its immanent dynamic. Since it is at the service of universal communication, natural law reflection must endeavor to clear away by means of argumentation all those differences that are due to defective presuppositions. On this level, ethical pluralism must be overcome resolutely, not only because there is only one truth but also a fortiori out of respect for the dignity of the human person who may not be deprived of his full existential possibilities in the name of "tolerance."

But this is only one aspect. Ethical pluralism can also be caused by other factors. The immanent historicity of ethical reason means that we must assume that risks will be involved. Lines of argumentation may have true premises and yet be erroneous; there is a risk of self-deception. We also encounter what we might call a noncontemporaneous rhythm of processes of insight in the sense that the time is not yet ripe for one particular insight. Here too the natural law reflection has a specific task that never ends, namely that of correcting and of achieving a balance. This too is required by tolerance, which includes the readiness to learn and an awareness of history as well as the ability to wait. Tolerance is a virtue of critical solidarity, a virtue of those who accompany each other *in via*. Tolerance must not be practiced at the cost of freedom; its basis is the unshaken trust that each individual is willing to embrace the truth. It is thus understandable that the strategy of communities of ethical communication includes a preferential option for the institutional preconditions of the knowledge of the truth and is less interested in proclaiming individual truths. This is due to the fear that instead of encouraging an increase in insights, one may in fact help to keep these on a low level.

Finally, we should mention that ethical pluralism can also be an expression of the creative imagination of ethical reason. The one undivided truth presents itself to the eye of the observer in the undiminished wealth of its many facets, and this means that the observer discovers many different paths to this truth. For this reason cultural patterns have an absolutely essential task of mediation. This contributes a further nuance to the natural law reflection and argumentation in the course of which we must undertake hermeneutical investigations into the relationship between the individual ethical truth and its specific cultural milieu. What is legitimate in the specific circumstances? This shows that ethical pluralism takes many forms. For the moral theologian, ethical pluralism certainly need not carry connotations of intellectual resignation, nor need it kindle suspicion that the unity of the truth has been surreptitiously abandoned. Ethical pluralism can express respect for the varying conditions under which people arrive at the knowledge of the truth, and can thus be regarded as a transitional stage leading to an ever better mutual understanding. The essential concern of the traditional doctrine of the ethical natural law finds expression in this humanitarian ideal, which it exists to serve.[25]

The phenomenon of ethical pluralism thus compels us to examine carefully the justification of ethical claims, especially in situations of conflict that demand an exceptional measure of active involvement. Let us begin by emphasizing that moral theology has a professional orientation to problems, so to speak. Moral theologians are active where new uncertainties break out, where hitherto neglected points of view dominate the discourse and make it necessary to nuance one's previous judgment. I hasten to add that this last sentence risks distorting our perspective, for the ethical consensus is in fact much greater than is commonly supposed. Certainly, the questions that are under discussion form an exception, but it is possible to ask these questions only because a basic undiscussed truth is present a priori, a truth that no one need justify.

This last affirmation implies that moral theology must always inquire into its own tradition. The first question, therefore, is whether the past contains models that we can apply to find a solution to contemporary problems. The moral theologian presupposes at the very least that he can discover in the tradition indications and clues that are worth pondering, even if these may be in need of further development. This is true of specific areas in which human beings are faced with challenges, but it is even truer of those views of life and fundamental attitudes that generate a kind of antecedent knowledge that allows us to live responsibly. This is a realistic formulation since the requirement to justify moral theological positions generates a great deal that lies outside the sphere of the daily experience of life with its unavoidable ordinariness (or indeed, its banalities) and that belongs rather to the sphere of a lofty intellectual ethos that touches the life of the individual only tangentially. This is no reason to drop the reins of the intellectual endeavor and dispense oneself from the responsible task of thinking; after all, it is usually via the confrontation with normal situations that we prepare ourselves to stand the test of border situations.

Attitudes to life that say something about the contents of one's own life must take shape. A person must know what she is living for before she gets actively involved; otherwise she will end up with a bitter disappointment that hastens on the progressive decline of her ethical vigor. This can be prevented by ideals for living that kindle her enthusiasm. We should not underestimate the appropriateness and correctness of individual normative solutions because this entails both certainty in one's conduct and respect for individual freedom. Intellectual honesty requires us to reflect on norms, especially in view of new situations that have not been evaluated hitherto. But this can be meaningful only where there already exists a basic certainty about the right way to live; in that case, the individual solution will not be completely wrong.

The Potential of the Tradition with Regard to Human Life Stories

The existing moral tradition is made up of life stories on which theologians have reflected. In this context, it would not be wrong to speak of the fates that have befallen human beings. These must never be forgotten. Forgetfulness of history is the death of ethical thinking; intellectual acuteness on its own does not suffice for the formation of ethical judgments. This is why the justification of ethical judgments includes remembering. It is all too easy for us to suppress the past; without the past, it is easier to think, but this does not make our thoughts any truer. This means that the moral theologian, as the representative of one particular theological discipline, cannot do without an immanent hermeneutic of his own discipline. He must know how the categories in which it is natural for him to think actually arose: What was their existential background, and what contemporary problems and urgencies are present in them? If he lacks this knowledge, he risks developing a faulty consciousness of the problems he is studying. And this may lead him to give answers to questions that have long ceased to be questions. This, however, is the death of an academic discipline, when it is oriented only to intellectual husks devoid of content and fails to respond to the claims made by the present day. This risk ought to inculcate a salutary unease. Anyone who remains untouched by this unease is not meeting the demands of his academic discipline. The awkward fullness of reality must rip open the limitations of our categories. One who does not take this principle to heart is no theological personality; at most, he or she is a learned scholar.

Another component in the work of justification is connected with a person's life story, because every moral theologian reflects nolens volens on the course of his own life and measures individual theoretical solutions against his own ethical praxis. Does he genuinely recognize his own self in this thinking? No doubt, a skeptical reserve is a good thing when one speaks of theology as a biography on which one has reflected, for this opens the door to an aggressive subjectivism that would veer off into tactlessness and achieve the opposite of what one (rightly) intended. This is why nothing is more beneficial to moral theology than reserved reflection; no one desires to be talked round or placed under constraint by another person's eloquence. Objectivity is a wholesome protective shield here, and it is more necessary the higher the authority of the person involved. Nevertheless, the link to one's own life story remains, for where does theology come from if not out of life stories?

This means that we must first consider the temporal dimension since the experience of time is the most original experience of all. The vividness of this experience increases as we grow older. What does this mean? If one is to recognize the ethical claim in a manner free of all falsification, every reflective person has an existential task that the circumstances of his life compel him to perform. There are key events that cannot turn out well without an ethical confrontation. They compel a person very forcibly to ask what the goal of his life is, whether he is able to mobilize any greater resources of strength, or whether he is living on the edge of his own possibilities so that every further step leads into the abyss. Are his expectations of what is commonly called a happy life unrealistic? Do these expectations distract him from essential reality? A life can miss its target—indeed, it can be utterly spoiled—because a person always passes himself by and has never found his own self.

The experience of time takes very different forms in the course of a life story. In youth, a person has a carefree relationship to her time, and she is far from thinking or feeling that time is the most precious human possession. This changes as she grows older. The end of her time compels her to an utterly honest truthfulness, and the approach of death urges her to live intensely, to make the most of time. This necessarily affects the purity of ethical knowledge. I am not thinking here so much of insight into ideas of ethical value: this insight must be considered independent of time since it depends at its source on the purity of a person's dispositions and on a person's relationship to the truth. Rather, the temporal dimension emerges clearly when a person tries to mediate between the governing anthropological ideas and her own life. The wisdom that is born of life is absolutely necessary here: ultimately, it is this wisdom—not thinking in the categories of purely objective laws, essential as this always is—that decides all the relevant evaluations of goods; this is all the more true when these goods are person-centered and thus bring the possibility of acting in a way that expresses our own self. The approach of death permits us to achieve a wholesome distance vis-à-vis inner-worldly ideas about happiness. We see our lives in contexts that go beyond the calculable moment and include the hope of immortality.

Normative affirmations are not capable of expressing all that such a process entails. This process cannot be directly universalized. Rather, the individual alone must take responsibility for it. Nevertheless, the spark leaps over to one's neighbor, even if only in the form of an invitation, an appeal. The spark communicates itself by providing food for thought. It gives an extra knowledge that does not insist on being translated into action but is like an unobtrusive friend who is there whenever he is needed. The wisdom born of life allows ethical reason to recognize the good more purely, and it empowers our freedom to do the good for the sake of the good. This does not in the least mean a renunciation, for an ethic of that kind would be inhuman. On the contrary, it means an increasing spiritualization. This affects our strategies for action, especially when we have to make sacrifices. The intellect on its own is incapable of discerning what makes life worth living; we must set out on a lifelong process of thinking that profits from the sapiential traditions.

Ethical Knowledge in the Medium of Time

The temporal dimension gives our freedom the possibility of growth. Everything takes time, and this is true on the level of ethics as well. Every attempt at justifying ethical principles will be unrealistic if it suppresses the factor of time in the history of the individual's development. Everyone experiences that he grows into the ability to respond to ethical claims. The internal consistency of his freedom grows, and his behavior is marked by an increasing self-confidence even when he must master difficult situations. A person becomes most clearly aware of this when drastic changes in his life story begin and obvious spurts of growth suddenly reveal the limitations of the past. Wherever someone takes responsibility for his activity in alertness of mind and eager anticipation, the possibilities for freedom are extended. Previously, his attention was directed to sore points, but now he is fascinated by new possibilities. This is comparable to a paradigm shift: all at once, he no longer understands the past; he glimpses better solutions to problems, and these solutions bestow automatically, so to speak, the consciousness of a fulfilled human existence.

A number of perspectives show us the wealth of facets in this process. Moral theological reflection has perhaps paid too little attention to the fact that an existential drama is unfolding here, in which the individual risks everything since the burden lies on his shoulders alone. Norms and institutions do indeed offer relief, but only to a certain extent since they always break down when we must venture out onto new ground. This means that we are not wrong to speak of the testimony of a life, a testimony that is put to the test above all when, in addition to the price we have already paid in terms of our commitment, we must also reckon on misunderstandings and even on serious trouble. In this situation, the strength of an ethical personality determines the outcome. If new insights are to win acceptance, we must be willing to think beyond our own death. Institutions, on the other hand, always move slowly, and they can lose their credibility because the relief that they provide is always linked to an abstraction. Unlike the individual, institutions risk nothing, and this makes them lazy and self-satisfied with regard to established ways of thinking and patterns of argumentation. Institutions are always the last to undertake the work of revision. Only the person who is obliged to think will actually do so, for he sees his personal identity vanishing, and if he does not think, he will not survive. This is why the degree of moral credibility is in inverse proportion to the amount of power that a person or institution possesses.

Experiencing time also means learning to live with one's own boundaries. Every life story contains what we might call a positive resignation; this is something that must be learned—painfully. The more clearly a person recognizes what is possible for freedom and what promotes her own existential project, the more will she be oppressed by the awareness of the impossible, that which will never take shape. The ethical élan would be crushed if this insight were to cause a person to lose the self-respect she owes herself; what we need here is a calm composure, and this is bestowed only on those who are masters of their appointed lifespan. The dialectic of the experience of time is in the background here. The inexorable passing of time brings about a wholesome shock and at the same time invites us to live with concentrated intensity, in our mind tasting to the full each moment of the life that we are given. There are experiences of happiness bound to one particular moment that allow us to ignore long periods of grief and renunciation—it is as if we were simply flying above them. Even a past that we seem to have made a mess of can be obliterated in this way, thanks to the staying power that leads us out of existential crises (whether these are our own fault, or are inflicted on us from the outside). One very important element in meeting the test of life is the refusal to abandon this hope. Without this hope, there will be no fulfilled life. And we can ask whether it is in fact possible to live with the mistakes we have made, whether there exists an art of "coming to terms" that tries to make the best of the remaining possibilities because the alternatives may entail higher risks.

At this point, however, moral theology enters realms that are not accessible to an abstract "drawing board" way of thinking. The only solutions are asymptotic, and this makes the reflex principles more important.[26] The presumption is in favor of continuity in one's own life project since this allows one to look for paths and modes that can make life easier; exceptions bear the burden of proof and are legitimate only when all the available possibilities for freedom have been exhausted. In this context, let us recall the axiom *facienti quod in se est Deus non denegat gratiam* ("God does not deny grace to one who does what is in his power"). The contents of the *in se* depend on the one concerned. The community of ethical communication can do nothing more for him—but also nothing less—than make proposals for action. This demands a high degree of truthfulness. Boundary situations of this kind reveal the ethical substance of a person. In the whole of his life story, there may perhaps be no more urgent test of truth. At the same time, however, truthfulness means that one never suppresses this experience.

Living with boundaries prompts reflection on the law of graduality. Is it possible to apply this law without succumbing to the obvious temptation of cheap self-deception? At any rate, a person cannot simply dismiss the risk of becoming an eloquent advocate in her own defense, so eloquent that she drowns out the admonitory voice of conscience. Her neighbor too is instrumentalized: he is of value only if he supports one's own prejudices. Everyone tends to seek allies of this sort, who spare her the annoyance of self-criticism, but she forgets here that the foe is often her best friend, since he possesses the freedom necessary to engage in a confrontation.

Even when this is admitted, however, the question formulated earlier remains valid. I have already said that reflection on ethical norms is indispensable: without the intellectual courage that precision requires, moral praxis declines into savagery, especially when inalienable legal goods must be protected. The concept of law is analogous here: it refers not only to individual goods, since the good of a meaningful life generates a much more fundamental legal claim. To renounce this claim would mean abdicating the respect one owes one's own self. Norms lend support to this claim, even if this support may be difficult to decipher. The word "law" is central here. Normative affirmations reflect the profound hermeneutical reference to that basic law, in which the law of graduality plays its own role. Accordingly, the precision of norms is ambivalent. It brings a relief from burdens since this precision allows us to know spontaneously what demands we can make of ourselves—for when substantial claims are made of us, these always include the claim that this or that may legitimately be demanded of us, and it is not possible to have direct knowledge of this claim. Nevertheless, we cannot completely overlook the burdens connected with norms since these burdens tend to emerge where the boundary between norm and ideal becomes porous (or even totally fluid).

Does not an institution all too easily yield to the temptation to extend the claims of ethical norms, even when this is done with the good intention of giving people certainty about the correctness of their actions? Ideals are transformed into norms because this is the only way to achieve a maximum societal presence, and the contours of one's own group identity are sharpened. However, this strategy is not without its problems. It forgets the fact that norms can never control more than a part of the processes that unfold in the course of a life story. Too much normativity brings about the opposite of what is intended. It blocks processes of growth instead of promoting them. It therefore seems more important to elaborate heuristic models and to investigate the guiding concerns that lie behind ideas about ethical values. Inspiration is the best moral help, since it *invites* people. And this is what we need when we must hold our own in the moral combat. A life story degenerates into triviality when a person no longer fights battles, when she is no longer irritated by boundaries. But this can be recognized in complete truthfulness only by a person who is inspired by hope to take hold of what is possible in the here and now, by a person who knows that a morality of small steps is more honest than a "drawing board" morality, no matter how irreproachable its façade may be.

The Perpetual Tension between Being and Knowing

We have seen that the justification of ethical claims may not suppress the dimension of time; that, in other words, experience is a necessary component in this act of justification. This however does not mean some vague "existentialization" of thinking that would sacrifice intellectual honesty.[27] Justification entails getting to the bottom of something on the ontological level and inquiring into the invisible foundations of phenomena. And since the phenomena are capable of a variety of interpretations, the decisive thing is the meaning that is attributed to them. Interpretation is the key word here: justifying goes together with interpreting, and this is what we must now discuss. The reasons put forward in support of the validity of an ethical claim must be utterly transparent, down to their ultimate ground.

Every science studies the question of this "ground." In moral theology, this question implies a further question: how do we understand metaphysics? What concept of Being are all the arguments based on? If Being is understood as the fullness of all individual determinations, we have already decided a priori how the work of justification is to be undertaken, for in this case, justification implies an act of metaphysical discovery that is antecedent to every deduction and that makes deduction possible. As knowledge progresses, it penetrates into the fullness of Being. If one wishes to justify an ethical claim, one must set out on this process of discovery. Justification demands more than tracing a claim back to ultimate, unchangeable axioms, for that would not do justice to this specific understanding of metaphysics; rather, one must investigate the meaning contained in such axioms. There is thus a process of mediation between the claim that is to be justified and its ultimate grounds. The claim is not simply measured against indubitable grounds: the claim prompts us to think about these grounds themselves. Have they been appropriately understood? Is there no possible doubt whatsoever with regard to their validity? These questions force us to think in a way that is not content with the guarantee of formal logic but accepts the risk of the act of discovery mentioned earlier. This is what is meant by the proleptic reaching out to Being. In this context, the word "intuition" denotes something that is indispensable whenever we seek to justify a claim, and intuition is followed by the work of reflection and argumentation. When we have grasped the ultimate ground (*Grund*), we must adduce many reasons (*Gründe*) in support of it; the *Grund* cannot be thought of without the *Gründe*, nor the *Gründe* without the *Grund*. This mutual dependence is because the act of knowing is subject to time: the reasons that are adduced must be transparent to what it is they are justifying. Deduction alone is inadequate here and cannot take us forward. Rather, we must look for correspondences that can be explained and checked and pass the test of general comprehensibility. This process never stands still but is continually prompted anew by experience.

The hierarchical relationship between the ontological *Grund* and the gnoseo-logical *Gründe* is ambivalent. The philosophy of science sharpens our awareness so that we seek to identify this phenomenon and eliminate fallacious inferences. Everyone knows that the reasons that are adduced may be unconvincing, leading to the dismissal of the claim to validity. However, this need not always be the case. Repeatedly, we see that a legitimate claim is supported by false or insufficient arguments; in this situation, academic honesty requires us to fill this vacuum. This is an indispensable service to the work of communication and benefits the matter at hand because the more weight the arguments can bear, the clearer will be the insight.

We also find specious arguments. At first sight they appear completely convinc-ing, but closer examination and lengthier reflection reveal how shaky they are. Taken by themselves, they may all be convincing, but their presuppositions are incorrect, or else they have been untouched by a significant historical change or a decisive development.

The moral theologian will pay great attention to this point, for it not only tests whether he possesses a developed methodological consciousness, but also tells him something about his own truthfulness. Let us mention some aspects, all of which concern the critical way of handling the intellectual tradition that is presupposed in each individual thinker. The most harmless aspect is the insight—with which no one will disagree—that ethically relevant circumstances can take very different forms, and that these indirectly affect the formation of an ethical judgment. The real problem does not lie in the de facto change of circumstances, and to remain on this level would not permit us to get beyond unhelpful platitudes. The challenge lies deeper and concerns the appropriate way to grasp this phenomenon: What is the relevance of the individual factors?

This brings us to another aspect. The history of thinking does not stand still. Changed circumstances compel us to reflect critically on our own intellectual categories to see whether they respond adequately to the new claims. Moral theology can get used to one particular set of categories, but when familiarity with this becomes too much a matter of course, one passes reality by. The same applies to established patterns of argumentation: habit becomes the enemy of truth. This confronts the moral theologian with a critical question: Is he at risk of becoming a prisoner in the edifice of his own thought? If so, he cannot avoid suffering under problems of his own making. Experience is needed here, since it snatches him ever anew out of this dungeon of the spirit.[28]

These considerations do not take us far enough; we must broaden our horizon. We cannot simply dismiss the possibility that a superficial reference to elements of the tradition may import false problems into the discussion. Individual portions of the tradition are broken off and used, without a thorough examination, to help justify some claim that is urgent at the moment. The question remains whether it is possible to make an immediate transfer of this kind from one context in the history of ideas to another. Does this not invite the risk of favoring solutions that pass reality by? Another risk is the fatal error of consciously tying one's own criticism of the past to the worst representatives of the tradition, for then one's contrary position will remain shut up in the same intellectual structures. The circumstances are indeed different, but one fetters oneself to the past, and a constructive growth that would go beyond the past is impossible. The contents may change, but the form remains the same.

It is easy to find examples of this. For example, we have the affirmation that the law of Christ is coextensive with the ethical natural law and does not add any further truths or claims to this. This proposition has its origin in Thomistic thought, which puts the New Testament law, the Ten Commandments, and the natural ethical law on the same level.[29] This was completely legitimate in terms of the epistemological interest that governed theological reflection at that time; the problem that Thomas investigated could not have produced any other answer. The same proposition recurs repeatedly in the manuals, where it makes an anti-Reformation point, and this continues into Neo-Scholasticism. Whether the same proposition can be maintained in the modern period without any further differentiation remains an open question. Has there not been a fundamental change in the understanding of the natural ethical law in the intervening period? The name has indeed remained unchanged, but the varying conditions of the history of ideas, which always entail challenges for thought, have given the matter a new significance. An intellectual approach that employs the categories of alleged objectivity is not the issue here; the principal problems concern the historical milieu that conditions our act of knowing, and this entails a shift in the relationship between faith and ethical reason. The decisive question now is, taking account of the epistemological interest that governs the reflection of the theologian, how can faith bring about a better insight into the natural ethical law? More precisely, in view of deficient levels of insight, how can faith contribute here the greater knowledge that it claims to possess? Patient, detailed work is needed if we are to fill out the contents of the formal program that is proclaimed in the context of the faith by the proponents of an autonomous morality. But this must not lead to a direct transfer of the problems of the Enlightenment to the present day since the expectations with regard to faith have changed, not least thanks to a renewed theology of revelation.

The Ambivalence of a Christian Humanism

The situation is the same when Christian morality is described as a completely human morality. Texts from the Second Vatican Council provide the basis for such a claim. The moral theologian is in good company when she thinks along these lines, for she is taking up concerns of the magisterium. Such a perspective may be justified at first sight, but it easily risks encouraging a humanist narrowing down. This fear is based not so much on the thesis itself as on the emphasis with which it is put forward. For was there ever anyone who actually maintained the opposite of this thesis? Is there anything in the moral theological tradition that might lead to the conviction that human beings are robbed of their lived identity, of their right to full self-realization, in the name of Christian morality? It is all too easy for such an association to be made, and then the lines of battle are drawn up—although such lines of battle are utterly unfounded.

This first affects the relationship between faith and ethical reason. In keeping with Enlightenment thinking, faith is accused of particularity, or even of an historical arbitrariness, whereas reason makes the claim to absoluteness and universality, and presents itself as the true advocate of the human person. This is a fundamental misjudgment of the Christian understanding of faith. Faith does indeed remain dependent on reason; at the same time, however, faith goes ahead of reason, opening the doors and showing the path. Besides this, ethical reason is also embedded in a faith (of whatever kind) that it follows, in the sense that it is not reason but faith that generates a basic relationship to the world.

The incorrect understanding that I have mentioned earlier bears its fruits in the way in that the normative nature is understood. For the Christian, the *natura elevata* is normative. The contents of *this* nature must be uncovered since it is a question of the divinization of the human person—his "humanization" is a triviality in comparison. After all, what is faith supposed to bring about if not divinization? A morality for supermen, perhaps, or for angels? We must also look critically at the image of God that is implied here. The fear is sometimes expressed, especially with regard to texts of the ecclesiastical magisterium, that an anthropomorphic image of God is being cultivated. But this simply ignores the facts. Such an evaluation reveals superficial thinking that projects remnants of nominalism onto the theology of the magisterium. Critics who think in this way provocatively ignore the essence of Catholic theology, which stands or falls with the doctrine of the analogy of Being. This doctrine, which is taken for granted by the Catholic theological tradition, excludes a priori any relationship of competition between God and the human person. The meaning and the weight of individual affirmations are decided by their unquestioned presuppositions. The person who overlooks this fact will inevitably make mistakes when she seeks to justify claims and will thereby overshoot the mark. Accordingly, the first question is always whether the supposed enemy against whom one is arguing really affirms what he is alleged to affirm. This is the only way to avoid the danger of falling into the same mistake.[30]

We must look critically not only at the image of God but also at the Christian understanding of the world. Justifications of moral theological affirmations will not succeed if they are based on a separation between the relationship to God and innerworldly spheres of life. There is indeed a conceptual distinction here, and it has a basis in reality. But how are we to think of the relationship between the things that are distinguished in this way? The decisively theological approach is rooted in the doctrines of the creation *and* the incarnation. This means that the theologian's principal question will always be how the relationship to transcendence changes the understanding of immanence. The task of moral theological justification is to make this plausible. To think in the opposite direction eventually leads to the impasses of a secularized ethic since one is taking the wrong course from the very outset. And the intellectual categories employed on this course cannot lead to the right outcome because they suffer from epistemological reductionisms: typically, they regard human nature as an object that must be subjected to an analysis that is methodologically free of any ideas about transcendental goals.

This type of thinking can be found in the Scholastic and Neo-Scholastic traditions, but it cannot be taken as a model for the present day with its specific challenges, for that would end up in an intellectual anachronism. Every epoch summons us anew to a critical reflection on theories of knowledge that were accepted in the past without question. An accurate analysis must be accompanied by the inspiration that comes from ideas about goals; both of these together, analysis and inspiration, are constitutive of moral theological justifications. We need only add that these ideas remained alive even in Neo-Scholasticism; mostly, however, this fact is overlooked. Naturally, this makes it more difficult to grasp what is intended by the texts of the magisterium. The magisterium thinks primarily in theological terms even when it argues in terms of natural law. It would be wrong, however, to accuse the magisterium of pushing its own authority in matters of faith too far. The *fact* that the magisterium enforces its authority should not be criticized, but the *way* in which it employs philosophical categories in the framework of natural law argumentation certainly does deserve criticism.[31] A claim made by the natural law, when correctly justified, is also the claim made by Jesus Christ.

We need not speak here in detail of the weaknesses of an explicit faith ethic. It is impossible to infer directly any norms for action from the word of revelation—and this principle also applies to religious obligations. When ethical claims are to be justified in the name of faith, this always necessitates reflection on the revelation and on the inspiring competence that has its origin in the revelation. And it is surely obvious that one must take account here of the whole spectrum of natural law argumentation. Therefore, we are not surprised to find that proponents of a faith ethic neglect the whole question of normative justifications; indeed, they do not even trouble to hide their reservations on this subject. When they do take up this issue, they tend to display a fundamentalist understanding of tradition that reminds one of the mentality of an archivist. Their preference for Thomas is surely a symptom of this. The expectations they kindle in their attempt to satisfy the human need for security pass reality by. An interpretation of Thomas may be exceedingly sophisticated, but it will not solve any problems. At most, it can offer some clues, but it is our responsibility to use our competence to take these clues further.

Thus, no theologian would deny that there exists a will of God and that this will imposes obligations, but Thomas himself would be the last to assert that he had recognized this will definitively and decisively for all future generations. Arguments from tradition are somewhat ambivalent. It is of course understandable when people look in times of upheaval for authorities that provide certainty, and every serious scholar will ask himself whether the tradition of his academic discipline contains viable solutions, or whether its epistemological potential is exhausted. But we cannot stop there. The work of justification entails facing directly the claim posed by the matter in question, and critically examining one's own categories to see whether they meet this claim. Otherwise one's thinking becomes fundamentalist. Without intending to do so, such thinking may in fact reflect the intellectual attitude of an absolutist society and of the exercise of authority that corresponds to such a society. This thinking can be maintained for a time, but a bitter awakening lies in store—especially when the attempt is made to suffocate fresh discussions by referring to the classical authors. This attempt may be done with great skill, and the argumentative weaknesses of modern critics may be exposed; nevertheless, this attempt overlooks the fact that the justification of new insights slowly but surely acquires solidity. This unfortunate impression is strengthened when, for example, texts of the magisterium draw on new philosophical categories to define doctrines that deserve discussion rather than taking the step—both possible and necessary—of presenting these doctrines in a more differentiated manner and attempting to justify them more convincingly. The supreme lack of honesty is reached when positions that once were vehemently combated are now defended a posteriori with equal vehemence. Such defenders forget that it was *others* who once put their head on the block for these positions; in such cases, the appeal to an allegedly unbroken tradition lacks all credibility.

Naturally, the opposite occurs too. One's own tradition is unjustly accused of making argumentative errors that it never actually made (and indeed could not have made, given its intellectual presuppositions). A classic example of this is the accusation of naturalism that is leveled at both the magisterium and Neo-Scholasticism. This is an "imported" problem, especially when reference is made in this context to David Hume and G. E. Moore, since the epistemological presuppositions are different in each case;[32] or else it is a simple error, since naturalism not only presupposes a reduced concept of Being that neglects the basic ontological tension between Being and the existent but also a naturalistic anthropology. This, however, is clearly a caricature of the situation. Positions are drawn up that dissolve when confronted with reality. This is why critical texts must be read with a critical eye—precisely in order to work constructively on one's own tradition and to develop this further.

Moral Theology—A School of Truthfulness

The Long-range Perspective of the Tradition

It is rightly expected of a theologian that he will be a theological personality. It is not surprising when the *moral* theologian finds himself particularly affected by this expectation since his discipline is the first to be assailed by the onslaught of the problems that concern both thought and action. Accordingly, he cannot evade the task of asking difficult questions and looking critically at the intellectual tradition to which he himself belongs. He will be driven by the secret fear lest the imperatives he formulates in the name of the faith might be unfounded. There is thus no cause for astonishment at the fact that the characteristic virtue of the moral theologian is restraint, and that moral theology is consistently willing to suspend judgment.[33] This, however, must not give the impression that the primary function is that of criticizing the tradition, for that can be a strategy for exempting oneself from intellectual responsibility and a sign of a lack of solidarity. Equally important is the function of consolidating the tradition. Indeed (despite what first impressions might suggest), the consolidation occupies more space than the criticism.

The moral theologian stands in a tradition that has proved its worth. When new insights emerge, it is highly probable that they will offer support to the positions that have been held hitherto. This is most likely the case where an insight of faith has determined the moral-theological discourse, where a potential for existential wisdom, which has been acquired in the course of history under the influence of faith, has played a role in the formation of an ethical judgment that is academically respectable. This must not leave the moral theologian unaffected. He is not a neutral observer of this context—in the name of a reason that would be detached from history. Rather, he belongs to this context and attempts to take intellectual responsibility for this belonging. Thanks to his experience of everyday life, he is conscious—and grateful—that his tradition generates a natural capacity to provide workable solutions to life's problems, and that one must not frivolously jeopardize this capacity. If one were to do so, moral-theological reflection would degenerate imperceptibly into a pacesetter of moral disintegration. Indeed, the greatly exaggerated criticism of individual points can be a pretext for a global criticism that necessarily congeals in itself because it cannot offer any constructive alternatives. Once again, the factor of time plays a decisive role. Experience shows that constructive solutions attain inner consistency only one step at a time. Usually they are exposed for long periods to the risk of dissolving into nothing, and the misunderstandings that arise in the social milieu help to intensify this process.[34]

This means that we must now point out a dilemma from which moral theologians today are not spared. There is necessarily a dominant tendency to tackle new problems based on a critique of one's own tradition and of the doctrinal teaching proposed by the Church's magisterium. Both of these are under suspicion (at least in the sense of a methodological supposition) until the opposite has been demonstrated clearly. Regrettably, this entails a fatal narrowing down. First, the spectrum of one's academic interests is reduced. Scholars want to see the confirmation of their critical prejudices, and they look for areas in which these prejudices can get to work. The result is that controversial themes predominate. This in turn leads to a virtually omnipresent monotony where all we hear are variations and paraphrases of answers that never change. The spark of the conflict then leaps over to the scholarly community so that the position of another scholar is of value only to the extent that it confirms one's own judgment. The community is divided into academic friends and foes, and this means the certain death of scholarship. It is however equally obvious that this manner of proceeding inevitably generates a preference for the beaten tracks: the results of protracted investigations are already known in advance. And this is even more tangible because the pressure within the Church (from all sides) is growing. An opinion of one's own is an excessive luxury since theology is subject to the dictates of a "political" calculation.[35] This inevitably leads to an attitude of partisanship. Whether or not this is consciously present, there is a process of assimilation to the authorities and the fractions that dispenses the individual theologian from the burden of intellectual autonomy. Usually this is accompanied by an academic overproduction. It is only seldom that one encounters anything original here, and still less anything that genuinely takes the discussion further.

It is therefore no cause for astonishment when theological reflection becomes remote from real life. Initially there was indeed an urgent problem, but now the discussion has taken on a life of its own and follows other laws rather than the only legitimate law, that is, the demand made by the problem itself. The unbiased Christian cannot shake off the disconcerting impression that what he is witnessing is the interplay of the dictates of theological fractions, and that theology is not something that actually serves *him*. At most, theology is at its own service since its reflection takes hold of ever-smaller sections of reality. The onlooker is co-opted: his function is to confirm academic positions, although he lacks the qualification of an adequate awareness of the issue that is at stake in these positions. Scholarship turns into a plebiscite, conviction moves perilously close to cajolery, and more weight is attached to the formal structures of the argumentation than to their contents. The consequence is a creeping loss of reality. The issue itself is no longer of interest: it is subordinate to the proclamation of one particular position.[36]

Theology as Reflection on Life Stories

These considerations show why we must appeal to the theologian to practice an ethos of truth. Truth needs the long-term perspective: it lives from the seeker's freedom to forego momentary successes. The more one succeeds in thinking time-lessly, the better is the guarantee that one can carry on an academic controversy in a constructive manner, contributing points of view that rescue it from intellectual impasses. This requires a high measure of self-respect, and the theologian must resist the temptation to let anyone deprive her of this freedom of spirit—whether in the name of ecclesial loyalty or in the name of the dictates of groups within the Church[37]—because this always makes her judgment less impartial. She will swim with one stream or another, without noticing that time is slipping away from her. This suffices to demonstrate the raison d'être of the biographical element in theological reflection. Only a theological personality is capable of filtering problems and arguments through the mesh of her own life story. Behind this lies the convic-tion that all theological questioning derives from the reflection on life stories and the mastering of them. This alone disposes of the charge that such a reflection will necessarily end in a form of subjectivism that imposes itself on others, or indeed that such a reflection deliberately intends to co-opt others to the theologian's own side, so to speak, and is merely a sublime form of the exercise of power with the secret agenda of ensuring that the theologian herself will not come to any harm. No, the intellectual integration of her own biography into her work is not some-thing she does on her own. It is in a living communication with other life stories, which form a critical corrective that widens the horizon and prevents a fruitless gyration around her own ego. Indeed, it is not presumptuous to affirm that theology is embedded in a continuous conversation.[38]

At this point, however, we must pose further questions. The first aspect concerns the courage to be modest. Spending time in reflection on one's own life story—naturally, in a communicative openness—is an effective protection against an arrogant mentality that thinks in terms of "recipes" and attempts to resolve intel-lectual questions as if these were factual issues. Such a mentality may of course be very acute, but it forgets that fundamental attitudes to life are incomparably more important since these constitute the humus for the resolution of problems. A reflection on the course of one's own life hitherto, with its ups and downs, pays more attention to this point without necessarily reducing thereby the objectivity of the argumentation. Theological thinking of a biographical nature also contains an element of therapy. It is close to an honest examination of conscience that is fully aware of the various ways in which we lull our conscience and dodge its demands, and it attempts, perhaps painfully, to wrest from these evasions something that is true. If a theological formula has an exonerating function, and dishonesty and evasion lie concealed behind it, does it not degenerate into an empty phrase? The question is whether the intellectual endeavor is "covered" by competence acquired in the course of a person's life story, or whether a wide gulf yawns between such competence and his own life story.

If such a gulf exists, moral theology will certainly suffer since it can condemn itself to irrelevance and thus fail to do justice to its genuine mission. Through its appeal to the human dimension, it may perhaps connive at human naïveté; in that case, hypocrisy is not far away. A person applies all his energy to the solution of problems that doubtless have their importance for a responsible structuring of the contemporary lifeworld, and that he must confront if he wishes to remain a reliable and constructive dialogue partner in the intellectual debates of our time; and yet such problems often lie on the periphery of everyday consciousness and have little to do with "passing the test" of his own life story. They belong to a lofty intellectual ethos, and the discussion of these problems can remain in a nonobligatory sphere. But despite all the intellectual exertions it may entail, the nonobligatory sphere leaves *me* unaffected.[39]

The existential problems under which people suffer silently tend to be inconspicuous. They remain in silence and play scarcely any role in the public academic arena. It befits the truthfulness of the moral theologian to pay the appropriate attention to these problems too. For example, there are the many forms of resignation from which no life story is spared; there is the entanglement in interpersonal and societal constraints from which one cannot extricate oneself, with all the will in the world; and there is the need to accommodate oneself, if one is to survive at all. It would be easy to add many such situations of conflict to this list, but we need not do so here.[40] It suffices to emphasize that factual issues of moral theology that are treated on the level of norm-theoretical thinking that establishes a distance between the thinker and the question continually require the supplement of action-theoretical reflections, otherwise they will end up in irrelevance and, hence, in untruthfulness. For this task we need the silence that bestows the watchfulness of soul that attempts again and again to encompass the whole spectrum of existential experiences and to reflect on these from an ethical perspective. One is repeatedly confronted by the critical question whether it is possible to live with solutions that are merely declaimed. A moral theologian who proceeds in this way is convinced that the conceptual instruments at his disposal are like constructs that must remain transparent to the reality of life, and that it is here that his own truthfulness begins.

The Principle of Vicarious Representation

There is a principle of vicarious representation in moral-theological reflection. A secret band of solidarity unites the members of a community of ethical communication. The experiences of all of them are received intellectually and then given back to them, and each one makes his own contribution here. This preserves the moral theologian from the deadening routine that tends above all to arise when his discipline threatens to descend to the level of a noncommittal "Glass Bead Game" (as in Hesse's celebrated novel), when it no longer causes him pain, when it no longer demands that he bear witness. He must have the courage to waken sleeping dogs—by giving himself a bad conscience before doing the same to everyone else. This makes him vulnerable, but at the same time, it prevents him from hurting others.

For this, a whole life is needed. A person must invest her best powers if she wants to identify the true claim that is made by the ethical dimension. This insight is sometimes lost to sight in the debates of moral theology. Doubtless, arguments must hold water—who would ever deny that? But this alone does not make them plausible. Arguments also contain existential knowledge of the highest quality; there is no quick route by which the understanding can gain access to this knowledge, nor can it be acquired by one generation alone. This gives new nourishment to the argument from tradition. The reflexive principle *in dubio pro traditione* never loses its validity, and the moral theologian must never lose his receptivity to it. He must not overlook the fact that ethical crises have their origin in areas of general disorientation, where a comprehensive framework of sapiential knowledge about life has been lost so that an emotional uncertainty robs action of its unquestioned spontaneity. There has always existed an ethical pluralism with regard to individual questions, and we can live with this provided only that the living substratum is ensured.

This sheds a brighter light on the principle of vicarious representation. The ethos of truthfulness demands of the moral theologian a personal lifestyle that compels her to confront the basic human questions against the background of her own life story. She needs the various areas in which she has stood the test: the experience of these areas continually throws her back onto the very foundations of her life. If this does not happen, she is already on the brink of the abyss of untruthfulness. An intellectual façade is constructed, but it proves to be unsound as soon as the well-trodden paths of a conventional morality are left behind and she is obliged to cope with situations of extraordinary stress. For this is the hour of truth, which shows clearly that all the superficial evaluations of goods (for which she can set up more or less unambiguous rules of preference) need the reference to that good that consists in a successful good life. Analysis alone cannot decipher what is meant by *this* good. Its meaning is disclosed only to the one who patiently undertakes the intellectual task of looking at his own life story, which is both shaped and borne up by the inspiring power of ideals and personal goals.

This means that one must have the courage to be different. One must be able to contradict a dominant intellectual climate that generates societal coercions and threatens to rob the individual of the freedom to make unselfconscious judgments. Often it is only too late that one recognizes that one has connived at a creeping trivialization of life: the fatal fascination of the quick solution drove one irresistibly to take the easy solution, thus depriving the human person of his best possibilities. Vicarious thinking attempts to resist this pressure. It ensures that the individual will have free spaces that protect him from pressure from the public sphere and that allow silence to emerge. If an ethos of objectivity, free from distorting prejudices, is to hold sway, it is necessary to reflect upon one's own life. And here, until the opposite is demonstrated clearly, the presumption is against the majority. Only a person who thinks based on an imperturbable interiority is able to endure these tensions without succumbing to intellectual rigidity.

Seen in this light, the moral theologian is an uncomfortable dialogue partner. His discipline possesses a fundamentally conservative trait. This is above suspicion, since it is born of an ingrained distrust of currents that come and go. Once these currents have passed, the individual who adopted them uncritically is left helpless, perhaps indeed cheated of his life. The tradition possesses an advantage in terms of knowledge, and this must not be squandered—especially when first appearances would seem to call this advantage into question. Besides this, moral theology treats its ideas more lovingly than any other theological discipline. The brittleness of its outward appearance must not lead us astray on this point since it should rather be considered a sign of a modesty that does not in the least lack the necessary self-assurance.

This is demonstrated in the respectful way one deals with dialogue partners of all kinds. To begin with, one must achieve intellectual mastery over the tradition of one's own discipline, and this requires honest mental work. What intellectual categories were employed to defend what justified concerns? One must also include the context in the history of ideas since moral theology has always been a child of its own period—that is what constitutes its inherent restlessness and vitality. Every epoch has left its traces, both in what was adopted and in what was rejected. Criticism must bear in mind that something that was later called into question may perhaps in its own time have been not only legitimate but also absolutely necessary. Later generations may feel drawn to engage in polemic against their predecessors. One is assured thereby of the favor of the public; at the same time, however, without noticing what one is doing, one abets a creeping disintegration of the tradition.[41] At the same time, one shrugs off the duty to make a constructive contribution—and that is dishonest. This is why one must be willing to put patient questions to the past. What can and must be salvaged for the present day? What concerns remain valid? Is it perhaps possible to maintain these concerns more convincingly? It is only once we have done justice to these questions that we may voice our criticisms, for it is only then that we may confidently reject whatever trace elements may remain of obviously false historical developments.

A glorification of tradition also exists that expects that the classical representatives of one's own discipline will supply perennially valid answers to all of life's questions. This position deliberately refuses to see that the history of ideas has moved on. This does not apply only to factual issues. Intellectual categories, too, are involved in this movement and have undergone a process of differentiation. It is sometimes claimed that insights of the past can be transferred globally to the present, but there is in fact no immediate recourse to something that belongs to the past.[42] First, we must answer the question of whether the problem area and the intellectual categories are truly the same today as in the past. If a person avoids this question, or indeed regards it as unnecessary, she risks all too easily getting lost in sham fights and bearing off the addressees of her own argumentation into a pseudo-world. She can, of course, have tremendous fights in a pseudo-world, employing lofty intellectual efforts, but the shots fly wide of reality. Untruthfulness of this kind brings about the death of an academic discipline.

The Promises of the Ethics of Conviction

Only an understanding of tradition that is purified in this way makes it possible for us to venture to tackle the true problems. The scholar will face up to reality courageously, instead of secretly covering it up. The first challenge, which never abates, derives from the ability of our own freedom to face conflicts, an ability that is experienced directly and is the fruit of suffering. Essentially, a conventional morality belies the fact that no decision is ever absolutely unproblematic. This is why norm-ethical reflections must be supplemented by perspectives from action theory: only this guarantees that one will grasp the whole of reality, instead of absolutizing artificially created segments.

In the center of an integral thinking of this kind stands the available power of freedom. What may one think oneself capable of? Indeed, what *must* one think oneself capable of? The moral theologian is exposed to the double risk of making excessive demands on the one hand, or insufficient demands on the other; in both situations, his discourse has a corrosive effect. Generally, one spontaneously associates the moral theologian with the first of these two variants since the suspicion of rigorism occupies what we might call an ancestral place in the moral-theological climate with which we are familiar: Jansenism and tutiorism (at least in their coarsened forms) were influential for a very long time. It is doubtless true that understandable concerns lay behind these tendencies. For example, there was a justified desire for certainty in one's conduct, and moral theology responded to this through a maximum precision in ethical norms. A "drawing board" moral theology was created under the aegis of the scientific ideals of mathematics, physics, and jurisprudence—ideals that were foreign to the discipline of moral theology. This certainly satisfied the demand for a highly articulated system of order, and there was no lack of intellectual responsibility;[43] but this was too much of a good thing since it is not possible to analyze the correctness of ethical decisions completely, down to the last little detail, and to define this correctness a priori. Improvisation is necessary because there is always an unforeseen element. Nor is it possible to offer the same kind of definition of *all* the human goods that must be realized: there is a spectrum of spontaneous expression that does better justice to reality than precise definitions (be they never so well thought out) can ever do.

A first form of untruthfulness begins here since such a conception of norm-ethical thinking remains tied to the dominance of the descriptive reason, which apprehends only that action that is empirically verifiable and understood as the fulfillment of a norm. This conception tends to block out the fact that the inner action is of equal importance; it approves of an ethical decision that corresponds as closely as possible to the dominant image of good order. We may remark en passant that this conception tacitly operates with an understanding of ethical norms that lacks the differentiated deep dimension—an inevitable tribute paid to the epistemological foundations that this conception chooses, resulting unavoidably in an alienation of reality. This kind of thinking is unmistakably characterized by an externalization and a mechanical application of the claim to universal validity. It is true that we find an ethical consistency here that eschews compromises; a logically coherent system enforces its claims *sine glossa*. But one cannot brush aside the impression that this is achieved at the cost of truthfulness. People are lulled into believing that their conscience need not reproach them, if the external correctness of their conduct corresponds to the criteria that this conception puts forward.

The conviction establishes itself in the world of thoughts and feelings. It includes in equal measure intentions and motivations. Everyday use of language does not always draw a precise distinction between these two, nor need it do so; but in view of the complexity of ethical truth, such a distinction is useful. Motivations refer directly to ideas about ethical value. Their original function is to ensure the goodness of one's conduct. The intentions have a different function: once ideas about values have been recognized, these must be translated into general and concrete goals of behavior. Consequently, the immediate object of the intentions is the correctness of behavior. Motivations and intentions are not simply juxtaposed without any connection; they are not to be regarded as hypostatized entities. Rather, a process of intellectual mediation takes place between them. Motivations are characterized by their rational structure. They resist a voluntaristic narrowing down because, in the last analysis, ideas about value possess a recognizable content and generate something that might be called a prior understanding. At the same time, intentions are also dependent on motivations, for otherwise ethical correctness will degenerate into a value-neutral objective correctness that is at best the object of the instrumental reason. Correctness is always a correctness that bears a value.

If this is accepted, light is shed on the relationship between virtue ethics and norm ethics. Of course, it may seem self-evident within moral theology that they cannot be detached from each other; still less can one construct a contrast between them, as we have already emphasized in other contexts.[44] Here we need only add some precision to the definition. Virtues are originally related to motivations, but not in an exclusive manner: they also share in the intellectual mediation with intentions. Norm-ethical reflections go in the opposite direction. Their starting point is the correctness of the individual action, but they do not stop short there. Rather, they include the deep dimension proper to virtue ethics, although sometimes only in a nonthematic manner. We must bear this in mind when we consider the problems we are discussing here. If the fundamental conviction is constituted by means of this mutual relationship between motivations and intentions, it is responsible for structuring the course of external action.

This is why it is mistaken to play off conviction ethics and the ethics of responsibility against each other. The goodness of the conviction ensures the correctness of the action. It is on this level that a person experiences both conflict and coping with conflict in the course of her life story, and truthfulness demands that she get involved here. She will then realize, perhaps very suddenly, that the external course of action is ambiguous—in more senses than one. It is possible, for example, that the correctness of this course of action does not provide sufficient information about the conviction that underlies it; this has often been pointed out, and it is obvious to everyone. However, it is questionable how such a discrepancy can be sustained. It is clear that the external course of action possesses a certain measure of autonomy vis-à-vis the inner conviction, and there can be a kind of phase shift between the two. In the course of one's life story, boundaries and constraints are generated by freedom's ability to sustain conflicts, and it is also possible for the individual to allow the confrontation with these boundaries and constraints to start in the inner sphere of her conviction: she begins by constructing an intellectual world that makes heavy demands, hoping insistently that her external actions will submit to this intellectual world.

This is the locus of the law of graduality (of which we hear so much today): the well-intentioned person grows step by step into the full truth that is the power of freedom. This process takes the whole of one's life, and if one wishes to make progress in knowledge, one must grapple unreservedly with the question of ethics. This is how an ethical personality is built up. He or she acquires a higher degree of certainty with regard to action, and this spontaneously influences evaluations of goods and strategies for conduct. Norm-ethical considerations do indeed remain indispensable. They establish a clear intellectual framework, but they prove limited in the face of the "surplus" that is generated by the emotional quality of one's conviction. The correctness of conduct, which is initially present in norms, receives its ultimately decisive form from the power of freedom—and from a purely norm-ethical perspective, this power can be taken hold of only asymptotically. To be an ethical personality means taking responsibility honestly for this process.

The endeavor to dispose of the suspicion of rigorism is understandable, but it can lead a person to make insufficient ethical demands. He lacks the courage to utter a lofty claim, or to bear a testimony that kindles enthusiasm in others. Indeed, he lacks the courage necessary for a supreme achievement that would consume all his powers. His thinking is dominated by a mentality of assiduous assimilation, where an intellectual strategy of providing reassurance never permits the emergence of any confrontation that would force him to face up to his limitations. This deprives the ethical life of its tension, and it is only with reluctance that he admits to himself that all this could end up in a fraud. What looks like a mantle of mercy encloses the addressees of ethical directives in the boundaries constructed by their sufferings—and robs them of the salutary possibility of breaking out of this prison.

It is surely undisputed that moral-theological thinking must not bracket off the dimension of time.[45] A timeless normativity, which carries the disastrous inheritance of an objectivistic essentialism, deprives the human person of the possibility of succeeding in his life story. It kills every ethical élan. Failure is inevitable for the person who possesses nothing other than this normativity. The awareness of this fact gives moral theology a function of accompanying that goes beyond the normative discourse, and only ethical personalities can carry out this task. The one who is struggling to break out of his prison needs to know that he is understood as he takes his little steps. He needs a hand stretched out to him if he is to experience what the essence of morality is, that is, that it means more than merely the fulfilling of norms and that it may present itself more purely in a commitment that is resolute and does not let itself be deterred when it falls back into its old ways. The meaning contained in the norms will be interpreted in the act of accompanying such a process with understanding. Before norms obligate, they invite. This is a test of truthfulness. The moral theologian must have the gift of discernment of spirits, which is oriented to the permanent transition between "not yet being able" and "being able"; this path must be taken. If this does not happen, a leaden hopelessness is diffused, and the individual will be ultimately even more alone. A person of whom others expect nothing will feel definitively abandoned—even when the others are acting out of sheer kindness when they expect nothing of him.

The Relevance of Revelation to Action Theory

The eye of the believer looks expectantly to revelation to see whether he may await constructive help from it. But as the recent debate about autonomous morality in the context of faith has shown, he must take care from the very outset to avoid errors of judgment. The outcome of the discussion depends on the underlying theology of revelation and on the theory of science that guides the scholars involved.

It has already been mentioned in another context that there are no formally revealed categorial norms of conduct; by now, this has attained the status of a moral-theological commonplace. Nevertheless, a consensus has also emerged that

this thesis does not clear up all the problems. Up to now, no champion of autonomous morality has ever claimed that faith is irrelevant to ethical reason. On the
contrary, there is general agreement that faith establishes a context of meaning
that generates indispensable affirmations about the human person's understanding
of himself and of the world. For this reason, faith is the natural point of reference for
moral-theological reflection. Faith provides ethical reason with food for thought.

However, to speak of categorial norms of conduct is unhelpful since it opens
the door to misunderstandings. It can even be taken as an example of an uncritical
handling of philosophical foreign elements. In general, this concept is taken to
mean those norms that refer to the structuring of innerworldly spheres of life in a
way that is immediately relevant to action. The price paid for this definition is an
abstraction with a theoretical basis that is at home in the tradition of the moral-
theological handbooks, that is, the distinction between the religious and the
earthly groups of obligations. As long as we remain on the level of methodology,
there can be no doubt about the justification of this distinction. On the level of
outward appearances, the different groups of obligations stand alongside one
another, and the fact that action is embedded in time and space obliges us to
consider them separately because it is only then possible to bring order into human
life. In the background, however, there is always the conviction that an abiding
tension unites the two groups of obligations: the methodological distinction does
not in the least mean an ontological separation. No one doubts that methodological distinctions are indispensable for moral-theological reflection, but this is only
one phase of the work, which must be supplemented by the continuous intellectual
mediation between the things that are distinguished—without confusing them.
This mediation is the real point, the epistemological interest that guides theological
work. One would inevitably fail to do justice to reality if one were not aware of
this. Here the theologian must demonstrate his intellectual honesty.

Nor do we overlook the fact that the concept of the categorial norm of conduct
contains a necessary schematization, as is made clear by the antithetical contrary
concept, that is, "transcendental." At the historical root of this pair of concepts
lies a problem concerning the metaphysics of knowledge that does not fit seamlessly
into our own philosophical tradition; or at any rate, it requires a clarification if
misunderstandings are to be avoided. The original context is marked by a problem
of formal reasoning against the background of very precise epistemological premises.[46] One would need to investigate individual instances to see whether the moral
theologian makes these premises his own, but where the intellectual tradition of
Scholasticism is presupposed without question, the assumption is that he does not
do so. If one's own thinking is rooted in realism—albeit a critical realism—one
will handle this pair of concepts with insightful understanding. The guiding interest
will be directed to the complementarity of the two concepts, and the decisive
question is how the dimensions of reality that they designate compenetrate one
another, how the one is always contained a priori in the other. This means that
the perspective differs from that of the original context. A deliberate failure to
mention this would be an offense against the requirement of intellectual honesty.

As soon as one must give an account of the substance of these concepts, this distinction offers little help. The mutual compenetration of the transcendental and the categorial dimensions of the one undivided reality is the relationship that is constitutive of all norms of conduct, and this relationship must be decoded. This must be taken into account, when the moral theologian as theologian—and what else is he?—engages in norm-ethical reflections. If, however, he is content to leave the distinction as it is, the transcendental dimension evaporates into a formal emptiness and becomes irrelevant to the task of discovering norms since this goes hand in hand with the task of substantiating norms; at the same time, the normative content succumbs to the heavy weight of advancing secularization.

Clarifications of this kind are necessary to dismantle unrealistic expectations with regard to the relevance of faith, and to propose criteria that are truly appropriate to this matter. Ultimately, what is at stake is the credibility of the theologian's intellectual competence, and the question is how this competence is to prove itself in practice. Moral theology's self-understanding is on trial here, and a satisfactory answer probably requires us to locate the origin of this self-understanding at the point where the affinity between faith and ethical reason is most concentrated (despite all the justified distinction between the two). This is the case on the level of action theory. When ethical conduct is defined as self-realization, as projecting oneself in the direction of definitive and comprehensive perfecting, this points first to the fundamental self-understanding of the agent. Naturally, one cannot dispense with norms, but these lie on a derived level. They are an objectivization of the personal basis from which they have their origin, and they offer direct guidance for conduct. One could say something similar about faith. The believer is directly affected by its reality: in Jesus Christ, he is confronted by God. The individual truths of faith lie on a derived level. They are an indispensable vehicle of a personal event that is antecedent to them.

We must bear this in mind when moral theology discusses the relevance of faith. If we were to take our starting point in the self-understanding of moral theology as a theory about norms, we would not grasp the full extent of the problem: logically, the antipode can lie only in truths of faith. This means that one is moving on a derived level, and this in turn has consequences for the methodology that we apply. The central question is whether it is possible to derive ethical truths from truths of faith. As the discussion of autonomous morality has unanimously emphasized, the answer to this question can only be negative because truths of faith and ethical truths belong to different epistemic levels and are characterized by different logical structures. An immediate transition between the two is impossible.

No objection can be made to such an argument, but the decisive problem remains unsolved. For what can a deduction actually achieve? All it can do is show that there is no contradiction in intellectual operations or in the steps in one's argumentation. It does not bring about an increase in knowledge because what appears in the inferences is already contained in the major premises. Everything thus depends on the substantial contents of the major premises. It is here that the decisive point lies—not in the guarantee of formal logic since this follows on the contents that have been recognized. It does not itself constitute these contents. The reductive methodology leads logically into a blind alley. No constructive solution is in sight; at best, the problem is simply postponed. If progress is to be made, we must cast our intellectual nets wider.

Contents are accessible only to insight: this is true in equal measure of ethical truths and of truths of faith. In both cases, we must avoid an objectivistic reductionism; we must refer back to the self-understanding of the one who gains insight, for it is here that all objectivization has its origin. The reality of the world that surrounds us does indeed possess a kind of rationality, but this must not be exaggerated. At most, it supplies hints to reason that perceives, understands, and interprets; these hints are received and decoded. Accordingly, it seems more appropriate to say that the reality of the world that surrounds us is constituted in its rationality by reason. And one can say something analogous of the reality of faith. Here, too, we need to refer back to the self-understanding of the believer: truths of faith are the objectivization of this self-understanding. The believer is not confronted initially by truths of faith but by God's self-communication, which makes itself known and consequently allows itself to be grasped in the believer's own subjectivity—a subjectivity that is oriented to transcendence. Seen in this way, the ontological status of truths of faith can be defined only when the appropriate requirements of the metaphysics of knowledge are satisfied.

It is easy to see what this implies for the problem we are studying here. Both truths of reason and truths of faith owe their existence to an intentional achievement of the knowing subject. This affirmation is not psychological but metaphysical. The two kinds of truth are not in the least confused, nor is the difference between them implicitly leveled down. But thanks to the subjectivity of the human person, which is oriented to transcendence, they remain related to each other. Indeed, these are two dimensions that compenetrate each other without any infringement of the autonomy of each one. For this reason alone, the appropriate model cannot be an understanding of autonomy in which reason and faith stand unlinked alongside one another. Rather, the autonomy envisaged here is a relational autonomy that comes to perfection when the relationality vis-à-vis the antithesis is activated. There is no presuppositionless reason since the dimension of faith is antecedent to reason a priori. Nor is there a faith that would not continually demand to be decoded intellectually by reason. It is obvious that we must avoid a rationalistic understanding of reason; at the same time, however, it is equally important that we avoid an understanding of faith that glides imperceptibly into something close to an irrational voluntarism. Both these positions fail to do justice to reality. This is how the decisive course to be taken by the intellectual work of the moral theologian is staked out. Ultimately, what is required is a transcendental analysis of the intentional basis that makes itself known as the fundamental self-understanding of the believer and is constituted by the circumincession of faith and reason.

Since moral theology is a science of faith, it is understood that it admits the supremacy of the dimension of faith. This is meant *in ordine perfectionis*. The most essential ontological and epistemological reality of the human person is disclosed through faith, and the theologian proceeds on this assumption. It would be a fatal misunderstanding to see such an affirmation as a limitation on reason since the opposite is true: this liberates reason to unfold its full possibilities. This is why it would also be wrong to employ quantitative demarcations to define the correlation between faith and reason: both are at work across the entire spectrum of ethical behavior, and it is here that the key to the correct understanding lies. Faith initially brings about a context of intentionality, and in this sense, faith must always be understood as an intentional achievement. There are good reasons for describing the basic elements of a theological anthropology as open meanings that the theologian works unceasingly to understand. Norm-ethical reflection, conversely, is primarily a task entrusted to reason, although one must not bracket off the reference back to the background of faith, which is mediated anthropologically. It is clear that this reference back to faith cannot be carried out by means of deduction, for this would silence and eliminate the productive power of reason. By allowing itself to be inspired by faith, reason unfolds its own dynamic.

But what is reason's specific achievement? The best way to describe it would be as an insight into correlations, not in the sense of simply noting what exists but in the sense of conceptualizing. It is only under this presupposition that we are justified in speaking of a growth in knowledge. The reason adopts guidelines that derive from faith and develops these further in a process of discovery in which perceiving and experiencing form an indissoluble unity, a process that is propelled in equal parts by intuition and reflection.

When this is granted, light is shed on the norm-ethical relevance of faith. When the anthropological implications of faith are described (as above) as open meanings, this does not in the least mean that they are nonbinding. The intention of such a description is to show how complex the mediation is. All the stages of the mediation are equally indispensable and important. The human person does not live from norms alone but just as much from the totality of what the norms presuppose. This means that one would narrow down the work of moral theology if one attached too much importance to norm-ethical considerations, and this would lead to an impoverishment of the ethical life. Norms are only the end product of many different and mutually complementary intellectual achievements. They do indeed record a consensus that has grown up, but at the same time, they point to the virtue of *epikeia*. Norms on their own cannot cover the totality of ethical action; they need to be complemented by the virtues. It is therefore not surprising that the virtues have an irreplaceable task of mediation between faith and the way in which ethical norms deal with faith.[47] All these reflections must be borne in mind when Christian morality is described as the perfectly human morality. As a purely formal proposition, this is both undisputed and worthless. It is only by means of a hermeneutical reflection on the effective history of the faith that it is possible to state more precisely the contents of what is meant.

The Salutary Tension between the Final Goal and Partial Goals

These ideas will become clearer if we look at the doctrine of the final goal of the human person since ethical action is characterized by its immanent dynamic toward the definitive perfection. A human being is an ethical personality to the extent that he allows himself to be captivated by goals and commits his best powers with complete consistency and without wavering to the realization of these goals, without heeding the losses he suffers on the way. This is true universally, even beyond the borders of the Christian faith. If one's own story, in all its fragility, is to endure, one must live for an idea and let oneself be consumed for it.

But what does this mean for the Christian? No one would regard the final goal as an immediately practicable criterion of action; to think in this manner can lead only to a theological illusion, and one would expose oneself to the suspicion of ideology. Conversely, however, the doctrine of the final goal must not be formalized since the consequence would be a total irrelevance to action. At best, this doctrine would be important in terms of motivation, but all the normative perspectives would be generated by an analysis of the immediate object of action and the structures of action. This is why we must cast our net wider. The doctrine of the final goal is intimately linked to a truth of faith, that is, to eternal life in the vision of God from face to face. This sheds light on its relevance to action. The human imagination is incapable of making objective definitions here, but these are not necessary if we wish to speak of relevance to action. It appears more appropriate to say that the final goal has a liberating power. A critical filter is established for the judgment and evaluation of the innerworldly goals of one's life and one's conduct.[48]

But what kind of "criticism" is meant here? If a global relativization or even a devaluation or a casting of suspicion on innerhistorical ideas about happiness is meant, that would be inadequate because this would fail to take account of the unity in tension between creation and redemption. Accordingly, a differentiated understanding of "criticism" is necessary. An orientation to the final goal means that a person is liberated from the compulsion to realize herself within history. She is capable of enduring boundaries, renunciations, and sacrifices without becoming impoverished in human terms. She has an increasingly realistic view of things. She is aware of the transience and the abiding ambiguity of all that is earthly. She would be untruthful vis-à-vis her own self if she wished to eliminate from her own awareness of life the consolation that holds out the prospect of life after death; in any case, as time passes, she knows very well what will never be fulfilled in her own life, and she must face this with calm. She might suspect that this is a covert attempt to cheat human fate, but this is not the case. The Christian is not like the sage who justifies the suspension of his own active involvement on the grounds that all is vanity, leaving himself with nothing more than a life empty of tension. The Christian has goals for her action within history and fights to achieve these goals; she identifies with them. But this is done in the superior knowledge that all these goals possess validity only to the extent that they help her to experience already in this life the happiness that God gives, and bestow the consolation of a good conscience. It is by this criterion that the human fulfillment of the Christian must be measured. All the individual goods are functional in relation to this criterion and can claim only a hypothetical value for themselves.

Nevertheless, it is impossible to overlook the presence of wisdom too. This derives from the evaluation of the course of a person's own life and generates a fundamental attitude to life that could most fittingly be described as openness to correction. The disastrous fascination exercised by the idea of self-realization at all costs inevitably leads at some point to shipwreck; no criticism is as merciless as the criticism of history. For plans do not work out smoothly; they are thwarted again and again, when one least expects it—but when one most needs this to happen. History is nothing other than a lived theology of justification. It demonstrates at close quarters the depths of the theological idea. The doctrine of the final goal cannot dispense with this. It is linked to a theology of history that measures all the implications of the Christian image of humanity against the experience of transience. This is not the fruit of an attitude of resignation but rather of a trust that God's kindly providence extends even into the extreme situations of life, a trust that everything that happens to me will turn out to be good for me, provided that I am willing to recognize the hint that these events contain and to orient my own intentions to this hint.

It is in this perspective that the relationship between final goal and partial goals must be seen and that the word "relativization" acquires its specific coloring. When the anthropological implications of faith are described as open meanings, this description contains a pointer to the dimension of one's life story: these meanings are open to correction in the sense that the partial goals that they generate pass through the critical filter of the divine providence one has experienced and on which one has reflected. The doctrine of the final goal has moral-theological significance only when it is accompanied by an anthropologically decoded theology of the divine providence over one's own life. The believer is profoundly convinced that all the events of his life will turn out to be good for him, provided that he preserves the gift of discernment and reflects on all the experiences he has gathered to see how they can help him attain a greater purity in his intentions. He wants to learn how to let go—not in the sense of an attitude of renunciation but as an unconditional commitment to such goals for action as express the perspective of the Gospel and the anthropological implications of faith. Seen in this way, the concept of "falsification" can take on a positive meaning. The life story of the believer, if it is reflected upon attentively, unmasks all the false courses taken, and encounters and apprehends goals for action that not only make possible but also imperiously demand an undivided commitment and an unreserved gift of oneself— without crushing or discouraging the individual. The believer's goals for action are always inviting and liberating. Openness to correction is at the service of this insight to prevent it from dwindling into a trivial demand.

This has repercussions on the underlying theology of providence. God does not act immediately in external events but rather in the ability of the human person to understand their meaning. The course of history depends on this ability—if one assumes that history is an intentional achievement of the human person. Equally, we now see more clearly what is meant by speaking of the ethical insight of the believer. The final goal does not have the status of an object that makes itself known to the reason that simply records it. Rather, the final goal opens up a horizon within which goals for action within history are projected creatively. This does not impose limits on human knowledge; rather, it dissolves the boundaries and liberates this knowledge to the full exercise of its possibilities. It stimulates ethical reason by presenting points of view that are worthy of consideration and are open to further development through a norm-ethical decoding. Seen in this way, it is impossible to misunderstand what is meant by speaking of a Christian intentionality; at the same time, however, this pointer is indispensable. The intentionality of which we are speaking here does not belong to the level of the psychology of knowledge; all the ideas presented here are active on the level of the metaphysics of knowledge, but now in the context of faith. Similarly, from another perspective, we see the limitation of the conceptual pair "transcendental/categorial," where these two concepts are envisaged according to the model of an unlinked juxtaposition. In that case, one never gets beyond abstractions. But the believer is interested in how the two concepts compenetrate one another, for it is only in this way that he can identify those imperatives that correspond to his fundamental self-understanding. And this is the moment of truth.

The individual Christian cannot refuse to face this question. He must shoulder the task of becoming a religious and ethical personality. Accepting this task means having the intellectual courage to be free from all intrahistorical coercions, among which the compulsion to a controllable self-realization and self-justification occupies a central place. The one who truly believes is convinced that at the end of his days, no matter what outward appearances may suggest, God will declare him just if his conduct is in harmony with the intentionality that governs his life. Only in this way can we achieve the imperturbable self-respect that is essential for consistent ethical behavior and that bestows freedom of conscience so that one is no longer subject to the judgment of other people. This self-respect also bestows the superiority of spirit that a person needs if he is to accept justified criticism with humility and to correct what is wrong in his life. But who can live in this way? Only the person who is grateful in the depths of his heart both for the gift of his life, which continually astounds him, and for the mystery of his eternal destiny, which continually overwhelms him. In this mystery lies the driving force of a self-forgetting behavior that is free of the anguished fear that one will be impoverished in human terms, or indeed be cheated of one's own happiness in the name of morality.

But what does this mean for the task of becoming a personality? In the course of his life story, a person who consciously lives his faith acquires a distinctive religious profile. A person who begins to reflect on God's providence cannot avoid linking himself to very specific insights of faith. No doubt, he affirms the totality of his faith, and he does not make an arbitrary selection; nevertheless, through his reflection on his biography he will inevitably encounter very specific truths to which he anchors his life. These truths inspire the inner world of his thoughts, the inner world that generates his actions.

From this perspective, every Christian is an existential theologian, indeed an existentialist thinker in the most original meaning of the word. She is able to make sense of her own history and to recognize the workings of God's providence without succumbing to intellectual short circuits, thereby perhaps ending up in an intolerable rigorism. Favorable and difficult situations both offer her tasks for her life, and she can discover these and courageously set about them. When someone says that God has put her in this particular place, this is the outcome of a noble reflection that never lets go of that person but presents a challenge to the power of her imagination. Naturally, such a reflection will not dispense with evaluations of goods, but the final word belongs to the degree of the person's emotional commitment, which is the decisive factor in accepting or refusing the demand that is made of her.

It is no longer possible to evade this test of one's truthfulness. It pushes the Christian out to the periphery of his existence, and the only possibility left to him is to profess his faith. In this sense, we are justified in speaking of a personal norm that obligates only the person involved; for everyone else, it is at most understandable, and thus the personal norm (obligating *one* person) has a right to the other person's respect. It seems appropriate to link the personal truthfulness that is understood in this manner to the verdict of one's conscience. God does not inflict violence on the human person. He invites him and makes it possible for him to learn the possibilities that are inherent in his existence, but this never happens at the cost of one's freedom. No matter how plausible an insight may be, it is translated into ethical behavior only when it gives a person the freedom to be himself, when it empowers him to take responsibility for his life story in the presence of the God who encounters him in the depths of his conscience—in that place where he is completely alone with God—as the source of joy, the foundation of his life.

This sheds a clearer light on the function of ethical norms of conduct. It is of course the task of ethical norms of conduct to regulate individual decisions, thereby relieving their addressees of a burden; but these norms also oblige one to search for that ultimate point where faith becomes an anticipation of vision, where God manifests himself as the Lord of one's own life story, as the Lord who steers through all dangers a course that accomplishes his plan of salvation—even if this knowledge is born only hesitantly or, indeed, in pains and crises. Norms are thus an appeal to the human person's freedom to open himself to this truth. They lead beyond the individual decision into a fundamental sense of security; it is only this security that makes ethical conduct possible. In a person's conscience, she takes responsibility for her whole life, not only for individual deeds. This involves a fundamental attitude, not just a righteousness measured in terms of norms, and it is out of this depth that a religious and ethical personality builds itself up.

The Moral Theologian as an Ecclesial Thinker about Existence

The moral theologian cannot be indifferent to all this since ultimately he too is one who thinks about existence. He must give an account to himself of his thoughts. His reflections and speculations are sometimes abstract—what are the existential problems that in fact accompany them? Are there realities that he sidesteps surreptitiously, realities that clearly get short shrift in his thinking? Does he perhaps sense, even if only dimly, that he lives on the run from his own self and attempts to suppress the knowledge of the truth? His willingness to get involved with moral topics that are on everyone's lips can easily contain an element of self-exoneration, or indeed of self-justification. What is not put into words is just as important, or perhaps even more important. And the moral theologian must not forget this, for otherwise moral theology decays into politics and is subject to the same public constraints as all the other forces in society. In a silence that is free of such constraints, thought will be fresh and unspoiled—qualities that are required if a salutary confrontation is to take place.

This means that the first self-critical question of the moral theologian must concern the dominant methodology of his academic discipline: is the guiding interest the liberation of ethical reason based on faith, and are all other reflections subordinate to this goal? We have already discussed the relationship between ethical reason and faith. One must recognize the points of correspondence and establish them by means of argumentation; this is a summons to the truthfulness of the theologian. It is undeniable that faith is the object of exaggerated expectations, and that these can lead to a dictatorship of the *ratio theologica*, but the opposite is equally possible, that is, a laborious moralizing that takes people's breath away and hands them over to the dictatorship of unbridled reason. Here faith must establish what we might call a critical reservation by protecting reason against itself.

The moral theologian must get to grips with this patient work of thinking. This alters the perspective. The decisive questions in life are not linked so much to individual problems of normative ethics. They lie on a deeper level, and one must identify fundamental attitudes that give a constructive response to the abiding centers of conflict in life since these are a continual source of pain. Free spaces and intellectual horizons must be opened up so that one need not keep on looking at the sore points. Human beings must be given the chance to grow out beyond their past so they can look at this past as something small, something that loses its threatening power to paralyze them. The psychogram of the believer must correspond to the intellectual substance of the faith, for otherwise morality only brings death.

The areas of testing are obvious. I have in mind attitudes such as an unlimited trust in the meaningfulness of one's own commitment, despite the repeated temptations to give up, to become weary, perhaps indeed to become bitter and cynical in the face of the powerlessness and lack of success that one has suffered. I have in mind the undaunted courage to make new beginnings despite all the setbacks one has experienced. I have in mind consistency, reliability, faithfulness, and confidence, which counteract the paralyzing experience of disappointment in oneself and in one's neighbor. I have in mind tolerance and the willingness to show understanding in the construction of interpersonal relationships, no matter how the other person may react. Every one of life's dramas is played out primarily in these depths, and it is only against this background that all the concrete directives for action take on a meaning. If each directive is taken in isolation, they are inadequate to cope with the task of coping with life as a whole—and *that* is the task that these concrete directives serve. Indeed, they can become dangerous because it is all too easy for the experience of guilt to be fastened to the wrong places since guilt feelings are generated that do not in the least correspond to genuine moral failure in the depth mentioned earlier. This is why the transgressions of norms are never more than the tip of the iceberg, like symptoms that point to a hidden disease, to unresolved existential conflicts that repeatedly elude one's grasp, or conflicts that one is only too happy to evade to save oneself from shouldering the burden of patient contestation.

The moral theologian must not deceive himself on this point, for otherwise—no matter how precise and free of contradiction the formulation of his normative statements may be—he will be conniving at a creeping untruthfulness. In the last analysis, the human person is more than a logical system, and inappropriate parameters of academic discourse risk distorting reality. Besides this, they help no one. If effective help is to be offered for the problems of life, we need healing perspectives that assist in the reconciliation of the conflicts that have caused pain. These perspectives have their source in the basic self-understanding of the believer, and they need the intellectual preparation of moral-theological reflection. Ultimately, a person can pass the ethical test only where it is possible, despite all the fear of losing herself, to grasp the promise of a fulfilled life, where the wounds she has suffered do not make her bitter but rather offer a welcome opportunity to reflect on the fundamental ideals involved in the project she has sketched out for her life.

It may surely be taken for granted that moral-theological work has an ecclesial dimension. When the question of authority attracts all the interest in this connection, this inevitably leads to a shortening of perspective, and one forgets that the community of believers *as a whole* bears responsibility for ethical knowledge and pursues the search for it, although there are always moral elites or competent moral judges who play a decisive role in this process. This means that, despite what may sometimes seem to be the case, ethical truth is not "administered." Rather, the Church is the privileged place of discovery of the truth, and hence the privileged place of truthfulness: this is the Church's task. This points us anew to the deep dimension of ethical knowledge that I have mentioned above. Human questions that emerge from this depth—human questions about which people do not speak—are taken up in the Church, where things that are usually veiled in silence are put into words.[49] It is certainly necessary to take a moral position on the problems of the age, and the Church would be unfaithful to its mission if it were to refuse this intellectual challenge. Nevertheless, this is only a part (and not the most essential part) of the responsibility that the Church bears. There is also the risk that the Church will overextend itself by failing to respect the different degrees of authority. This will mean overdoing things on the level of the Church's authority to issue moral directives, by succumbing to the temptation to issue excessive definitions that settle like a burden on the individual's conscience instead of setting him free.[50]

This already indicates one initial critical question regarding the dominant idea about public order in the Church. Which criteria are applied to this idea, either explicitly or implicitly? One fundamental principle must be that the ideas about order in the sphere of the life of civil society cannot be transposed to the sphere within the Church. This sphere follows criteria and perspectives of its own. Even to speak of an "analogy" between the two orders risks causing misunderstandings when this evokes the association of "similarity." At most, one can speak of a "negative analogy" where the dissimilar elements outweigh the similar. Similar reservations are appropriate in any discussion of public morality, irrespective of how close or loose a link is intended between the legal and the moral orders.

If we accept this, we can draw a first boundary line. The endeavor to attain precision in normative affirmations is understandable because what is involved is not only security in one's action and in life in society but also the effective protection of vulnerable and perhaps irreparable human goods. Nevertheless, it is possible to issue detailed regulations only to the extent that this is allowed by the specific character of the goods that need protection, and of the ethical actions that are oriented to these goods. This boundary line is drawn by the nature of the case, and to transgress it implies untruthfulness: one gives the impression of certainty, but such a certainty goes far beyond the possibilities of one's own intellectual achievements. The intention is to ease people's burdens, but instead, as if by a sleight of hand, it actually imposes a burden that has a paralyzing impact on the joy involved in taking ethical decisions and on the free spontaneity of action. This is tragic because the courage to speak plainly and commit oneself, instead of being content with wishy-washy exhortations, deserves all our respect. The Church is in fact an uncomfortable dialogue partner that does not abandon its ability to utter contradictions or hide its own convictions, although the question—once again, a test of truthfulness—must still be asked: Does this really happen with the same consistency in every sphere of life, or is there an arbitrary construction of particular emphases?

The Second Vatican Council stated that an ethical pluralism exists in the Church too. This phenomenon seems so familiar by now that it is not necessary to discuss it any further. But the almost thoughtless way with which this topic is treated, as something taken for granted, is perplexing. Is the dissent in the Church truly as great as it appears? Has not dissent always existed? Is not the characteristic mark of the present age that one ascribes an official status to this dissent, instead of suppressing it? *E contra*, is not the consensus greater than some people are willing to admit? Where are the decisive causes of an existing ethical pluralism? Do they lie in different anthropological presuppositions for the formation of ethical judgments, which sometimes accompany cultural or subcultural patterns? Do they lie in different temporal rhythms of the processes whereby ethical insight is attained? Do they lie in divergent external conditions of ethical action? Or do they lie in erroneous normative deductions? Such questions need to be cleared up before a normative position can be taken. And such a position may perhaps include a demand for tolerance. The decisive factor is always the extent to which the manifestations of pluralism are justified. Truthfulness means tracking down the real causes without prematurely breaking off the search for a consensus; otherwise, one gives rise to the suspicion that one is putting the unity of the truth at risk. Any dissent that erupts can never be rooted in the truth itself. It has its origin in the diverse historical conditions of the knowledge of the truth, whether these conditions lie in the external milieu or in the knowing subject himself.

As I have mentioned in an earlier context, this must be borne in mind especially in the case of the argument from the natural law. The natural ethical law is characterized by its inherent dynamic, which makes toward a growing unity. Before it is possible to work toward unity, there must already exist a comprehensive horizon of that which is held in common. For how would it be possible to recognize pluralism if not against the background of an existing agreement? To affirm that this agreement must never be understood mechanically (that is, at the cost of the varied expressive power of the *humanum*) may seem a commonplace since we find the same problematic—in a manner completely free of suspicion—when we seek to apply meaningfully the principle of equality. It is up to the differences to demonstrate their worth; they draw their justification from their ability to confer a meaningful expression on the unity.

Moral theology, as an academic discipline linked to the Church, can find inspiration in this example when it assists the magisterium in grappling intellectually with pluralism. Tolerance becomes untruthful as soon as it surreptitiously abandons the search for consensus; freedom's right to search for the truth also includes an obligation to accept the truth. Nevertheless, there is one thing we should not forget: a dissent that is endured in honest tolerance is certainly a better basis, and is easier to live, than a forced consensus that fails to respect the fact that one must freely accept the burden entailed by the processes whereby knowledge is attained.

This draws our attention to the existential emergency of ethical pluralism, which always occurs whenever the limits of the ability to withstand stress become obvious, that is, when a person comes to the limits of his strength and every further step would be a destructive excessive demand. This tension will be experienced as especially painful where there is a clearly developed consciousness of the prophetical dimension of Christian morality and of the way in which the Church speaks of this. What the Church proposes is not primarily a system of norms, for such an idea would fail to do justice to its task. The Church endeavors to develop better alternatives for action by cutting a path through the undergrowth of compulsions that have come into existence as a result of human guilt, both on the level of knowledge and on the level of freedom. The Church always addresses higher demands to the human person. Processes of ethical insight always remain unfinished, and it is here that the Church attempts progressively to resolve the conflict between grace and concupiscence by elaborating liberating objectives that almost imperceptibly establish themselves as norms. This process must not be stretched out on the Procrustean bed of a triumphalistic rigorism, for in that case hypocrisy would be but a single step away. This process is truthful only when it also sets one free to exercise a greater clemency. For ethical truth is always a disputed and oppressed truth. It cannot be established by force; in addition to a better insight, it needs the testimony of a person who accompanies one on the road. Ethical progress means creating space equally for the challenge and for the sympathetic understanding; the scandal begins where this does not occur. All ideas about "order" must find their orientation in the same perspective.

Notes

1. See Schaeffler, *Die Wechselbeziehungen.*
2. Lotz, "Zur Thomas-Rezeption der Maréchal-Schule."
3. Demmer, *Deuten und handeln*, 131–68.
4. Demmer, "Natur und Person"; and Thomas Aquinas, *Summa theologica* I.29.3 c.
5. Schockenhoff, *Das umstrittene Gewissen*, 99–114.
6. Demmer, *Moraltheologische Methodenlehre*, 34–52.
7. *Gaudium et spes*, 22.
8. Schaeffler, "Zur Anthropologie und Ethik der Hoffnung."
9. See Bujo, *Die Begründung des Sittlichen*, 123–36.
10. Virt, *Epikie*, 261–66.
11. Demmer, *Moraltheologische Methodenlehre*, 136–41.
12. Demmer, "Erwägungen zum 'intrinsice malum.'"
13. For an historical overview, see Müller, *Die Wahrhaftigkeitspflicht.*
14. See Simon, *Wahrheit als Freiheit.*
15. Hedwig, "Die philosophischen Voraussetzungen," discusses the analogy of the concept of truth and reflects on this with regard to objective truths and truth *in actu.*
16. This is emphasized by Schüller, *Die Begründung sittlicher Urteile*, 162 and 308.
17. *Summa theologica*, I.79, 11 ad 2.
18. The distinction commonly made in normative ethics between goodness and correctness tacitly assumes a metaphysics of action that remains tied to the external performance of actions. For a sketch of the historical background, see Pinckaers, *Ce qu'on ne peut jamais faire*, 20–66.
19. See, among others, Rhönheimer, *Natur als Grundlage der Moral*, 312–16.
20. Mieth, *Die neuen Tugenden.*
21. Puntel, *Wahrheitstheorien in der neueren Philosophie*, 29–31; and Bender, *Ethische Urteilsbildung*, 66ff.
22. Thomas Aquinas, *De veritate* I.1.

23. *Summa theologica*, I-II 94, 2 c.

24. Habermas (1981); Apel, *Diskurs und Verantwortung*; Höhn, "Vernunft—Kommunikation—Diskurs"; and Bucher, *Ethik—eine Hinführung*, 210–20.

25. Schüller, "Zum Pluralismus in der Ethik."

26. Demmer, *Moraltheologische Methodenlehre*, 136–41.

27. Lotz, *Transzendentale Erfahrung*.

28. One relevant example is the relationship between law and morality, and the underlying understanding of the state.

29. *Summa Theologica*, I-II 100 and 108.

30. It is, however, possible for texts of the magisterium to have recourse all too glibly to the supposed will of God, especially when appealing to the necessary bond between faith and the ethical reason.

31. For example, the introduction of personalistic categories ought to lead to a more differentiated view of the relationship between nature and person. Demmer, "Natur und Person," 79.

32. Wolbert, "Naturalismus in der Ethik."

33. The moral theologian who has studied the philosophy of science is aware of the abiding tension between hypotheses and theories.

34. Innovatory achievements of ethical insight derive from the willingness on the part of ethical elites to bear a testimony that goes against the dominant trend—and to do so for the whole of their lives.

35. In its document "On the Interpretation of Dogmas," the International Theological Commission speaks of a hermeneutic of suspicion. English text: *Origins* 20 (May 17, 1990): 1–14.

36. In this context we are often told that there is closeness in terms of the history of ideas to the epoch of nominalism.

37. Experience shows that trench warfare leads to a narrowing down of perspectives, where people lose sight of the escape routes that could set them free.

38. Demmer, *Sittlich handeln aus Verstehen*, 39–43.

39. One can draw up a list of subjects that swallow up considerable amounts of intellectual energy—for example, ecology, bioethics, or economic ethics—but that affect only in a peripheral manner one's awareness of life and the way in which the individual leads his or her life.

40. See Weber, ed., *Der ethische Kompromiss*, 113–46.

41. One can make the mistake of a bad reading of bad tradition. Criticism should always be directed at the best representatives of a position, for then it automatically relativizes itself.

42. The current euphoria with regard to Saint Thomas is a relevant example here, especially because this recourse concerns questions of the modern lifeworld such as contraception and bioethics.

43. See, for example, Wolkinger, *Moraltheologie und Josephinische Aufklärung*, 77 and passim.

44. Wolbert, "Wozu eine Tugendethik?" 249–54.

45. Höver, *Sittlich handeln im Medium der Zeit*, 313–31.

46. The original Kantian text encompasses a problem that is not necessarily the problem of the scholastic thinker; see the reflections by Thönissen, *Das Geschenk der Freiheit*.

47. Schockenhoff, *Bonum hominis*, 349–51.

48. The consciousness that all earthly goods are subject to temporality is antecedent to the analysis of the individual object and makes this analysis possible. This is important for every evaluation.

49. Of its very nature, the Church brings reconciliation and therefore also healing because it gives ethical action a place in God's redeeming act. See Hünermann and Schaeffler, eds., *Theorie der Sprachhandlungen*, 130–49.

50. Schuster, *Ethos und kirchliches Lehramt*; Römelt, "Glaubende Kirche und Ethik," 144–54; and Müller, "Was ist kirchlicher Gehorsam?" 26–48.

CHAPTER THREE

Truthfulness as the Basic Attitude of the Ethical Personality

Simplicity of Insight

E VERY ETHICAL ACTION is a self-presentation of the agent in which he displays himself fully as he truly is. It is therefore only right to see ethical action as the touchstone of truthfulness. There is a very intimate reciprocal relationship between morality and truthfulness. Our own tradition has occasionally lost sight of this link; the decisive reason for this is inherent in the system and lies in the conception of the manuals of moral theology, most of which were constructed according to the structure of the ten commandments or of the various groups of obligations. The obligations vis-à-vis the truth stood alongside other obligations that were equal in rank. It was scarcely possible to discern any person-centered structure—neither was such a structure intended. The primary interest lay in the compilation of the material, and thinking in terms of the system took priority over thinking in terms of the person.

The newly awakened interest in virtue ethics has brought an obvious change in perspective. Now it is the person, defined as a personality, who occupies the central place. Fundamental attitudes, which derive from the fundamental positions taken by the person, delineate his intellectual and ethical profile. These are far from devoid of content. In these fundamental attitudes, an existential situation relevant to action takes form in the shape of a preliminary understanding that subsequently seeks to be translated into concrete deeds. The driving force here is the fundamental self-understanding of the agent. This begins by taking the form of virtues in which it can find the safe starting point for each specific individual action. Accordingly, it is not at all surprising that the intellectual virtues— especially prudence—assume a leading role in Saint Thomas's thinking. This leading role is fully bound to the subject, for it is only so that it is possible to examine and come to know the ethical object.[1] The agent projects himself into his world of objects, and this empowers him to apprehend the claim that is inherent in these objects. The intellectual virtues thus establish an intellectual horizon within which individual acts of knowledge take place. At least in most instances, the certainty that is present in this horizon is greater than the certainty that attaches to the particular act of knowledge directed to an object, although unique situations are also conceivable in which (independently of the degree of their inherent complexity) the state of affairs is self-evident, and compelling imperatives take hold of the individual and indeed force him to act in one particular way, since there are no longer any other alternative possibilities of action which need to be taken seriously. Such a certainty is not unfounded: it occurs above all where the intellectual virtues authenticate an indubitable basic orientation of one's own life and at the same time help one to attain the ability to make a concrete judgment. The more the individual allows himself to be captivated by this image of virtue, the less probable it is that he will err. We see here in a very compelling manner that ethical knowledge is essentially free; it can be realized only as truthfulness, that is, as the fundamental attitude that fuses into a conscious and intended synthesis both the burden that is laid upon the subject and the orientation to the object.

If the specific object of ethical reason is the good with regard to its truth, and if this is grasped (despite all the ramifications of an intense reflection) in one simple act of knowledge, this reveals to us a first characteristic of the truthful person: the attitude of an indisputable simplicity or sobriety of thought that has an open mind and allows itself to be captivated by the truth. This is the most natural thing in the world. Everyone who has the courage to say "yes" to his own ego desires spontaneously to be truthful, for it is only thus that he is fully himself. Otherwise, he will lead a life that passes his own self by. Behind this lies the conviction that the real goal of ethical truth is that the human being should become a person. Ethical truth helps us to lead our life on the basis of the meaning that it discloses to us, and it preserves us from leading a life at second hand, a life lived (consciously or unconsciously) at the expense of others—for such a life cheats one sooner or later of the self-respect that is required if one is to act with any kind of consistency.

Such an attitude can stem only from an ultimate certainty, an undaunted trust in the meaningfulness of one's own life, regardless of all successes and failures, and independent of all the affirmation that one may have experienced at the hands of one's fellow human beings. The truthful person is moved by only one concern—not to fail in his life's project with all its claims, ideals, and promises. This concern consumes all his emotional energy. He is kept spellbound by all those necessary things on which he lavishes the best of his powers, driven by the deep-seated fear lest he might not have filled the days of his life to the full, lest he might have failed to recognize the promise that these days contain. It is easy to see that the truthful person can only be one who shapes his life on the basis of an inner life orientated to transcendence, one who has the gift and the strength to enter into the silence of this inner life and to find there all that he needs. The truthful person dwells in his thoughts here. He calls an inviolable inner space his own. Since no one else can assail this space and wrest control over it from his grasp, it can be the basis of his freedom. The moral-theological topic of the right to a private sphere has a number of more superficial aspects, but it points beyond these to this basis: one must be truthful, for only so is it possible to unfold oneself and to lead a life that one has freely chosen for oneself, a life free of all heteronomy.

Nothing is as true as death. No one can escape its clutches, and it always has the last word. Only the person who understands how to die, who does not fritter away her life in the permanent flight from death, is able to be truthful because she possesses the power to block off the many superficial (indeed, banal) possibilities of flight that are open to her, and to achieve mastery over the time that is available to her. But this is possible only where death is not understood as a threat, a moral catastrophe, or the definitive seal set on human failure but rather as a passage to eternal beatitude in the vision of God from face to face.[2] To carry out this transformation in the course of time is a task for the whole of one's life, a task with which we are confronted openly in situations of obvious loss. Only the person who lives out of the invisible has mastery over the visible.

It is important to underline this point because this entails preliminary decisions about the elaboration of a theory of action. These decisions concern the relationship between the final goal and partial goals, which we have discussed earlier. While there is surely a basic decision in favor of the final goal, there is no basic decision in favor of death. Death is not chosen: death is undergone. How this happens depends on the meaning given to death—and this in turn depends on how the final goal is understood. All the individual decisions are located in this perspective: in the sphere of temporality, they are interpretative extensions of the basic decision into the material of the reality of the world around us. In this way the decisive course is set for the understanding of individual goals in keeping with the fundamental attitude of the agent, which is built up in the inner world of his thoughts, wishes, and aspirations. We always approach the objects of our actions with a preunderstanding, for it is only thus that they receive the status of goals of action. At the same time, the specific object of action is recognized in its indissoluble ambivalence: in its finitude and transience, it reminds us of the ineluctability of our own dying. Only with this reservation is it possible to aim at this object; only so can it attract the dynamic of the human will, only so is it true. And only the person who is willing to accept this ambivalence can be called truthful because he does not fall victim to any delusions about what lies in store both for him and for what he does in this time. Rather, he endeavors to extract from the transience something that endures, thus identifying and structuring the goals of his action in such a way that this can genuinely take place.

This has consequences for the attitude of truthfulness. Death is a precursor, antecedent to everything that exists. This generates in us an attitude of "precursory" commitment: we have no illusions about our own fragility, and we anticipate the needs of our neighbor and help him. It is not so much death that is the threat but rather our own inability to cope with the experience of transience. It is therefore not surprising that others find the truthful person attractive. Fear does not make him power-mad since he has already confronted the power of death. He gives his neighbor space to breathe. He does not seek to gain influence and to establish interpersonal dependencies that merely lead him to forget his own weakness. The truthful person is very much aware that he does not need any of this to have a fulfilled life. He knows, on the contrary, that if communication is to succeed, it must be characterized by powerlessness.

Purity of Attitude

The truthful person is a conviction ethicist in the most original sense of this term. She begins by imposing order upon the world of her thoughts because this is her most essential lifeworld. There must not be any discrepancy between the inside and the outside, between thinking and action. If the unity of the personality is not to be broken up and gradually destroyed, she must establish an equilibrium that is open to the future. Naturally, this ethical requirement has a programmatic character. In other words, it cannot be realized overnight, but needs lifelong attention. If excessive demands and setbacks are to be avoided, it may be a good idea to speak of a *dominium politicum*; but this must not dilute the seriousness of the requirement because the person who does not hold her thoughts in check makes herself open to attack and easily becomes the plaything of momentary impressions, feelings, or moods. This leads to an increasing self-uncertainty because she cannot resist these attacks and hence succumbs to them. The pact with the enemy is already made, and all that is needed is the external occasion—which will indubitably arise.

The truthful person instinctively admits to herself that she is fragile, thanks to the coercive force of her thoughts. Accordingly, she has a vigilant sensitivity with regard to this danger, which erupts from within her own self. Conviction ethics means building up a discerning world of thought that keeps in mind the best of what one has become conscious of in the course of one's life.[3] Only the best is good enough for the truthful person; without self-respect, she perishes. The person who can relate lovingly to her own thoughts, who genuinely takes care of them, can feel certainty about her decisions—she will retain full control over them. The intellectual climate is determined by her calm and her mastery. A harmony unfolds between attitude and behavior, a harmony that is strong enough to endure conflicts and ensures the success not only of individual decisions but also of an entire life. The truthful person knows that an intellectual culture is a helpful presupposition of ethical consistency. It makes her able to pursue goals of action using the strength that is in fact available to her. Incidental evaluations of consequences do not weaken the goal but seek to discern it all the more purely.[4] A precarious procedure of evaluation of this kind, which introduces an element of strategy into ethical behavior, can elude the danger of self-deception only if one has practiced the formulation of "unbribable" verdicts in one's thoughts well in advance.

This implies a question that must be posed with regard to the exact situation analysis that leaves nothing out. It is indeed true that one must take intellectual responsibility for the goal of action at which one aims; a lack of analytical incisiveness leads either to excessive demands or to irresponsibility. Nevertheless, in this exercise of intellectual acumen, the thoughts do not get bogged down but also reflect on the power of one's own freedom. Once again, this is where conviction ethics comes into its own. What one considers a reasonable demand is the fruit of an inner truthfulness that consistently blocks off every intellectual escape route. The emotional commitment of a person's own freedom decides what is possible, and he bears intellectual responsibility for this freedom since it is not something that simply occurs naturally. Rather, it points to a background in his life story that must be recalled and reflected upon, and that addresses an abiding appeal to his willingness to learn.

The strength of an ethical personality depends on the extent to which a person integrates his own past in ever-new attempts. In each decision that he takes, this background in his life story is present. The ground is prepared gradually for changes because changes do not fall like a bolt from the blue. It is possible to notice the signs that point ahead to them, and an ethical personality retains a vigilant sensitivity to events of this kind so he is never caught unprepared by challenging situations. The ethos of prophylaxis begins in the sphere of his inner life.

The truthful person is characterized by simplicity of thought, naïveté, or indeed foolishness that is far removed from weakness or simple-mindedness and is in fact the opposite of this. The truthful person is well aware that the good is exposed to contestation in this world, and he notes with a vigilant eye the obvious pointlessness of many a well-intentioned effort. To flee from this reality leads to self-deception, and he is not in the least inclined to this; at the same time, however, he retains his basic optimism because he is profoundly convinced that the good never happens in vain, even if its fruits may ripen in a place where he does not expect it. He thus approaches his own history with a preliminary decision and remains resolved to interpret all events and experiences in keeping with this preliminary decision. He constructs his own reality by means of an interpretative achievement.

We must look more closely at this. The Western philosophical tradition has made us familiar with the theorem of the *reditio completa*, in which elements of the metaphysics of knowledge and mysticism coalesce.[5] When the knowing mind enters into itself, it discovers its capacity for the truth. In the knowing agreement with itself lies the ontological reason for the agreement with the surrounding world of the objective and the empirical. Truth thus occurs where the act of knowledge forms the details of its object and thereby makes the person capable of knowledge. It is impossible to separate the theory of the truth from the theory of knowledge since each determines the other. This is why a person is justified in affirming that truth is constructed by the knowing mind. This is the case, at any rate, when we reflect on the empirical knowledge of the object from the perspective of the context of the theory of truth.

It would obviously be fallacious to introduce such fundamental reflections directly into the topic we are discussing and to draw ethical consequences from them. Nevertheless, such reflections are relevant to ethics because they permit us to reflect on the metaphysical conditions of truthfulness in the knowing and acting subject. To form the details of the world of objects through the act of knowing means introducing into this world of objects a preunderstanding that is present in the subject. In its capacity to do this, the human mind displays its function of imposing order. This has obvious consequences for the way in which the ethical question is posed: truthfulness means the readiness to interpret the totality of human experiential reality in such a way that it is at the service of one's own ethical consistency. This reality is true to the extent that it allows one to recognize the possibilities of better conduct and to grasp these possibilities decisively—in short, it is true to the extent that it exposes itself to the ray of light that is shed by ideals and objectives.

The capacity for conflict in our life story leads to hurts and disappointments, and if these are not to become a pretext for bitterness, it is necessary to establish truthfulness on these epistemological-anthropological foundations. The truthful person makes himself vulnerable. He accepts the risk of human communication without reserve, and there is no "breastplate" of intellectual compartmentalization to shield him. He identifies himself spontaneously with what he says and what he does, without needing any special reflection, still less any explicit intention to do so. Whatever he does takes on inevitably the character of an expressive action in which his innermost dispositions are revealed. And this must be so, for otherwise life in society will be continuously marked by tactical considerations and protective measures. At some point, the rearguard battles become second nature, and one no longer knows who the other person really is. Where people encounter one another without trust, interpersonal relationships are doomed to die since this is then not an encounter between personalities but between people playing roles in a play.

The Life Story as an Interpretative Framework

We have not yet exhausted the significance of the interpretative achievement that was mentioned earlier in connection with the epistemological-anthropological foundations. Further perspectives will take our reflections deeper.[6] We shall look here at the underlying existential project that affects everyone, provided only that he lives consciously and consistently.

The ethical stature of a person is shown in the honesty with which he approaches this task. The epistemological realism is translated into an existential attitude that flows into every mode of communication. Here the word "interpretation" takes on a specific coloring. It dispels the suspicion that a subtle subjectivism is at work; rather, it presupposes insight into an objective meaning of life as the very thing that makes interpretation possible. But this insight is not completely present from the outset. It discloses itself only in the course of a lifelong process that must go through ups and downs, through certainty and contestation, if the end result is to be a completely mature personality, one whom his neighbor experiences not as a burden or as a source of fear but as a support. A person discovers himself, in his possibilities and in his limits, and he grows into ever more spacious rooms of the inner life—provided only that he opens himself to this process without reserve.

Many situations give an impetus to this process, but the decisive tension is kept alive by the imagination of a person's own ego: the personality is itself the law that governs its development in the course of the life story. It is thus only logical that both self-respect and the claim one makes on oneself increase. In this way, a filter is set up in the inner life. Its meshes admit only that which can be integrated into the logic of this development—everything else is excluded from admittance to one's own inner world. This is not a censorship that distorts things. It corresponds to an intuitive need to develop one's best powers and not to lag behind the de facto possibilities, for that would entail a creeping untruthfulness.

But where are we to find the interpretation mentioned earlier? How does it come into operation? If one extends the epistemological-anthropological access route by analogy to the dimension of a person's life story, we see that the specific object of this interpretation is events that generate experiences. Here the entire wealth of the word "experience" comes into play. It includes not only the dimension of the empirically vivid but also the transience of time. This is the raw material into which the human person interprets a life project. It is true that the world of the given supplies indispensable clues, which are registered by the observing reason, but these do not suffice for a life project—this requires transcendent criteria that derive from the creative imagination of reason. A horizon is opened up, within which all the partial elements are in movement, although this takes place in a varying acceleration. Freedom has a constitutive share in this process.

Because ethical truth is personal truth, it has an expressive quality that can be discovered and translated into action only in the course of a lifelong process. The richness of a personality, a person's sapiential insight, the congenital gifts and acquired abilities, the nuances of her worldview—all of this requires a temporal sequence if it is to be brought to light and realized. The various modes of communication must expect this to be the case; they never stop short at the superficial information because the background in the person's life story always flows into them. She can of course endeavor to prescind from this methodologically, and to let pure objectivity dominate. But in order to do this, she needs the capacity for abstraction, and this is acquired in the course of her life story. It has its origin in an overflowing wealth that never imposes itself but gives her neighbor what he rightly expects. The more differentiated and distinctive a personality is, the more will she succeed in achieving such a pure objectivity.

But the laws that derive from a person's life story and govern communication go even deeper than this. Dialogue partners always go together along one part of the path. Their encounter is never limited to one isolated point in time. If it did not go beyond this, and this happened deliberately or because of carelessness, the encounter would be unnatural. This observation contains considerable ethical implications that in turn concern the interpretative achievement that is required here.

This applies first to the situation of the one who speaks since he makes the gift of himself, in all his vulnerability, to such a situation. Communicating himself always means exposing himself, and this is why he quite spontaneously feels the need for self-protection. This ambivalence attaches to all speaking. If communication is to be successful, trust is necessary. The richer a personality is, and the more ramifications the background in his life story, the higher are the demands. In comparison with this, the individual points in time, which demand no commitments, inevitably look like a barbarous lack of culture; culture requires time, not only to perceive commitments but also to participate actively—and this is a question of intensity rather than of frequency. However, a certain length of time is necessary since duration is always the indispensable medium of personal self-disclosure. This duration requires closeness, but it also demands distance since the partners in the communication need a space to discover themselves, a sphere of personal intimacy into which the other must not intrude if the communication is to succeed. Where one partner imposes his will on the other, the presuppositions for a high-quality fellowship will soon wear out. Where people no longer understand how to be silent together, where silence is felt as a threat, the spoken word has already lost its power to unite them. Emptiness spreads out, and all the spoken word can do is to fill this gap. Solitude is something completely different from the isolation that kills, and only the one who is able to bear this solitude is capable of communication. Every fellowship lives out of this power—for otherwise it only oppresses the individual.

This means that we have now identified one first object of interpretation. The question is what demands the speaker can make of his own self. What degree of trust has been reached so that he can give another person a share in his own lifeworld? There must be a reciprocal correspondence between the intensity of the encounter on the one hand and the contents and extent of the disclosure on the other; this is where the registering reason meets its limitations. Where communication does succeed, it is ultimately up to the speaker to decide freely what world is revealed to the hearer. The expectations of the hearer must be measured against this criterion.

Interpretation does not in any sense contradict the demand for unambiguousness, but it protects us against fatal simplifications that can have negative effects on the speaker, the hearer, or third persons. We cannot apply the model of an action that brings about particular effects to communication on the level of verbal disclosure.[7] It is indeed true that fellowship is brought about by means of speech, but this effect cannot be separated unambiguously from its cause since it is already present in this cause. And this is why speech tends to take on the characteristics of an expressive action. The speech act is not functionalized but retains its own value. In speech, the speaker is entirely present: he presents himself as he genuinely is. This is a test of his truthfulness: there is a seamless transition between what he is and what he does.

A person who is willing to take part in verbal disclosure will be concerned to achieve a harmony between means and ends, making the tension between these two as transparent as possible. From the perspective of the speaker, and with regard to his ability to communicate, this means that his overriding concern must be to translate in a consistent manner the unambiguousness of his life project and of his fundamental attitude into the spoken word. Justice vis-à-vis his dialogue partner demands this because it is the word that offers him the immediate access to his own person. No doubt, what the speaker does continues to stand alongside what he says, and everyone will agree that his deed gives information about the seriousness and the weightiness of his word. This, however, does not invalidate what I have just said because the deed also demands the word that accompanies it, interprets it, and opens it up. At any rate, the dialogue partner wants to know whom he is encountering. He demands certainty.

In many situations, it is legitimate for his dialogue partner to demand certainty, and this will in fact be his wish. And it is relatively easy to grant this wish because everything comes down to the question of what the other person is entitled to demand. But the demand for certainty cannot be limited to the unambiguousness of the information that he owes to a dialogue partner: communication that is more than information goes deeper than this. The corresponding right to unambiguousness aims to protect human vulnerability at one of its most sensitive spots, that of unfeigned trust. Everyone treats his neighbor spontaneously as a potential friend— the axiom *homo homini amicus* is an apt expression of this inclination—and no one feels more humiliated than the person who is let down by a "neighbor" who abuses the trust that has been placed in him. The material damage that may be involved here is not the decisive factor. Rather, one feels hurt in one's self-respect, and this undermines the quality of dependability in the life one shares with others in society. Against this background, information remains "functionally" oriented to communication: in principle, the disclosure of individual truths is embedded in the self-disclosure of the truthful person.

From this we can infer a preferential strategic rule: the presumption is in favor of the fullness of information to the extent that this serves communication. The burden of proof lies on those who would maintain the opposite position. The expressive character of language shows clearly how precarious it is to keep silent about things, and a fortiori to make a false statement, since spoken words are not interchangeable like the instruments one employs to attain some particular goal with the greatest possible efficiency. Here more than anywhere, the goal at which one aims is already virtually present in the instrument employed! It is the privileged status of language, that is, its immediate relationship to the person, that resists every tendency to functionalization. The speaker is himself directly affected in the act of speaking, and it is utterly impossible for him to distance himself from his language. Indeed, his act of speaking has an immediate repercussion, whether positive or negative, on his intellectual and moral state. This means that truthfulness in speaking is, not least, something that protects the speaker himself. Situations of speech must remain transparent, for otherwise human fellowship is irreparably sundered.

Key Situations of Communication

What is true in general of the broad spectrum of life takes on an explicit and concentrated form in key situations that demand maximum trust if a person is to pass her test unharmed.[8] Let us first consider the speaker. When irrevocable conditions for living are to be constructed, she must invest trust. Her future life-partner has a legitimate desire to be shown her own lifeworld and to be told about the thoughts, problems, and questions that preoccupy her. There must be a dialogue that touches on all the subjects that are central to her life and brings to light her opinions and fundamental attitudes, though in a manner that is open to correction. For it is only thanks to the challenge of a dialogue that each person reflects on that which moves her most profoundly, on that out of which she lives. She reveals herself to her dialogue partner, and she is able to do so only when she knows that she is protected in her vulnerability, that is, only when she is met with respect. This brings out a singular feature of human relationships that usually only touches our consciousness tangentially, namely that mutual respect is the indispensable presupposition of love. Where mutual respect is preserved, love possesses a safe point of contact, irrespective of all dangers that threaten. The presuppositions for this are inculcated in a dialogue where the partners encounter one another in freedom and thus grow toward one another without taking possession of each other. It is then absolutely right for a person to let himself be guided by love when he assesses how far he should go in revealing himself and to what extent there remains a sphere of the inner life that belongs to himself alone—though without entailing any breach of trust. In that case, the only decisive criterion is the capacity of his dialogue partner to bear what he tells him or her.

It is easy to see that despite all the closeness that is offered and sought, a dialogue conducted in a spirit of trust erects a protective wall that prevents the accompanying experience of bodiliness and sexuality from becoming a continual source of unease and that prevents this experience from deteriorating into triviality. The physical gesture needs the spoken word, for otherwise it becomes aggressive and even restricts the freedom of choice since it makes an impartial judgment impossible and creates emotional bonds that lack any basis in an understanding harmony. This can never have a happy outcome, for the moment of truth will come at some point in life, the hour that demands a person to nail her colors to the mast. Then she will be obliged at last to do something she wantonly neglected at the proper time—and this never happens without pain.

There are, however, also situations in which the hearer is just as vulnerable, just as much in need of protection, as the speaker. Frequently an introduction step by step into the full truth, taking account of the law of growth, is necessary. Once again, key situations that demand complete trust are conceivable. It is indisputable that the basic right to the truth is at the service of freedom because only the person who has an unrestricted access to the truth can form a judgment in freedom and thus lead a life for which he himself takes full responsibility. This demand has its source in the dignity of the person: at its root is the principle of autonomy. The right to the truth is very close to the right to life, provided that the word "life" is understood to mean a life that is worthy of the human being, that is, as a fundamental anthropological category.

Here too, the principle of what can reasonably be demanded comes into play: while the truth itself cannot impose on the hearer a burden that goes beyond the limits of his strength, this can certainly be done by an incautious introduction to the truth, an introduction that is remote from reality. This entails a lofty responsibility on the part of the speaker, who must empathize with the situation of the person whom he is addressing. He must ask himself what the foreseeable effects of his speaking will be. Is the other person capable of coping with these effects? Is it possible to limit or indeed avert harm by reducing the communication and accommodating it to the hearer's ability to receive it? There are many imponderable factors in a reflection that is based in suppositions and is forced to take into account the incalculable freedom of the hearer. Perhaps he is much stronger than one is willing to admit, and perhaps he might feel humiliated if this kind of consideration was shown him. Even the best of intentions cannot eliminate this risk. Evaluations of goods do not lessen this risk; they only help to define the reality involved.

The classic example that is generally adduced here is the relationship between doctor and patient, especially in extreme situations of incurable suffering and certain death. To hand over this problem to the sensitivity of the doctor alone, so that she would have to find an acceptable solution while absolving the sick or dying person from *his* responsibility, would be short-sighted because truth always comes into being between equal partners, and everyone involved has a share in this. This is why it is supremely important to practice truthfulness in every period of one's life story. This can never begin too early, and no life is immune to situations in which truthfulness may be put to the harshest of tests. The calm acceptance of one's own dying is the high point that sums up everything that one has courageously practiced in the course of a whole lifetime. There are people who—on closer examination—have in fact always led a parasitical existence at others' expense by evading every painful confrontation, thus leading a life at second hand in an illusory world. This will inevitably end in a catastrophe, even if only in the hour of their death; and perhaps this attitude was in fact already a hidden flight from the death that manifested itself in all its premonitory signs. This means that the doctor is faced by an earlier history, most of which is unknown to her. She can communicate only so much of the truth as the sick or dying person explicitly or implicitly allows.

Even if we admit all this, it is nevertheless an undeniable fact of our experience that the communication of the full truth usually has the effect of liberation and release. The burden of uncertainty is lifted from our shoulders, and we can more easily receive the consolation that consists in being able to die. Ultimately, everyone has the right to prepare himself consciously for his death. This too—and not only the greatest possible freedom from pain—belongs to the dignity of dying. However, such demands are meaningful only if they encounter an understanding of death that is dictated not by a hopeless terror but by a calm acceptance. The capacity for truthfulness is acquired where a person grapples in the inner world of his thoughts with the irreversibility of dying. He must not only expect death; he must also think about death, for then he is able to bear truth at every point.

Nevertheless, there are situations in which a person consciously keeps silent and avoids mentioning certain things. The patient need not be told about all the medical details since this does not help him. It will rather tend to make him uneasy, and this will not at all promote his healing. It is understood that the doctor must not undermine the patient's willingness to actively collaborate in the healing process. Equally, it may be that the doctor avoids speaking about incurable sufferings if the knowledge of this situation would only cast a cloud over the remaining time available to the patient.

This may appear obvious, but do not completely dismiss the danger that the doctor exercises her power in a manipulative fashion and keeps the patient in a state of dependence. In other words, the doctor implicitly reduces the patient to the status of a child and then exercises the sovereign power to define what the "quality of life" is. This is why we must carefully inquire into what the other person truly wants; and this in turn must be examined to see to what extent it is justified or if it perhaps stands in the way of better alternatives. Since the sovereignty of one person over another has its starting point in the word, it is also through the word that this sovereignty must be overcome. The alternatives here are a nightmare or a demand for action, and no situation can dispense itself from making a choice. In the last analysis, therefore, the morality of every communication is measured against the competence to bring about freedom and the autonomous acceptance of burdens: does it empower the one addressed to perceive his basic right to an unhindered self-realization? And this is the original perspective of our thought. It is only at a second stage that we must ask whether and to what extent the one addressed must be protected against his own self. We must aim at equilibrium between these two perspectives. On the basis of what I have said here, it is obvious that the first perspective merits a strategic preference and that the presumption of the speaker must be in favor of this perspective, as long as the opposite is not unambiguously proven to be the case.

This introduces a provisional quality into many speech acts. Placing limits on what one says and avoiding speaking about certain things are never more than hypothetical acts in the sense that they are oriented to a necessary transcendence toward fuller forms of communication. The phases of education, of the pedagogical introduction into the truth, are all classical, so to speak. This must indeed adapt itself to the ability of the young person while at the same time spurring him on. Naturally, the situation is more complicated when one cannot be content with a purely objective communication, that is, when this must be accompanied by interpretation (e.g., in the case of sexual education). If facts (as in this case) do not remain firmly integrated into an interpretative context, the young person is exposed to them unsheltered. He cannot cope with them, and they will lead to his downfall, humanly speaking.

This reminds us of the many comparable situations in which the communication of truth is in fact linked to a profound interior convulsion. In the act of speaking, one must take heed not only of the measure of the intellectual ability to receive what is being said but also of the emotional state of the person who is being addressed. Obviously, a person can make excessive demands of her dialogue partner and drive him to the limits of his ability to cope with stress if she fails to take into account his psychological resilience. Often a person needs a distance in time from unsettling experiences before he can speak about them or permit another person to speak to him about them. Time must heal the wounds that have been inflicted before a verbal objectivization is possible. Indeed, there exists what we might call an encapsulation of centers of conflict. A liberating process of forgetting and suppressing them is necessary over a lengthy period before one can come back to them in words. This is especially the case where a person must come to terms with the guilt he has incurred, or with the harm he has suffered at the hands of others. It cannot be too strongly emphasized that each individual has his own very personal time here, both for speaking and for hearing.

In this context, the first thing one thinks of is probably the confession of sins in the sacrament of penance; this situation certainly applies with regard to the moral impossibility of completeness. The criteria that are to be applied to sacramental confession are the same that apply to every demanding encounter. There is nothing mechanical about sacramentality; it does not bring independence of the network of human conditions, nor does it override the need for intimacy. At the same time, however, we cast our net more widely to take in those situations in which the confession of guilt can impose a heavy burden on human relationships that have been laboriously built up. What can the other person cope with emotionally? He may indeed see a confession of guilt as proof that a person trusts him, but such a confession also tends to poison his thoughts and to rob him of the impartiality that is indispensable if human bonds are to work successfully. Why should a person impose this heavy burden on him if a guilty past is long over and buried, and has no more significance for the present day? And yet doubts arise as soon as this is said, and the arguments in favor of the contrary position are obvious. If a person keeps silent, does not this amount to practicing deceit? Indeed, is it not an abuse of the other person's trust? For example, would someone have taken the decision to link his life to another person if he had known about the guilt incurred by his partner at an earlier date? Or would he feel that his partner underestimated his readiness to forgive generously? There is no easy answer to these questions. Certainly, one must limit the damage as much as possible, but it is not clear a priori where in fact the lesser damage lies, whether in keeping silent about a fact or in risking the end of a relationship. A person may feel that her right to lead a life free of the shadows of the past is more important than the other person's right to complete information; she will tend to think first along these lines, and those who are involved in the situation must respect this. Nevertheless, this contains an implicit reproach of her partner, for either she does not trust him or else she thinks him incapable of bearing the truth. Accordingly, it is not hard to see why people decide to confess their guilt and ask for generosity.

Other questions: How do I see such a relationship? How essential is it for my happiness in life? Can I do without it? Can happiness be bought at the price of keeping silent when such silence could be interpreted at the very least as a breach of trust? All these reflections apply in the other areas of life as well, and the fact that we cannot escape them sometimes confronts us with utterly insoluble problems. On occasion, not only the happiness of one's life is at stake but also simple physical survival, or at least survival in a manner fit for a human being. How strong is the other person's right to the truth? Are the conditions that he imposes on me just? A person cannot forever remain a prisoner of her past, especially in situations where her professional existence is at stake, when the price to be paid for what lies in the past turns into an intolerable burden for the future. The situation is different when the open admission of her religious or moral conviction entails a high professional risk. Since keeping silent could be interpreted as a denial, the presumption is in favor of an open admission.

Truthfulness in Relation to One's Own Self

The praxis of truthfulness is a paradigm, so to speak, of the fundamental problem of the relationship between ideas about ethical value and the ideas that guide anthropological reflection. A successful life demands more than a livable balance between one's own interests and those of others: certainties, hopes, and suppositions likewise determine the process of arriving at equilibrium. This cannot be a matter of solutions to individual points; when conflicts erupt and must be reconciled, fundamental attitudes are required. As I have noted, these attitudes do not take the place of normative solutions to individual cases, but they do possess the ability to guide developments and to initiate solutions.

This means that we must look once more at the sensitivity of the one who acts. Hermeneutical interests will guide us here. It is in the quiet of a person's own conscience that he prepares for the truthfulness of encounters and relationships.[9] He must be able to admit to himself, impartially and humbly, where in his life a silent struggle is going on and where he must prove his worth in a manner that does not attract attention, since otherwise the consequence would be a creeping untruthfulness. He must have the courage to reflect on himself and to see his life story as a perennial story of learning as well as a story of conversion; and he must have the courage to grasp every occasion to do this. No one is spared the painful experience of "too late." Doors that close and relationships that break up remind us of losses that no one perceives but that can be decisive for the course our lives. The unbiased eye of the reflective person attempts to grasp the true reasons for such events. Why did things have to come to this point? Is it possible to alter the tracks on which the individual decisions take their course? It may be relatively easy to identify obvious guilt, especially when it is linked to clearly defined actions.

Things become problematic when a person enters the half-shadows in which guilt and innocence seem to glide imperceptibly into one another, in which semidecidedness allows him to recognize dangerous tendencies that shrink as yet from taking the decisive step.

Truthfulness penetrates into these depths, attempting in far-sighted prudence to anticipate the course of events in order not to be taken unawares by history. How will a life finish? That begins here. How will communication succeed? That depends on the ability to face an unflattering confrontation with one's own self. A person must be able to distance herself from her own self, for then she receives the strength to put up with her neighbor without being crushed by him while at the same time modestly "taking a back seat." This shows us one source of untruthfulness, namely, the disturbed equilibrium between the communication partners where one constrains or is constrained. This begins in the hidden world of the thoughts; the obvious untruthfulness in speaking and acting merely seeks to cover up what one is thinking.

Truthfulness vis-à-vis one's own self demands that a person is clear about the motivations for her conduct. The phenomenon of action is never fully expressive since, although it reveals, it also conceals. Similarly, the intention that directly guides an action gives only limited information because it concerns only the idea of the concrete goal of action but says nothing about the deep roots in the life story of the agent. Here more comprehensive perspectives are required, and there is no rapid access to these. The real motivations lie on a deeper level, and they display an inclination to hide themselves and to deflect attention from themselves, leaving the individual in a half-intended unclarity about herself so that her emotional equilibrium may not be disturbed. This state of affairs can be remedied through a patient reflection on all those circumstances that have formed her own ethical profile, including both fulfilled and unfilled expectations of her own life as well as the ideals she has taken up and the projects she has envisaged for herself.

It is from this depth that decisions emerge, and the person who examines his conscience inevitably encounters sore points that he would much prefer not to see. This need not necessarily be a sign of guilt: there are a whole range of wrong attitudes, innate weaknesses of character, and basic patterns of contact that are both immature and unrealistic, and these can grow into permanent moral centers of conflict that poison his life again and again. He must be willing to soberly acknowledge his own frailness. Many people are insufficiently aware of how often they are moving on the edge of their strength—indeed, on a knife's edge—and the salutary reminder of this comes in the form of small or great tragedies. All too often the external correctness of a person's conduct gives a false impression here. It is like a treacherous lake that keeps its dangerous shoals and eddies hidden from sight.

In other situations a yawning gulf opens up between the external and the internal, between reality and thoughts. A person compensates for external losses, disappointments, deprivations, and frictions by secretly indemnifying herself and building an internal pseudo-world that remains untouched by all these negative things. Her precariously maintained equilibrium is purchased at the price of an increasing loss of the sense of reality. A creeping untruthfulness is at work, sneaking corrosively into the construction of sustainable relationships. This could have been avoided, if only she had had the courage to be herself. This is why truthfulness requires a free space of silence. There must be an honest confrontation with herself: she must not live tacitly at the expense of others, nor take refuge in the consolation offered by an illusory world that can take on downright bizarre forms and merely distorts reality. In such a case, the individual communication may still be true, especially if it occurs on the level of objective information, but its root in her life story is already corroded. Eventually she will maneuver herself into situations of blatant falsehood, above all when she must endure strains, but the presuppositions necessary to cope constructively with them are no longer present. Falsehood is a symptom of this fundamental breakdown. Something in the past that went wrong has grown, imperceptibly but all the more effectively, until it erupts through the surface. In this case, the spoken word is every bit as remote from reality as is the substratum in the person's life.

It is, however, also possible for a person to make excessive demands of herself all the time. This will inevitably lead to the collapse of her ethical life since, even with the best will in the world, the resulting tensions become unendurable. A compulsion to be perfect is generated, making her addicted to the flawless façade. She does not dare to admit to herself that she is overestimating her own possibilities in an intellectual presumption that flees from even the slightest trace of imperfection. The emotional energies are misdirected and are consumed in external correctness while neglecting the consistent construction of a motivational stratum that is capable of bearing strains. This is unsustainable in the long term. She must learn to live with the errors and limitations from which no one is exempt. If this does not occur, false frontlines will be erected and battles will be fought in places that do not deserve this while the true problems vanish unnoticed from sight. Often the individual herself is unaware that at the root of all this lies a profound lack of self-assurance; she is content with things that can be taken superficially under control—that is, her world; thus she ineluctably misses the opportunity for truthful communication. She fails to see that one element in every encounter is an invisible "surplus" that has its origin in an unlimited trust.

It is only with difficulty that the perfection of the verbal expression conceals the human malfunctioning, which is often dictated by anxious concern to employ this perfection to chain her neighbor to herself. Ultimately, this amounts to an aggression where she is primarily interested in herself rather than in the other person, and she is intent all the time on enforcing her own wishes. This brings a perspective of latent untruthfulness into what she says and does. Her neighbor is of value only to the extent that he is useful for her own purposes; he is in fact nothing more than a pawn. Therefore, it is not out of place here to put in a plea for the courage to be imperfect. The person who accepts herself in her limitations and is aware of the provisional character of her endeavors encounters her partner in freedom, and so she sets her partner free. The situation of speaking is uniquely suited to shed light on how the human person becomes an end in herself. No other action is as disinterested as that of speaking, and it is in verbal communication that we see most clearly what the dignity of the person means. And here we also learn that speaking is the noblest form of service.

The Demand Made by the Goals in Life

Truthfulness requires goals to which it is worth committing one's life. All individual actions must be integrated into this perspective; they are expressions of the meaning of life that one has accepted and taken hold of. In addition to doing justice to their immediate objects, evaluations of goods in terms of loftiness and urgency, and strategic considerations with regard to the individual steps to be taken, must continually pose this ultimate question, which is the very measure of their truth.

Goals in life have an unavoidable limitation. No one can exempt himself from being forced to make choices, and only the experience of temporality is able to wrest positive possibilities from what is otherwise a threat. The secret of relevance to one's life story lies in the art of self-limitation, which affects every individual decision. These individual decisions can be successful only when the gift of moderation influences the way in which these decisions envisage concreteness.[10] But a person does not do justice to the reality of human action if the empirical factual sciences supply the exclusive parameter for dealing with the concreteness of a life story because he then forgets that this concreteness is wrested from time. And since time is continually disappearing, this concreteness, which shapes history, represents an achievement of the most original kind. The person who acts identifies with the goals of his action, for it is only so that his life story endures in the face of all transience. Naturally, it is only through many trial runs that he grows into such an attitude of mastery, where everything comes together like the stones of a mosaic, the plan becomes clear in the course of its execution, and a total vision is formed—imperceptibly, but all the more effectively. The details are not determined in advance; it is the task of the creative imagination to bring them into the correct order, and this imagination does not limit itself to the immediate scrutiny of successes but attempts to decode the overarching ideas about goals to see what possibilities for action they generate. In this way, the purity of a person's attitude begins in the resoluteness of his thinking. It is linked to the experience of an indestructible happiness that utters its promise even when appearances suggest the opposite. The person who wishes to achieve something lasting must be able to think beyond his own death. A high and risky price must be paid, and this can be done only by the person who is happy in his thoughts since he possesses the wholesome distance, united to self-respect, which is necessary if he is to see through the deceptiveness of all ideas about success. For as a person thinks, so he speaks—the word is the first bearer of his thought. The word accompanies the developments in the course of a life story, which always include turning points. By analogy, therefore, it would be logical to say: As a person lives, so he speaks.

Truthfulness includes an impartiality in one's expression that is superior to all claims that would appeal to plebiscites. Truthfulness refuses to swim with the stream or to go along with prevalent opinion, although at the same time it is well aware of the many kinds of dependence and compulsion to which even the most fearless person is subject. These include the slowness of processes of insight. The time may not be right for the implementation of an insight that has long been available, and the truthful person is the first to suffer under this discrepancy, which may impose an extreme burden on his power of resistance. He needs courage to take an unpopular stance, for it is only so that he preserves the ability to identify problems and to differentiate, to acknowledge without prejudice the existence of elements of the truth in the errors that he combats, and to seek a constructive balance between contradictory positions. And if there is one thing that truthfulness demands, surely it is the art of knowing how to wait! The person who has mastered this skill will most readily find the opportunity to escape from the many intellectual "three line whips" and to dissolve the contradictions in a higher unity. This means that truthfulness takes the form of the proven ability to resolve conflicts.

Truthfulness and impartiality go hand in hand.[11] The truthful person continually lets the world of her thoughts be torn open by reality. She is self-critical and knows how much she can be led astray by falling in love with the paths she has always trodden in the past. Often what one says may be correct, but her words do not meet with success because she has already assigned her neighbor to some particular category before he has even been given the chance to justify himself or to clarify his position. Indeed, her neighbor ought not to get such a chance, because she greatly prefers the suffering caused by supposed misunderstandings, or perhaps by injustices or mere thoughtlessness—since this helps to increase her self-esteem. The malfunctioning of the communication is due to a lofty egoism, a vanity in ethical terms, where she has ceased to be aware of how much her own behavior has contributed to this state of affairs. She can fall in love not only with her own ideas but also with unnecessary problems that often bear the mark of being her own fault. In such cases, truthfulness must give her the courage to seek a clarification and to demonstrate that the suspicions cast were without foundations so that communication may become possible and she may not perish because of the isolation that she has chosen for herself. This usually takes place in the little steps of everyday life, and this is why it is correct to speak of confidence-building measures. She makes an advance payment, so to speak, in the hope that the reality will follow on. One important reason for the disappointments incurred in relation to her neighbor is her own failure to develop the capacity for encounter and initiatives.

What are the reasons for such an omission? An initial supposition points to her own guilt. This allows the creation of a strategy of action that anticipates what her neighbor will do—and that liberates her. In this context, we are not wrong to speak of a nobility of the heart, which preserves an infallible sensitivity to atmosphere and enables one to concentrate her approach on the kind of people whom she can trust, people who also take initiatives of their own to ensure that the verbal communication will be successful. It is assuredly no exaggeration to identify the starting point of truthfulness in this depth. The ideas that she has about her goals play a decisive role here, and these will become clear in the course of the conversation.

There is an obvious parallel to the life story of the individual: just as there is a process of growth into the form that is her own, so too there is a growth into the demands posed by all those encounters which aim not merely at an isolated contact but at something lasting. In many ways, such processes have their privileged moments. The other person is gradually discovered, and situations of exceptional stress usually reveal to us the true value of our dialogue partner. All at once, something that she had only dimly guessed at in so-called normal situations emerges into the light. Her fears may be confirmed, but they may also be completely dispelled. More important than this, however, is the fact that the continuous flow of time is needed to dismantle unrealistic expectations. Nothing is as strongly oriented to the truth as time, which sooner or later reveals the innermost dimension of a person since no one is spared from mobilizing her ultimate resources. It is impossible to evade this, and no form of human cooperation is spared this test of the truth.

In situations in which people must be accountable, they cope in the ways in which they speak with each other. The spoken words are transparent to the testimony of the speaker's life. For speaking to be truthful, a salutary disillusioning is necessary. At some point, the speaker must simply throw away the entire bundle of deliberate or tacitly approved deceptions; stability comes where he does not refuse to look squarely at this challenge (which he always unconsciously assumes as a possibility). The person who accepts this challenge possesses the rare ability to embed every individual situation of speaking in a framework of safety that has its ultimate, unshakable foundation in an existential attitude of critical realism.

A person's own ego is no exception to this rule. The humble acceptance of his limitations generates an autonomy that is far removed from self-sufficiency, and a fortiori from an unacknowledged thinking in terms of hegemony. Besides this, he bears in mind the effect that his way of speaking has on others, and any potential self-overestimation will very soon be put in its place.

Truthfulness will profit from this awareness since it cherishes no illusions of any kind. Once he has recognized a path as true, the lack of illusions gives him a new freedom to take this path consistently and to the end. The obstacles mostly turn out to be products of his own imagination, without any backing in reality. Suddenly it seems perfectly natural to stand by his conviction and to speak the truth; this does not require any long-winded reflection, and still less any justification. This entails a preliminary decision about the outcome of the evaluation of goods in situations of conflict. Everyone creates for himself situations in which he can prove his worth. Freedom's spontaneity and the truth of the communication are two sides of the same coin. Conversely, strategic reflections on how to limit or suppress truth are by nature derivative.[12] There is therefore no cause for surprise that such reflections must overcome completely natural inhibitions.

To ask the truth of someone resembles a regulative idea that governs all verbal disclosures. The initial presumption is that the strength that is necessary both to speak and to bear the truth is present; this presumption is based on a theology of history that is not content to reflect on the courses of events but penetrates through to the causes of these events in the intimate sphere of knowledge and of freedom. Ultimately, it is here that the course of history is decided. The conviction that a person is sheltered in God's benevolent providence prevents him from taking refuge in the inner sphere. This conviction does not lack the courage to look outside and discover in apparent catastrophes the unique chance to prove his worth. When he looks at a situation in this way, he can see the truth it contains. There is a realism that is based on a theology of history and that indicates what the contents of true communication will be by contributing the perspective that will guide such a communication. It is indeed true that it is impossible to completely settle the conflicts that erupt; an unresolved remnant always remains, and he must have the courage to live with this. No very great experience of life is required to grasp this. Unrealistic expectations with regard to the precision of normative propositions must therefore be scaled back. It seems much more realistic to live and to act with strategic preferences, and the most momentous of these is surely the employment of the basic good of interpersonal trust as the criterion for all the evaluations one makes. To the extent that it is possible to envisage and calculate the consequences, what promotes this most immediate, most spontaneous, and most natural need of the human person? Every word that is spoken is true to the extent that it faces up to this question.

Untruthfulness as a Source of Personal Disintegration

Running Away from the Conflict

Successful individual decisions stem from fundamental lived attitudes. Normative ethics demands an antecedent virtue ethics if directives for action are not to congeal into hard and fast rules in their endeavor to be objective. A person's intellectual attitude provides training for ethical action. An immediate existential relationship to the matter at hand generates a comprehensive intellectual certainty, even if it is not possible to eliminate every doubt. In this way, an ethical personality acquires stability in himself. The different stages of life have their own specific emphases.

The converse is also true: unsuccessful individual decisions are the logical fruit of a process of deterioration. Wrong attitudes (commonly known as "vices") allow us to see where this process begins. An intellectual uncertainty spreads, generating a dynamic of flight from the salutary claim made on one by the truth. Unsurprisingly, the consequence is an increasing uncertainty in decision making. Our own moral-theological tradition speaks here of "hypocrisy." This contains an intellectual and ethical lapse that only rarely comes to light because it is skilled in adopting disguises. There is complete agreement between the content and the form, but this has taken a negative turn.

We must look more closely at this phenomenon for the simple reason that no successful life story can evade the imperative of ridding oneself of one's illusions. A person must learn how to bear the truth about himself, and if this does not come about through his own initiative, external circumstances will ensure that it happens. If, however, he runs away from this lesson, an imperceptible corrosion of his thinking will certainly ensue—with his own ego as its first victim. He builds up and lives a relationship to himself, but the ethical identity that he had once embraced slips inexorably from his grasp. It is only with difficulty that the façades are upheld while behind them a nightmarish emptiness spreads out. And although people's dealings with one another are often externally correct, they resemble a game of hide and seek. Is it not obvious that the individual spoken word will share in this process of deterioration and will degenerate, in a process of which the speaker himself is no longer conscious, into an open lie?[13]

This process tends to begin unobtrusively, remaining on the periphery of one's consciousness—there are so many distractions, and no one achieves 100 percent self-control at all times. The impulse generally comes from the little repressions of everyday life. These are dangerous precisely because they bring relief that is definitely salutary and is valuable for one's mental equilibrium. Indeed, they are necessary to one's health: a person must be able to forget if she wants to free herself from the shadow of the past. There is, however, a disadvantage, namely, that she can disregard the need for an intellectual confrontation in which she comes to terms with the past. In that case, it is easy for new situations that resemble the past to awaken without mercy memories that have not been purified. The past refuses to release her from its clutches: it is like a maelstrom that relentlessly drags one down.

The person who does not investigate the reasons for his failure robs himself of the chance of continuous healing; at most, he cures symptoms. There is more to this malfunctioning than a harmless sin of omission. It is here that a story of creeping self-deception begins, which leads logically to a story of consistent self-justification. He constructs an illusory world in his thoughts, and he finds this so fascinating precisely because it removes the harsh and humiliating confrontation. He keeps himself safe in his thoughts. This kind of flight reduces to an easily borne minimum the tensions that erupt between the ideal and reality.[14]

Evasive actions of this kind too easily tend to be reflected in the way a person speaks about moral topics. The insatiable desire to erect a flawless façade drives him into a verbal radicalism in ethical matters. The beleaguered ego hides itself behind big words, thus making itself invulnerable to attack; it cannot be caught and forced to take a definite stance. A widening gulf yawns between word and reality: when we meet an ethical personality, we are immediately certain that his words are "covered" by his life story, but here this is not the case. A first step out of ethical responsibility has been taken, and he has already abandoned surreptitiously all hope of coming to terms with the past in a constructive manner. At most, all that remains is what we might call a selective commitment, especially in those areas where he can be sure that he will get applause and that he will not have to endure any invisible struggles. The tattered scraps of a conventional morality that sometimes pass through people's heads without greatly disturbing them do indeed find a way to prompt action that does justice to the moral idea involved, but these ideas no longer get under such people's skin, and they are very far from being integrated into their life story.

The truthful person is refreshingly different. His intellectual modesty gives him the courage needed for a morality of small steps that begins in the silence of his own solitude, without attracting notice, but all the more effectively. Such a person is indeed a blessing when he speaks. He has accepted the demand that is made, and this impels him to formulate his utterances with reserve, with precision, and with controllability. It is above all his mastery of normative language that teaches him a modesty of this kind, since normative language is oriented immediately to obvious reality—although this need not be in any way disadvantageous to lofty ideals and goals for life. The truthful person has so much self-assurance that he can make himself vulnerable to attack since he lays all his cards on the table and does not shrink from confrontations. This is possible because (with all the reservations demanded by the matter in question) he takes a stance.

Key Situations of Untruthfulness

Untruthfulness generates a kind of naïveté in human terms that can have an oppressive impact on how people deal with each other.[15] There is a sharp contrast between the big words and the context of a life that has never been exposed to risk. One makes no commitment and slyly evades any test of his own integrity and steadfastness in order to speak all the more unrestrainedly. In this way dependencies are created on a high level. It is impossible for the other person to resist this diktat, for the price to be paid would be a merciless exposure. A high degree of decisiveness is required to do so since we all know only too well that the resistance put up even by the best of us is "unsecured," whereas the untruthful person develops a sure feeling for the weak points of his counterpart and sinks his claws into them. In this way he gives himself and others the appearance of superiority, and anyone who has dealings with him lives by his grace and favor. This is all the more oppressive when the emotional ties are stronger and the trust on which he draws is greater. Although the untruthful person may not be conscious of what he is doing, he exploits feelings—the weakest point of the human person—and abuses the unquestioning trust that is placed in him.

This must lead to human catastrophes if the truth ever becomes known and the person who is exploited in this way becomes aware that he is the victim of chicanery. A person never feels more humiliated than at such moments. He realizes then that reliability is ensured only where selflessness holds sway, for only the selfless person has so much distance vis-à-vis his own self that he need not pretend to possess certainties that are not "covered" by his own commitment. If he knows that emotional ties cannot be sustained—either because he lacks the will to do so or because the appropriate external conditions are lacking—he does not build them up in the first place. He possesses so much existential prudence that he is able to estimate future developments. He can envisage what will happen to himself but also (and especially) to his neighbor. He thinks on behalf of his neighbor too. In short, his assessment includes a calculation of the consequences of his actions. Even more significantly, he does not leave his neighbor alone since truthfulness and solidarity are relational concepts. It goes without saying that interpersonal guidelines are needed, if one is to speak and act truly. The untruthful person is very different: he thinks in terms of isolated moments, he shrugs off the responsibility he has assumed, and he is unconcerned about the damage that he does. He does not feel himself obligated by the requirement that speaking with another person entails accompanying him on the path. No wonder that the hearer feels bitter—and it is a life task to ensure that this bitterness does not degenerate into irreconcilability.

It is possible to instrumentalize the truth and to "politicize" it in many ways. There is a "politics" of speaking that seeks to exploit every situation in view of one's own advantage. The power politician says only as much as he can afford, not out of consideration for his neighbor's ability to bear stress but to enforce his own interests. And the highest of these interests is the calculus of power: the guiding consideration is always whether his counterpart is a factor to be reckoned with, or whether his counterpart can be integrated and used as a welcome and perhaps submissive pawn on the chessboard of his own strategies. The dialogue partner does not notice that he is being pinned fast and examined to see what his weak points are. Because of this assessment, the power politician already knows his counterpart better than he himself does.

It is perfectly clear that interpersonal relationships can never succeed in this way, for despite all his trustfulness, the truthful person will instinctively sense that the other is playing with him, that he is not being taken seriously as a companion on the path who freely takes responsibility for his own life story, but that he is in fact being used as a means to an end. It never occurs to the power politician that truth is possible only in freedom, and that for its own sake, truth needs an absolutely free space; he sacrifices truth on the altar of his own interests. It is therefore only logical that he does not let himself be pinned down. His convictions are of such a kind, and are always formulated in such a way, that they cope with every change of the wind. He is always on target, come what may, and he is always proved right—if not thanks to his arguments then thanks to circumstances. This is why he does not need the self-correction that is a painful duty for everyone else. His own empty formulae survive every shift in circumstances. He need not reckon with any setbacks since he has already secretly entered into a pact with any potential adversaries who might turn out to be dangerous.

It may seem trivial to point out that all this is sometimes done in great style. In this way the truthful person is suddenly confronted with societal coercions and commercial interests that hopelessly transcend his own limited powers and possibilities of exercising influence and ineluctably force him into situations of conflict. It is essential that the truthful person develop strategies for action, but he cannot determine in advance how much of his convictions he will be able to put into words, or even what kind of free spaces for the truth can be created in such a situation.

Here too we must draw a distinction since we will encounter many situations in which a fundamentally legitimate "interest" will not necessarily falsify the truth but will generate a guiding perspective that functions as a principle of selection. The mass media are the context par excellence of such processes, but such processes are found also in politics and the economic sphere. The problem for the ethos of truth is then whether such a guiding perspective serves the truth. Is it willing to accept correction? Does it still admit the free utterance of the truth?[16] There are, however, more oppressive coercions in which the truth is fundamentally distorted; the only question here is whether (at least in individual instances) the truth is possible and resistance has a chance of success (at least in the long term). This points us to a cluster of ethical problems that make the transition from the ethos of truthfulness to the sphere of cooperation.[17]

Truth can be at the service of one's own prestige. The decisive concern for the speaker is the publicity he hopes to gain. Intellectual vanity, usually accompanied by resentment, doles out the spoken word in such a way that each of the hearers gets his money's worth since he is told only what he himself had always wanted to say but without ever finding the right occasion.

The informational value of such speaking is usually small since there is no opportunity for a differentiated presentation. The speaker is looking for the fascination of a quick solution that deliberately avoids the task of patient examination. Simplifications are always overwhelming at first sight, and they appear so attractive precisely because they offer to relieve one of a dreaded burden of thought. The vain person is very well aware of this; thus he appeals to the presumed vanity of his counterpart and to his lack of willingness to weigh things up—a gift which is bestowed only on the modest person. Behind such a strategy lies a subtle form of violence: the vain person crushes his neighbor and refuses to give him the free space that is necessary to take a position that is justified by arguments. This obviously comes close to "politicization." The weak person is exploited in his real or imagined weakness, and the vain person's own prestige is assured because there is always a majority who support such proceedings and, indeed, demand them. The vain person can always appeal to this majority.

Such a false attitude is all the more oppressive the more strongly it is protected by institutions. The individual basks in the radiance of his institution (be it ecclesiastical or secular) and encounters everyone who does not belong to it based on a feeling of superiority that lacks any underlying human or professional competence. His self-satisfaction dispenses him from the need to acknowledge the autonomous value of every dialogue partner. He implicitly measures his dialogue partner according to demanding criteria that inevitably mean that the partner's life will appear mediocre. In this way communication is obstructed. The lack of respect for the fundamental principle of equality—which can be realized more purely in a dialogue than in any other context—drives his partner onto the defensive or even into flight. Truth is then at best a chance hit, certainly not something that can be taken for granted. This outcome is all the more oppressive the higher the moral claim with which the institution in question presents itself. The interest in moral questions then turns to areas that are far removed from those in which one could in fact be put to the test, to areas where the danger of personal failure is reduced to the minimum—but that offer a person the chance of looking good. The good is at the service of a person's own reputation. He is always flawless, and this is both painless and satisfying. He dispenses himself in this way from the need to acknowledge his own limitations and to live patiently with them. No wonder that human beings' dealings with each other are ambiguous, for the realistic acceptance of one's own self is an essential presupposition of truthfulness.[18]

The Failure to Accept a Share in Intellectual Responsibility

The theologian, and especially the moral theologian, cannot evade the task of a critical self-examination. Her public responsibility in Church and society stands or falls with her truthfulness. Untruthfulness becomes a serious threat when her discourse follows academic ideals that are inappropriate to the matter of ethics. This can occur in ethical rhetoric, when discourse is put forward in a manner that cannot be translated into action. It gives the impression of articulating norms while in reality it is presenting ideals, goals, or guiding concerns. Such an inclination becomes particularly disastrous when a high level of commitment is demanded, or when a painful confrontation accompanies the path on which one is put to the ethical test.[19] Another possibility is a flight into erudition, which eschews the need for confrontation. It is of course true that we need pure research, where the potential applicability cannot yet be envisaged; and it is precisely the humane disciplines that require such a free space. Nevertheless, this state of affairs cannot continue indefinitely, for there is always the risk that academic work will be noncommittal. A person who does not submit to the constraint of concreteness is fleeing from the truth, and here it is of little importance whether the preliminary decisions that lie behind such a malfunctioning are rigorist or laxist in nature. Such a flight is especially obvious when she refuses to give her counterpart an account of the specific degree of certainty that attaches to insights and propositions; not even the differentiation in the factual argumentation can cover this up. This is why the normative discourse is a salutary school of truthfulness, especially when it is equal to the epistemological demands that are made of it.

It is here that the share in responsibility for the Church's magisterium has its origin. It would be untruthful if this were to consist only of the criticism of individual texts of the magisterium since that would amount to the attempt to burden the ecclesial authority with the task of discovering the truth while preserving one's own unassailable façade. This is why criticism, which is necessary, must be united to the willingness to present constructive alternatives. It must become clear to the ecclesial authority that when the situation in the history of ideas changes, its concerns are better taken care of intellectually, and indeed that this is done not only better but more convincingly. It is understandable that the magisterium is afraid to move out onto insecure terrain. No matter how unfinished the tradition may be in individual aspects, the magisterium fears losing it or exposing it to misunderstandings.[20] Moral theology must show that these fears are groundless. It must demonstrate that differentiation is not the same thing as backsliding. The texts of the magisterium are only as good as the prevalent bogeymen and contemporary theology allow. Sometimes these texts expend energy in places that do not deserve this; the magisterium continues to speak about problems that have long since been resolved, and rearguard actions are fought that can only distort the necessary awareness of the problem involved. If a person were to accept this in a mood of resignation, this would be untruthful, but to engage in polemic against it is to succumb to a seduction since one can be certain of applause (usually from the wrong side). All that remains in the name of truthfulness is the patient middle course of constructive proposals. This course requires freedom and time since the "three line whip" makes thinking rigid, and pressure of time leads to exaggeration so that one ceases to do justice to one's own tradition.

Things against which one rightly fights today may perhaps have been required in the past. Truth is always soft-footed; suddenly one discovers that problems of the past have ceased to be problematic because intellectual developments have grown beyond them. Conversely, it would be dishonest if one were to restrict the critical partnership with the magisterium to the conduct of individual conflicts while bracketing off the intellectual presuppositions of the confrontation. The person who remains conscious of the limitations of his categories will begin by working on his own scaffolding before entering the fray, and he will offer his counterpart a better set of instruments, for then it will be possible to see whether the contrasts still remain or have already been dissolved. Dialogue in the Church would be untruthful if there were no space to exercise this responsibility.

Untruthfulness can spread where the Church and the magisterium succumb to the creeping temptation to a laborious moralizing. Although this is well intentioned, it obscures the Church's salvific task. This impression is given very strongly when detailed normative requirements are formulated and the appeal is made to faith, or more precisely to God's plan for the human person; we are told gratuitously that these requirements will make obvious sense to the individual in his conscience. No one seriously suggests that the Church's magisterium can be content with general guidelines and recommendations since that would mean renouncing responsibility for the link between faith and morality that is so often underlined; the faithful are dependent on solidarity, which means that the magisterium must have the courage to make concrete definitions. And yet questions remain. How comprehensible is this link between faith and morality? Does it admit of alternatives, or does it present itself with a claim to exclusivity?

There is universal agreement that a natural law claim based on good arguments is not identical to the claim made by the Christian proclamation; the burden of proof lies on those who would assert such an identity. There has been sufficient strife on this point in the recent past, and it is not necessary to discuss this question in detail here. It would be untruthful to attempt to gloss over the differentiated character of the process of mediation between faith and reason, either by means of a solemn pronouncement by the ecclesial authority or with a reference to a presumed unbroken tradition. One who refers to the conscience necessarily operates with a critical filter, and this is impossible without tolerance.

But the decisive problem lies elsewhere. It is surely more important to ensure that the Christian form of thought is not secretly shortchanged. This is connected to the underlying theory of truth. There is no universally consistent structure of ethical truth if one prescinds from self-evident aspects such as the absoluteness and universality of its validity. Rather, the ethical truth participates in the totality of its relevant presuppositions, whether of a theological or an anthropological nature, but this does not curtail its autonomy (which is in any case always understood as a relational autonomy) since the various dimensions of human existence do not in any way impose limits on each other. This participation entails both substance and form. This is why the correctness of ethical conduct is not defined exclusively by means of ideas about ethical value; the presuppositions just mentioned are a contributory factor to the definition. Current societal premises alone do not tell us how a person will tackle the coercions that arise in the history of a conflict, what expectations develop with regard to the conflict management at which he aims, or which systemic categories implicitly guide his thinking; a genuinely theological reflection is also needed, and this takes its starting point in the most meaningful affirmations of christological anthropology. In the context of faith, ethical truth unmistakably bears the signs of contradiction since the Church is essentially a contrasting society. The Church is never content with a verifiable consensus; its testimony consists in the implementation of better alternatives. The Church's criteria for action lie in the future. Always conscious of eschatology, the Church purifies its ideas about intrahistorical fulfillment.

Nor is this all. In the context of faith, ethical truth also bears the traits of mercy because it is based on the New Testament understanding of God, which makes truth and mercy complementary concepts. The limitations on human freedom that have been suffered are accepted and not glossed over: this is essential if these limitations are to yield better possibilities for action.

The systemic categories that guide the Church must pass through the critical filter of this dialectic. The Church must not be confused with an ethical fellowship of communication and solidarity that establishes a consensus and implements a system of order with a positivistic reference back to a religious superstructure. Nor is its authority comparable to a sovereign bearer of morality who authentically presents and interprets a natural ethical law that is understood to cover every area of life. Such models do justice to a part of reality, but they miss the real point. By setting false accents, they generate corresponding expectations that inevitably lead to an untruthful understanding of authority because it is impossible for such expectations to be fulfilled. At the end, we must ask the question (which may perhaps seem odd) whether this is not a veiled form of humanism, which is more dangerous than the form found in the autonomous morality against which battle is waged in the context of faith.

The primordial authority of the Church lies preferentially where faith leads people out of compulsions that are determined by a history of guilt, out of entanglements and conflicts; where liberating visions of action are elaborated, visions that the instruments of a normative ethic can never fully cover. This is particularly important at the present stage in the history of ideas. Normative systemic categories are sustained by many societal forces, which draw in varying degrees on the inheritance of Christianity but also contribute autonomous reason. The Church's task is to transform these categories from within, to open the doors onto better possibilities, and to keep these categories in motion. The Church's truthfulness is evidenced in its competence as a source of inspiration. In the name of truth, however, it must be said clearly that ideals are not norms, and that there will always be a need for the virtue of *epikeia* on the basis of faith.[21]

The Refusal of Solidarity

The refusal of solidarity means there will be no lack of situations that pose a dilemma. Indeed, they will be inevitable, and one must learn to live with them whether one likes it or not. Such situations always occur when someone encounters the limits of his strength, when he must face the test of catastrophes in the course of his life story. These cannot be foreseen or integrated into any plan; they can occur at any time in a person's life. What can he cope with? Can he imagine situations in which original decisions for his life become insubstantial, because they have lost the foundations that were self-evident up to that point?

There are more than enough examples, from marriages that break down to hopeless conflicts in the lives of priests and religious.[22] Let us leave aside the question of how far such situations are the result of guilt (although in normal cases, the presumption will be that people have neglected to do what was right). It is likely that in the beginning, there was the unconditional will to make an irrevocable decision; but when a person stands before the ruins of the past, he can be maneuvered into a situation that has broken out of the logic of the beginning and indeed seems to be moving in a diametrically opposite direction. Realistically speaking, he has only one choice, unless he wishes to commit a new and perhaps even more troublesome wrong. To think in terms of a moral system offers no further help here; a moral-theological discourse must be continued with other means if it is not to be exposed to the accusation of being remote from real life. Such means are not of a purely normative nature, although this must not be understood as a fundamental renunciation of norms and of their validity—in other words, one cannot speak of arbitrary decisions here. Nevertheless, the accent shifts, at least with regard to the ethical reflections that are to be undertaken. These revolve around the one crucial question of what is still possible in such situations, and what is reasonable to expect of the persons involved. A person can be untruthful here, and close his eyes to this question—with the result that he drives people into utter ruin.

This occurs in a manner that is beyond suspicion, that is, by means of the undifferentiated reference to a potential in the norms that has grown up in the course of tradition. This is beyond suspicion because in every situation of conflict that erupts, the first thing a person does is to look at the tradition. Does it offer sustainable solutions? Does it give the certainties that he needs, if he is not to lose his footing completely? Such a proceeding also has the appearance of wisdom, for ultimately, no situation is so new that it was *never* the object of reflection in the past. And yet, a closer look is needed because the tradition may have reflected in a more differentiated manner than is usually admitted. For example, the doctrine of *epikeia* has always existed, and it is worth examining the moral systems to see whether they contain elements capable of further development.[23]

It is true that *epikeia* originally belonged to the context of positive human law, either as the virtue of the sovereign or as the virtue of the citizen who took his share in responsibility, a virtue that fills up the unavoidable gaps in legislation in keeping with the total intention of the body of laws. *Epikeia* demands hard hermeneutical work. In contemporary reflection on the foundations of moral theology, we also encounter a broadened understanding of *epikeia* that locates it in the context of ethical norms. It does not in any way call into question the exceptionless validity of ethical truth. All it does is admit doubts about whether ethical truth has been appropriately formulated in propositions that do not omit any relevant points of view. Such points of view include both objective and subjective factors. Has an ethical norm been evaluated with regard to all the existential preconditions? To put the question in this way implies the methodological assumption that there can exist situations in which excessive ethical demands are being made because (at least at the present moment) the necessary strength is lacking. To judge whether this is the case demands the utmost measure of truthfulness on the part of the person who is immediately affected since the danger of self-deception threatens here in a manner virtually unparalleled elsewhere in human life. The presumption is initially in favor of the norm, which is the repository of a potential to experience not only the external situations of one's life but also the power of the freedom that must generally be assumed to exist. It is not without reason that there arises quite spontaneously the suspicion that a person is failing to realize his own possibilities because he is deceiving himself. But the stronger the fear of a looming self-deception, the less justified seems the suspicion of untruthfulness since the person involved is in fact willing in principle to shoulder all the burdens resolutely. But the person who is quick to make a judgment in his own favor, and thus against the norm, will easily succumb to the temptation to untruthfulness. He declares that he is his own best advocate, perhaps because in the depths of his heart he senses that he is deceiving himself but he desperately refuses to admit this—since he must not lose the façade that he erects both before others and before his own self. This is probably most likely to occur when there is no doubt about his share of guilt in the situation; in that case, the well-known mechanism of self-justification comes into operation. Conversely, the person who is guiltless (if it is not an unacceptable simplification to speak in such terms) will tend to make a judgment to his own disadvantage, and thus in favor of the norm. But does he perhaps overestimate his own strength?

This reveals the whole drama of *epikeia* in the context of ethical norms, for it is ultimately not a question of realizing individual goods, which may possibly be interchangeable, but of one's own life in its uniqueness and unrepeatability. This is a fundamental value protected by law; it is not in the least restricted to the dimension of bodiliness, but it always envisages the best possible success of life as a whole. It is, however, of little help here to point to the moral system of tutiorism since the question is precisely *where* the inalienable value protected by law lies. Perhaps the only thing that helps in such situations is to turn one's eyes away from oneself and to investigate the needs of one's neighbor. Besides this, the guarantee of greater mercy is found where the greater need prevails.

It is certain that open untruthfulness is present when the ecclesial community—no matter by whom it is represented—lacks the necessary solidarity. This can happen in various ways. In addition to the positivistic reference to norms of which I have just spoken, there can be a lack of willingness to ascertain the degree of certainty that attaches to current norms and is content with undifferentiated norms that admit only of a schematizing thinking. This is justified with a reference to the general need for certainty when one acts. It is all too easy here to sacrifice the individual on the altar of a principle that is perhaps insufficiently differentiated. Perhaps what the general need for certainty in action requires is in fact a critical reflection on the individual instance. Nor does *epikeia* ever lack the reference to the common good.

However, untruthfulness can equally well clothe itself in the garment of an overhasty acquiescence that immures in his own situation the person who has failed, depriving him definitively of any hope of breaking out of this situation. At first sight this looks like a gesture of mercy, but closer examination shows that it is merciless or even cynical. This is always the case when the ecclesiastical authority is overhasty in making use of its ability to grant a dispensation. It is all too easy for the impression to arise that it is getting rid in this way of its responsibility for the one who has failed. The fact that something is legally correct does not in the least make it morally correct. This is why the first and most essential duty is to accompany a person in solidarity. At least for the moment, this enables one to make peace with a situation of failure, accepting this with composure and humility. Nevertheless, more is required than this: the prospect of a complete restoration of the past situation must not be lost, at least in principle. This entails a task for moral pedagogy in boundary situations of this kind, in which the rule that applies everywhere in life has a particular importance, namely, that one must honestly acknowledge the guilt one has incurred. If this does not happen, any dispensation that may be granted has merely the status of a legal act. All that a person does is to acquire a good conscience via the devious route of canon law.[24] This is flight from the truth in a pure form, and the Church offers its services to bring this about. But the act of granting a dispensation does not even remotely dispose of the moral problem.

This suggests a number of considerations. First, we can conceive of situations in which silence is a sign of sympathetic solidarity since even the best-intentioned words could be understood as implicit blackmail. A silence of this kind is certainly not to be interpreted as consent. It only takes seriously the fact that a free space is necessary if one wishes to liberate oneself from the clutches of the past. Understood in this way, silence is eloquent, and it will always turn into speech as soon as there is a hope of offering constructive help. This rule applies to silence and speech in the Church in general, and these situations put it most sensitively to the test. The granting of a dispensation is only the final step. Accordingly, it is not hypocritical to make the criteria of a justified dispensation as demanding as possible—provided that the person who has failed uses more than the criteria of canon law to measure his membership in the ecclesial community of grace but knows a priori that he is included and accepted in the fraternal solidarity of the Church.

Besides this, the Church's act of clemency is not the kind of sovereign act of favor that would be appropriate to an absolutist prince. Rather, it is a reconciliatory gesture on the part of a community whose self-understanding derives exclusively from the word of the prevenient divine grace. It bears witness to the mercy from which the Church itself lives. Ideas about order in the Church must be measured against this criterion unless they want to aid and abet the creeping untruthfulness. The Church is a community of saints and sinners, of those who have mastered their life stories and those who have failed to do so, and one cannot apply to such a community the categories of order that are more suited to an absolutist state and to the interpersonal bonds, the law, and the morality that such a state assumes. Within the Church, none of this is needed.

The States of Life and the Life-lie

States of life in the Church can exercise a magical attraction on untruthfulness. Poverty and celibacy are privileged places of this phenomenon. One might even say that poverty and celibacy directly challenge people to take a critical look, and poverty and celibacy can generate an atmosphere of unease when the onlooker encounters phenomena such as the obvious discrepancy between the claim made by the ideal of poverty and what official pronouncements generally make of this ideal. The Church's orders put this ideal into practice in a way that makes it impossible to live poverty in the sense of beggary, and there is no point in discussing this particular question.

If, however, the impression is given that no challenging testimony is being given in the content of today's society, the reasons must lie deeper than this. A disappointment (sometimes unacknowledged) at the religious orders finds nourishment in the social security offered by the religious life. Indeed, one could speak of an excessive provision since the individual member of a religious order is completely insulated against the normal risk of life. This applies to all the details of life, from the competitive struggle with all its demands for self-assertion down to the banal considerations a person must make in everyday life (for the simple reason that he is on his own and must stand up for himself). The orders present the appearance of powerful institutions that offer the individual member not only a life free of risk but also the best working conditions. Some religious have no hesitation about being carried along by the heavy structure of their order. Privileged situations are created—for example, with regard to possibilities for work or for special training—that other people can attain only at the cost of tremendous efforts. In this way a societal difference arises, but because it is festooned with the pretense of poverty, no one dares question whether it is justified.

It is here that the subtle untruthfulnesses begin. Not to have taken risks generates not only thoughtlessness but also a human naïveté. A person makes a claim about herself that is not covered either by professional or by human competence, and a gulf opens up that becomes especially incredible when she makes high demands of others. This disguises itself as idealism, but it is essentially hollow. Where her professional achievements attain top quality, this is only because the best technical presuppositions for her work are available. And where something of the quality of testimony still remains present, this is due to the institutional guarantee that conflicts will be reduced, that is, that the individual will not be pushed to the limits of her strength—she is like a trapeze artist who invariably works with a safety net. Besides this, institutions are always right. She can hide behind their façade with no need to justify herself. The Christian in the world cannot afford such a luxury, and he must not only acquire his social prestige but also maintain it. This keeps him intellectually vigilant because he cannot afford to meet other people in the attitude of superiority that he himself has not merited but that was bestowed on him as an unquestionable possession, antecedent to any achievements on his part. Poverty then easily degenerates into an artificial life at second hand. Indeed, it decays into an open life-lie when the individual exploits to the full the possibilities that are available to him, when he asserts himself, when he himself becomes a powerful factor whose idol is his own desire for success and who employs his own luxury criteria to evaluate all the others who are not as privileged as he.

A person can of course win successes in this way, but this is not in keeping with the Gospel. The platform on which she acts has no room for truthfulness. Normal encounters are always distorted when the necessary self-criticism is lacking. Solidarity vanishes; the claim it makes on her is transformed surreptitiously into arrogance, and the principle of equality is subtly violated. Her counterpart automatically occupies the position of the weaker partner. Indeed, in reality he is no longer a partner at all but an opponent. Self-criticism requires her to seize thankfully the possibilities that are available for action, and to use these to the full in a spirit of modesty. Truthfulness allows her to understand the other person on his own presuppositions and to assess him in view of the options that are available to him.[25]

Celibacy is not insulated against the same risks of untruthfulness. In the context of a Christian anthropology, there can be no doubt that this is a meaningful way of life. It is usually affirmed that celibacy has the character of an eschatological sign, and that it reminds us that the Christian existence has a structure of hope. For the unmarried person, God is the entire fulfillment of his life already here and now, and the center of his thoughts is the richness and happiness of his vocation in which he finds his satisfaction. At the same time, however, his life is a gesture of solidarity with all those persons who suffer in one way or another, whether in body or in mind, because of the catastrophes of their life stories. His life gives them a hope that even a fragmentary life can be lived in fully valid manner, and that the structure of hope that characterizes faith gives him the power to accept limitations resolutely, to live with them, to reinterpret them and transform them, and thus to turn the story of conflict into a story of reconciliation. Understood correctly, celibacy gives him the self-assurance that is needed if he is to be capable of undisguised communication. It makes him open, sympathetic, and sensitive—but not in such a way that he hands himself over to other persons.

The temptation to creeping untruthfulness begins in the same deep strata. For example, communication is distorted when a lack of self-assurance leads to false attitudes that no longer admit any true counterpart. This can happen in very various ways. An elitist mentality can be cultivated, which consciously or unconsciously maneuvers the celibate into the position of the stronger partner, generating a feeling of superiority that nips in the bud any relationships of trust. His own advantage is always certain, and it is not surprising that the other person sees this as coercion: he is defenseless against such a claim since he cannot match it with anything of equal value.

Untruthfulness can also disguise itself more ingeniously by developing a manner of thinking that isolates the sexual sphere and attributes to this torso of a phenomenon a meaning that it does not possess in the complex and often conflictual reality of life—for in reality the experience of sexuality is woven into a multiplicity of overlapping and mutually conflicting experiences; in joys, fears, and compulsions; in contrast and reconciliation; in dependence and freedom; and in distance and closeness, solitude and fellowship. All this will elude the person whose thinking divides it up into segments. Such a way of thinking necessarily remains out of touch with life and gives the thinker a whiff of naïveté that affects the world of his feelings since these are not subject to control by any coherent life project. But such a life project is needed when the act of communication intersects with the life stories of other people, for otherwise it will not get beyond the stage of imparting superficial information. Only the person who assumes that his neighbor has achieved the integration of his feelings is able to build up mature emotional ties; only such a person escapes the obvious danger of playing with feelings. The celibate becomes profoundly untruthful as soon as he brings into play the immature and uncommitted world of his feelings in a manner for which his life story provides no "covering," for then it is easy to impose emotional ties on the other person, or even to exploit him. Often, such a phenomenon conceals a weak ego that flees into a role, plays this role, and imperceptibly becomes one with it. This does indeed make a person rationally predictable, but it does not domesticate his feelings, which can fluctuate freely and cause disasters.

Untruthful manners of speaking and of behavior are symptoms of this malfunctioning at the roots. The other gender is inappropriately over- or underestimated, and one looks either up or down but never straight ahead. The mode and contents of his speech will necessarily be either deferential or lacking in distance but never characterized by the respectful naturalness that is customary in every area of life. It is easy for misunderstandings to arise since the celibate fails to bear in mind that the married person too was once unmarried and that he or she remains so to some degree, even in the most successful marriage. One can also transform celibacy on the quiet into a bachelor existence that deprives one of the human tact in dealings with other persons that is possessed only by those who are aware of the vulnerability of feelings and the risks to which feelings are exposed—both in himself and in others. Such deformities derive ultimately from his inability to cope with the solitude that he has chosen. He cannot bear the silence that spreads out around him. He refuses to recognize that the integration of all the powers of the mind, which is a characteristic of an ethical personality, depends on thoughtfully holding out in that inner sphere that remains reserved to the ego in its joys and its fears, in its possibilities and in its limitations. It is here that the origin of all truthfulness lies; but here too lies the origin of every lie.[26]

The Principal Features of a Metaphysics of Ethical Action

The Conscience as the Origin of Every Decision

The story of the freedom of the believer before the face of God is a story of the interior dimension that begins in the depth of the conscience and then unfolds via a great number of individual decisions. The conscience is the privileged place in which the connection is made between the discovery and the formulation of the ethical claim, the place in which the identity of the acting person is constituted. Only thus is coherent action in history possible. This is an ontological affirmation with a gnoseological intention, and it belongs to the metaphysics of knowledge. It can be regarded as programmatic for all that follows. The metaphysics of ethical action that we seek to elaborate here must remain free of objectivistic and neutral reductionisms, and we shall consistently employ personalistic categories.

This demands a convergence—which is not the same thing as an identity!—between the ontological and the gnoseological questions. Only in this way is it possible to rebut the suspicion of subjectivism or relativism. The reasoning presented here offers no fuel to such a suspicion; indeed, it must be emphasized that only this way of connecting the discovery and the formulation of the ethical claim guarantees both objectivity and absoluteness. From this point of view, no suspicion can attach to the affirmation that truth is the agreement between the conscience and one's self, and that this occurs where the acting person is completely at home in himself.[27]

It is therefore unsurprising that there is a family resemblance between the theorem of the *reditio completa* in the metaphysics of knowledge and the theory of the conscience as this is understood by the metaphysics of action. This does not lessen the autonomy of the ethical truth, which in fact attains its full validity only in this way. This is in complete accord with the specific character of the ethical truth, where we see the original connection between goodness and rightness. This connection is antecedent both to the conceptual distinction and to the further subdivision that is genuinely possible; indeed, it is thanks to this connection that both of these are feasible.[28] In the conscience, the human person projects himself in view of his ultimate goal. He does not "have" a conscience: rather, he *is* the conscience. The Scholastic tradition calls the person *actus primus*, in distinction from the actions of the person, and this designation becomes an immediately lived and directly recognized reality in the conscience. The conscience is the person in his or her self-enactment with its reference to transcendence.[29]

The conscience, understood in this way, is the starting point for an appropriate understanding of truthfulness, which presupposes self-consciousness as a freely affirmed identity. The acting person is completely present to himself in his conscience. He sees through himself, down into the ultimate depths of his being, although this does not dispense him from the labor of patient reflection. The cultivation of the conscience takes place in this referential context, which is not open to further scrutiny, and which provides the relevant criterion for its cultivation. It is only at a subsequent stage that norms appear as concretized aids to orientation. This takes place in a lifelong process that aims to make all his insights and experiences transparent to this connectedness. Naturally, he cannot do without information, formation, and education, but even the best external conditions cannot generate anything more than a consciousness of the role he plays if they are not underpinned by the self-consciousness of the acting person. For it is not a question of ensuring the objective correctness of concrete individual actions—that is only one aspect. Rather, it is a question of correct ethical action per se, and more precisely, of ethical action for which an autonomous conscience takes responsibility. We might express this by means of the image of a circumincession in which the various dimensions converge and compenetrate one another in the conscience.

It is a commonplace of moral theology that mental activity of various kinds takes place in the conscience—from simple insight to highly complex inferences and argumentations, with all the risks to which these are exposed within history; from the preconceptual act of apprehension to the act of formulating and pronouncing judgments in concepts and propositions; from the intellectual responsibility for norms to the investigation of concrete behavior to see whether it corresponds to these norms. When the relationship between ethical reason and the conscience is called dialectical, this is meant in the sense of both release and connectedness.[30] In the contemporary intellectual climate, it is no longer possible to maintain the unquestioning sublation of such a conception within a comprehensive idea of *ordo* (ordering)—the glory of the conscience is also its great disadvantage. This is not to deny the existence of an ordered structure. However, it is the task of the conscience, in the complex actions that it performs, to take the existing empirical realities in their inalienable referential character and fill them with the meaning that it has grasped in such a way that an anthropologically grounded image of *ordo* is generated. This image then serves as a criterion for concrete action; and the concrete action in turn interprets and develops this image. We are therefore justified in ascribing to the conscience an integrative function that guarantees the unity in tension between the person and his or her world. In that case, the affirmation that the conscience discovers God's plan for the human person is not open to misunderstandings, but we must add that this process does not consist only of looking at situations and "reading off" knowledge from them. Rather, it possesses the character of a project. In the act of knowledge, the conscience projects itself into its possibilities of existence and of action, thereby creating the transcendental conditions that make categorial projects of action possible. It is only under this presupposition that the act of introspection is possible.[31]

This has far-reaching implications for the truthfulness of the conscience in its acts of perception and judgment. In every individual critique, the dominant question always looks for the deep dimension of the underlying attitude, which is driven by the insight into meaning to fuse goodness and rightness into a rooted unity in action; this takes place in a process of anthropological mediation. This inevitably means that cherished ideas about happiness pass through this purifying filter, for otherwise they will succumb to the tendency of a naïve eudaemonism. The chief task and competence of the conscience is to remind us that there is no such thing as happiness devoid of all criteria. How then is happiness to be understood? This depends on the verdict pronounced by an anthropological preunderstanding that allows even suffering of every kind to ascend to the status of a positive possibility.[32] It is only against this background that a person can bear the anxious question whether she has done enough, whether she has reached the limits of her own strength, or whether it is pointless to think in these terms. The purity of her attitude is revealed in the fear that she has failed to live up to her full possibilities, that she has not exploited them to the full—and hence that she has led a life that passed her own self by. Neither authorities nor norms can allay this distress fully; at most, they can tone it down and make it bearable. To overcome this distress is surely a fundamental problem of the ethical personality, and this demands an indestructible trust in the meaningfulness of her own life story—even though she has no means to check this.

There is thus an existential doubt that cannot be removed by any rational endeavor. The classical moral systems too are of no avail here since they were conceived in relation to the indubitable validity of norms and thus remained in the sphere of a morality of individual actions. The only path forward is offered by an understanding of the virtue of *epikeia*, which unites the degree of commitment that has been recognized as meaningful to the hope of a good outcome, the hope that one will grow into the ever-fuller possibilities of what it is to be human. The presumption is in favor of the verdict of one's conscience, as long as a person does not refuse this fundamental openness. We need not be disturbed by the fact that this inner rhythm is slower than the individual actions that succeed one another quickly because this is how continuity is introduced into one's own story of freedom, and action becomes calculable (even if this calculability refers only to the broad outlines). Accordingly, self-assurance begins in the conscience, provided that it bears testimony to this kind of freedom. This gives one the courage to put an end to fruitless and self-tormenting rumination and to discover the path that leads to action. Theoretical doubts will accompany a person all through life; at the right time, they can open up new spaces for the mind. But practical doubts must remain manageable, and this skill will be bestowed above all on a conscience that knows how to unite prudence and wisdom. Prudence makes a person circumspect in evaluating all the important circumstances attaching to her action while wisdom gives her the staying power she needs in the face of all that she experiences.

The Theorem of the Fundamental Decision

If it is out of the depth of the conscience that ethical actions emerge, it follows that the depth of the conscience is the place where they must be evaluated. The moral theologian is therefore obliged to apply a differentiated concept of action if he wishes to do justice to this reality. Often, people argue at cross-purposes because their discourse is determined by different starting points and cognitive interests, but they do not inform one another explicitly about these factors. Bearing this in mind, we must emphasize the multilayered character of ethical action. The phenomenon of the action that can be externally observed and that presents itself to the descriptive reason is like the tip of an iceberg, most of which remains hidden under the surface, concealed from a hasty glance. Only a reductionism that completely misunderstood reality would be content with the visible. And this would be disastrous since the invisible is much more real and effective. Moral theology has devoted much thorough reflection to this in recent years. As a result, terms such as "fundamental decision" and "preliminary decision" now belong to the core vocabulary of the moral theologian. My intention here is not to repeat things that are already well known since this would not take the discussion forward. Nevertheless, I wish to shed a little more light on some important aspects in the hope that this will lend greater coherence to the ideas presented up to now.

The theorem of the fundamental decision takes up all the criticism that was leveled at the prevalent interest in the correctness of the individual action when seen in isolation. There is a unifying bond that gathers together the multiplicity of actions in their varying intensity and depth, in their free spontaneity and forced necessity, in their actively doing something and passively allowing something to be done; and this bond imprints a homogeneous form on these actions.[33] These are always actions by the same person on his or her path to personality. The self-interpretation of the story of a person's freedom is performed in action: the *actus primus* communicates itself to its *actus secundi*. Here we already require an initial clarification, which concerns the underlying metaphysics of action. What does the term "self-interpretation" mean in the context of this metaphysics? Since the approach chosen here concentrates on the above-mentioned mediation between the ontological and the gnoseological categories, one must also speak of a participation that is understood in this way. The metaphysics of the ethical action is done in the style of a hermeneutical ontology, in personalistic categories, as opposed to the kind of metaphysics of action that begins with the individual external performance of actions.[34] Here let it suffice to say that preliminary decisions determined by the intellectual context not only favored such thinking but actually demanded it. The dominant concern—provoked not least by all those societal imperatives that were linked to the emergence of the administrative state in the modern period and that found expression in the legal thought of that period—was to ensure certainty in action. The scholarly ideals of the natural sciences also left their traces: the primary focus was on the precise compilation and cataloging of the particular field of research, guided by the methodological reduction of the scientific strategy to its exactly delimited area of competence, to the exclusion of everything else that did not belong to this object of study. Academic endeavors were directed to the concrete and the particular, which were the starting point and the point of reference for every generalization based on the "laws" that the scholar discerned.

Once again we must point out the strange meaning of the term "concrete-particular," which is defined by the underlying and unquestioned epistemological realism. All knowledge begins with the empirical and the sensuous, moving thence to the essence under the guiding principle of the *intelligibile in sensibilibus*, that is, that the general reveals itself in the concrete; I do not wish in any way to question the basic validity of this epistemological option. It is linked to a representation theory: in the act of knowing, the mind reproduces a faithful copy of its object in its own idea. In this sense, it assimilates itself to its object. This does not mean a complete passivity. Our own Scholastic tradition always drew a distinction between the *intellectus agens* and the *intellectus possibilis*. For a representation to arise in the act of perceiving and knowing, the empirical-sensuous object must be made knowable, and this takes place through the activity of the *intellectus agens*, which goes ahead and prepares the way. In the act of knowing, the mind structures reality before it takes notice of it. Only under this presupposition is it possible for empirical knowledge to have an effect on the mind; and we should note that this is an ontological condition of the possibility of knowledge.[35]

Nevertheless, this epistemological option, which is infiltrated by elements of the metaphysics of knowledge, still has obvious limitations. The activity of the *intellectus agens* as the ontological condition of possibility of the *intellectus possibilis* is considered only in a formal sense, and no attention is paid to the question of whether or to what extent this activity may contribute content to empirical knowledge. As soon as contents come into question, the predominance of the objective remains characteristic, and the metaphysics of action that is elaborated under these presuppositions bears the consequences. One single way of thinking about the objective remains dominant: the performance of the action is objectified and reason examines it and "reads off" its content. The ideal to be pursued is the highest possible precision in recording and formulating, and the culture of the concrete—an enduring achievement of nominalism—is united to the analytical acuteness of the understanding, to conceptual unambiguousness, and to consistency of argumentation. It is utterly out of the question for moral theology to go back to some earlier stage; this applies also to the level of the metaphysics of action. Nevertheless, desiderata remain. These are sparked by the cosmological preliminary decisions that tacitly contribute to the understanding of metaphysics. The natural scientist regarded nature and the cosmic order as immutable. Only knowledge was subject to change, but it attained its perfection in taking hold of and recording that which is immutable. This offers a key to the understanding of metaphysics. What is commonly called objectivistic essentialism is the reflection of a mechanistic worldview. Scholars have often enough underlined the fact that this entailed a flattening down of metaphysics, which affected the metaphysics of action in equal measure.

This background makes it somewhat easier to understand the theorem of the fundamental decision. When applied to the theory of action, the theorem of the fundamental decision signals the transition to the subject in the modern period, which can be seen most unambiguously in the various versions of transcendental philosophy. The moral theologians of our own days are aware that existentialist philosophy and personalism in its various schools of thought have also exercised an influence—to say nothing of the dogmatic-theological background. This knowledge makes it possible to study the problems themselves in greater detail, and the first area to be affected here is the understanding of "person." When the person is understood as a substance in the enactment of its orientation to transcendence, the "fundamental decision" expresses this ontological state of affairs with regard to the quality of freedom that is inherent in the person. The natural inclination to the good appears as a personal affectivity that not only challenges a person to take an explicit position but can also take on varying degrees of thematization in the course of her life story. The process of becoming a person is linked to this process. This could also be called a reaching out on the part of freedom to Being qua good. In this transcendental quality of freedom lies the ontological condition of possibility for the categorial free act.[36]

However, the moral theologian does not gain much help from this proposition, which remains colorless and lacks profile without further clarifications. One initial clarification lies in the reference to an undisputed element of the Scholastic tradition, the doctrine of transcendentals. The reaching out to Being qua good is characterized by the other transcendental definitions: it includes both unity and truth on an equal footing. Accordingly, a reaching out on the part of knowledge corresponds to the reaching out on the part of freedom. It is this convergence that awakens the interest of the moral theologian, especially because the underlying concept of Being is filled with content. This observation allows us to rebut a widespread misunderstanding in the metaphysics of knowledge. The fundamental decision is not a formal entity devoid of content. As the ontological condition of possibility of the categorial individual action, it already bears in itself a dimension of transcendental content, which mediates itself into categorial content. The content of the individual decision is brought about by this mediation; the idea of an unmediated juxtaposition would foment the suspicion that mechanistic categories were being employed, and would not do justice to the unity in tension that characterizes personal actions. Equally, it can be seen that this reaching out to Being is characterized by the mutual compenetration of knowing and willing in equilibrium. Naturally, these are conceptually distinct, and this distinction has a genuine basis. Nevertheless, one must bear in mind the varying degrees of interiority; in the fundamental distinction, which is their highest concentration, the undivided mutual compenetration prevails.

The theorem of the fundamental decision is thus taking on contours that can be helpful to the moral theologian in his reflections on the theory of action. This theorem encompasses the dynamic that comes about from the earlier-mentioned mutual compenetration of knowing and willing and enters into each individual decision like an existential, positing the individual decision in its own specific mode of existence. This is why we are justified in speaking of foreknowledge *and* preliminary decision: these are two aspects of one single reality. Every individual decision has its origin in this depth, and this is why every judgment that is content with the external appearance of the decision fails to do justice to reality. What is needed is a kind of hermeneutical labor that seeks to grasp and decode this deep dimension. This gives us a decisive keyword: a theory of action must first of all have a hermeneutical orientation. The question that guides our analysis is, what cluster of presuppositions is present in the acting person himself and makes the individual decision comprehensible and therefore assessable?[37] Here I have in mind the basic elements of the anthropology that has been assumed. In a first step, these define the parameters, which then demand to be filled out in greater detail. There exists a recognized correspondence between these two steps—otherwise the decision that is taken lacks the necessary immanent consistency and is no longer coherent. Doubtless, external factors play a role too, but everything must be subsumed under one common form, and (as I have emphasized) this is not to be understood as empty of content.

The tension between nature and person discussed earlier thus returns in the context of the theory of action. The person brings a preunderstanding to his or her nature without dualistically breaking apart the essential unity of the two, and this is what the fundamental decision does in relation to the individual decision. The unity of the action is not broken apart but acquires a more differentiated foundation. One must bear in mind that this preunderstanding—defined as a reaching out on the part of knowledge—also encompasses the ultimate goal of the human person. The basic elements of an anthropology that has been assumed look toward the final goal; we come to know them not as a static current reality but as a dynamic orientation to their perfected form. To omit this immanent teleology would be a fatal reduction. The individual decision is subject to the demand made by final forms that gradually become clear in the course of one's life story.

This, however, entails an intellectual problem with which the Christian must grapple since his ethical discourse operates with the idea of perfection beyond history, when we see God face to face. It is a theological commonplace that every form of fulfillment within history must always be measured against the eternal final goal of the human person. But how is this to be done? Is it possible to find directly serviceable criteria for this, or even to formulate such criteria in propositions, so that they present an unambiguously defined authority that judges and evaluates? It is not pointless to put the question in this way since this sheds light on the specific epistemological status of the fundamental decision, which is characterized by being antecedent to normative definitions. The assessment of human goods and the establishing of an evaluation of goods that will offer direction to the normative discourse both derive from a prereflective or nonthematic knowledge *in actu* of the fullness of meaning, knowledge that defines the prospective balance between gain and loss, between happiness and pain. This, however, already points to the underlying power of freedom.

The Biographical Dimension of the Virtues

The fundamental decision gives birth to a decisiveness of freedom with an immanent dynamic that enters into every individual decision and predetermines its outcome in a *moral* manner (i.e., while fully preserving freedom). This generates a spontaneous basic security that makes possible a relaxed action that flows from one's own "surplus." It thus seems obvious that we should link the fundamental decision and the virtues. The relationship between these two is one of mutual circumincession, and the virtues are the configurations taken by the fundamental decision in the many different spheres of life. Basic patterns of action are established that provide an initial intellectual orientation and guarantee stability and constancy in action. The dynamic identity of the ethical personality finds expression through this interrelationship, as recent publications on virtue ethics strongly underline.[38] Accordingly, the significance of the individual actions is not in the least devalued, as if the only thing that mattered was the fundamental decision—for that would be the logical extension of an anthropological dualism to the level of the theory of action. In reality, every individual action, in its success or failure, has repercussions on the fundamental decision. It may give it an increased consistency, or it may cause it to fade away imperceptibly but inexorably, so that in the end all that is needed is some trifling occasion, and the fundamental decision breaks down completely. And that is the silent death of the soul, where "soul" is understood as the lived relationship to God, the consistent fundamental orientation to the ultimate goal.

Irrespective of the dialectical interrelationship of mutual influence between the fundamental decision and the individual decisions, there are displacements in the rhythm between them that cannot be grasped directly but nevertheless have a long-lasting effect. An increased vigilance is needed, when one must look ahead prudently over one's own life story in the great variety of its constellations: something that begins on the periphery in inconspicuous symptoms tends to make its way into the center, where it will be accommodated. The fundamental decision takes over the impulses supplied by the individual decisions, even where these are very slight, and encounters them on its own initiative, for better or for worse. The clocks of the fundamental decision tick more slowly in this process than the clocks of the individual decisions, but this does not make them any less effective. This image helps to illustrate the specific laws governing the story of freedom, where there are no direct paths but rather an intricate interlocking of all the various dimensions. This is why the individual action can never be understood on its own terms alone. It remains tied to the basic condition of the acting person, and it is here that the ultimately decisive hermeneutical key lies.

One further perspective deserves a mention here because it can help to clear up a widespread misunderstanding. In connection with the fundamental decision, we keep hearing a proposition that is taken to be self-evident, namely, that the acting person identifies totally with the fundamental decision, or that this decision is taken in the center of the person. Other criteria are applied to the individual decisions. It is presumed that these are located on the periphery and that the acting person does not identify totally with them; the burden of proof lies on those who would dispute this. In individual instances, it is certainly possible that one individual action is so serious that it can abolish a fundamental decision that has stood firm up to that point. But if this is to be understood correctly, some additional clarifications are required. For such an instance to occur, a preceding history is needed: a fundamental decision must already have been hollowed out to such an extent by numerous acts of omission and infringements that the total collapse becomes virtually inevitable. The tendency that already exists looks for a trigger, for a suitable occasion that will confirm it. A contrary story has begun a long time ago, all the more dangerous for being unnoticed; the terrain is prepared and the disposition has been created. The final step is the identification with this preceding history, not only with some clearly definable matter. This is because the preceding history cannot be evaluated with the same criterion that is applied to the individual action when understood in isolation—that kind of reductionist metaphysics of action makes a realistic evaluation impossible. The meaning possessed by the matter of an action is revealed by looking back over the context in a person's life story in which this action arose. The metaphysical definitions produced by an objectivistic form of thinking do not do justice to this reality. At best, they can give indications, which must then be filled out through deep hermeneutical reflection.[39]

This affirmation bids farewell to an intellectual tradition in moral theology that employed metaphysical categories in the attempt to attain objective certainty but that made excessive demands of these categories so that the whole endeavor was doomed to failure. To cope with this malfunctioning, we need to bring together the metaphysical dimension and the dimension of the life story, and the theorem of the fundamental decision offers intellectual stimuli for this task as well as an initial framework for orientation. We are surely not wrong to see this as a kind of paradigm shift that replaces the collaboration between objectivistic metaphysics and rational psychology, which was typical of some of the moral-theological manuals with a new thinking on a level that is best described by the term *psychologie réflexive*. One who does not bear this in mind has failed to understand what this theorem intends and what it can in fact do—he will regard it as a relapse into an uncontrollable subjectivism.

The metaphysics of action that is our aim here thinks from the inside toward the outside. Its methodological point of contact lies in the highest concentration of action, not in its secondary manifestations. In this way the method and the subject matter coincide completely. This, however, indicates an intellectual program that is both philosophical and theological. It is philosophical, in the sense that it consciously picks up the *reditio completa* of Saint Thomas: in the act of knowing, the mind grasps not only the truth of its objects and the agreement with them but also its own inherent capacity for the truth. Only in this way is the mind truly at home in itself and at the same time present to the other. The mind's knowledge of God is also located in this interiority, and the reaching out to Being qua true and good (of which we have spoken earlier) now means, in the theological context, the reaching out on the part of knowledge and freedom to God as the author of one's salvation. I mention only in passing that this act of reaching out is not an achievement on the part of the human person but a gift of God's grace. This is taken for granted in theology: it is the theological interpretation of a philosophical insight.[40]

This allows us to clear up a number of misunderstandings that are sometimes found in works of moral theology concerning the correct way to employ a Scholastic concept that seems to have an oscillating meaning, the *finis operantis* ("the goal of the one who acts").[41] In the context of all the clarifications present up to this point, this concept has originally nothing to do with a way of positing a goal to which the empirical work of psychology has access; this level is defined by the *psychologie réflexive* mentioned earlier. The *finis operantis* encompasses the reaching toward Being with all that this requires. Theologically interpreted, this is the reaching out toward God as the ultimate goal in whom the human person will find all his bliss. God is usually designated as the *finis remotus* of action, but this phrase is not opposed to the idea we have elaborated here. All it does is manifest another form of thinking that begins with the concrete, empirical goal of action. Here, however, things are different. The *finis operantis* aims at God since He is more inward to the human person than that person is to himself (the heritage from Augustine and Neo-Platonism is unmistakable), but this first indication is insufficient. At the same time, the *finis operantis* includes all the goals of action within history in their orientation to the final goal. It is thus a reality *in actu* that was constituted by the acts of understanding and interpreting. It is the outcome of a complex intellectual achievement on the part of the acting person, who constructs a bridge to the varied individual decisions by imposing upon them one single highest form. For the believer, this highest form is identical to the Christian intentionality since this must be regarded as the "matrix" of all action.

The Variants of the Fundamental Decision

The fundamental decision displays variants with which it cooperates in the generation of individual decisions; we could say that it creates for itself initial forms of mediation that make the transition easier. This is closely connected with the process whereby an ethical personality comes into existence. The more single-mindedly this process is undertaken, the more clearly do preferential decisions in favor of very specific ethical values emerge. This is not an arbitrary selection, nor does it in any way qualify the absolute claim made by the ethical truth since its obligatory character is identical in all times and places—but without necessarily excluding particular accents that are connected with a person's life story. A person who posits ideals for his life, and *a fortiori* one who associates his life with a vocation, makes a decision in favor of preferential values that posit one very specific idea for his life. All the individual decisions are at the service of this idea. They fit into a form of life and give it expression. The individual takes on an ethical profile. His life story is governed by a dynamic. He goes through his life with open eyes and is always on the lookout for opportunities to translate his ideal into specific actions.

At the same time, this obliges him to develop a strategy for action to avoid the fragmentation of his strength. He must make a selection among the human goods that he seeks to realize, for not everything is equally possible. Once again, this entails a preferential choice (also known as a preferential option). It is true that the dominant ideals make their contribution to this choice, but the choice takes place in coordination with the possibilities that are available to one's freedom. In the last analysis, the most paralyzing experience of all is to see one's own life sinking down into irrelevance. This experience is the root cause of many kinds of moral dissolution.

Each person is responsible for the success of her own freedom. For this, she needs not only a life but also an attitude of unconditional truthfulness vis-à-vis her own self. The tasks that this involves are ultimately dictated by self-love and self-respect since it is in the ability to undertake these tasks that the ethical personality reveals itself. In what follows, we shall touch on some aspects of this process.

The Adventure of the Decision about One's Life

I have already noted that the construction of an ethical personality begins in the inner world of the thoughts. Responsibility for the success of one's freedom demands that the world of the thoughts be cultivated in view of attaining joy, a sense of well-being, and harmony with oneself and with the aims one has set for oneself in life. Sometimes people suffer not so much because of reality as because of the thoughts and feelings they have about it. This leads them to create a pseudo-world, but the encounter with this world produces a friction that consumes their best energies. They do not dare to admit that they themselves are the cause of their adversity since the business on which they ought already to be concentrating is their own life—a life that does not get weary in situations of unavoidable disappointment, of the lack of success, or even of the obvious loss of one's own self. As time passes, people learn in any case where the sources of indestructible happiness lie—in the calm consciousness that they have done what they could, irrespective of applause or criticism.

It is always possible to discover positive possibilities for life that bestow the inner freedom that is needed if the ethical construction of one's life is not to be bogged down in compulsions and fears. Naturally, everyone knows that a life lived with high ideals will inevitably encounter misunderstandings, and this is why a superior calm is required. Self-love and self-respect are two sides of the same coin. Both presuppose an unshakable confidence in the meaningfulness of a person's own commitment, a conviction that nothing in his life has been in vain—a conviction, in other words, that it does not matter whether or not particular goods were realized in his life since in either case the outcome was a continuous purification of the expectations of happiness that were linked to these goods. And this means that the story of his freedom becomes as it were naturally a story of truthfulness, and he develops a sure instinct for the perception of those goals of action that are most profoundly in accord with his own self. It is then no cause for surprise when his path through life leads to encounters with people who prevent the self-assurance he has developed from degenerating into self-satisfaction. They do this by making truthfulness possible and by unmasking all the secret devices he employs to protect himself from the claims made by this truthfulness. The more fulfilled a person's life is, the more do questions about gaining and losing himself sink down into the periphery. The mind's attention is directed consistently to the tasks for his life that he has recognized; he avoids a fruitless rumination on all those things that did not work out, whether through culpable failure or through adverse circumstances.

Self-love and self-respect are indispensable presuppositions for the success of interpersonal relationships, among which life-long bonds occupy a privileged position.[42] The breakdown of these relationships is usually programmed in advance by the fact that a person chooses a partner to compensate for her own weakness and lack of self-assurance, and leads a life at the cost of her partner. This makes all proofs of love fundamentally untruthful because they transmute surreptitiously into a secret coercion. The partner is aggressively taken captive and "occupied"—his emotions are no longer free because his counterpart (who in reality is not a "partner" at all) cannot endure his freedom. The true goal of a relationship ought to be the liberation from being fascinated by one's own self, but this does not happen here.

True unity with one's neighbor bestows distance to one's own self, but this can be borne only by a person who loves and respects himself thanks to his consciousness of the uniqueness of his life story, and who thus finds it completely natural, indeed a matter of course, to tie himself down, to give his life an unambiguous form, and to defend this form against adverse circumstances and inappropriate demands from his fellow human beings. He will also find it natural to implement this unambiguous form, thereby bearing testimony. Self-respect always requires the courage to put up a constructive resistance when demands are made (no matter what kind of demands, or by whom they are proposed) which seek to undermine this basic right. Ultimately, all the subjective rights are based on specific individual goods in one common legal right—the personal right par excellence to lead a life for which one takes responsibility in untrammeled freedom.

This is far removed from self-assertion. The only point I am making here is that the best service of one's neighbor consists first and foremost in one's own self-assurance since freedoms do not impose limitations on each other; rather, they dissolve the limitations and liberate each other. Encouragement is necessary here since committed relationships are like an adventure with challenges and opportunities that one must not refuse because of a lack of resilience. When a conflict is waged honestly, each person must know how to yield to the other. But if one person does not take intellectual responsibility for this yielding, it leaves behind a feeling of humiliation that is the source of subsequent bitterness.

Because it is moral theology's task to give help with people's lives, moral theology must reflect on these questions. As a sapiential doctrine, it draws on the experiential potential of many life stories, which include a good portion of common sense and knowledge of human nature. We find classic examples of this in the sapiential literature of the Old Testament. One ought not to dismiss too readily the help that these texts offer, for life stories were not mastered because a perfect system of norms existed but because a treasure of the knowledge of life, of prudent rules, and of perfectly natural patterns and strategies of action was available. These provided a basis for life because they gave people a comprehensive and certain orientation. Besides this, they make life easy, and this too is a perspective that concerns the moral theologian unless he wishes to expose himself to the charge of being remote from real life. Excessive ethical demands, especially in situations of conflict, arise when moral-theological reflection has nothing other than imperatives to offer. The imperatives crush all those who lack the sapiential security that enables them to take their lives into their own hands.

The experience of the inexorable passing of time confronts the human person with all his fragility and frightens him with the possibility that his life is meaningless. He must tie himself down. He must impose a project on the raw material of his life. He must confirm his personal identity by means of a choice with which he can be one, a choice in which he recognizes himself totally, a choice that sets up an irrevocable goal for his life to which all the partial goals are subordinate. The decision about one's life corresponds to this longing. It must be constituted in such a way that it challenges one to undergo a permanent story of purification without ever giving oneself up. All events, insights, and experiences are welcome opportunities to form oneself ever more perfectly; their concreteness belongs to a process that integrates into itself obvious transpositions of emphasis that move imperceptibly from the yearning to gain oneself to the calm acceptance of losing oneself. With the passing of time, he thinks more and more of what he still has to do. The examination of conscience automatically becomes a reflection on the indissoluble bond between his life story and the things that life reserved for him. What lessons has life taught him? These lessons can take very varied forms in the individual states of life, but there exists an affinity between the problems involved.

Thus, both marriage and celibacy equally demand a wholesome disillusionment. A person who cannot endure truth cannot be faithful; at some point, he will fail. But nothing is as truthful as definitiveness since it is no longer possible to escape. Similarly, tolerance is required since every choice is linked to the milieu of a partner, and this means that there is no evading the claim made by his neighbor. He can prepare himself mentally for this, especially by a basic attitude of respectful friendship that is willing to experience and to accept the other as an enrichment, not as a threat. Nothing is so well suited to cultivate such a climate as a confidential conversation among equals that ranges over the entire spectrum of life. Every fellowship lives from this because the way in which we speak with one another trains us in the culture of dealing with one another. People get to know each other and learn what kind of persons they are. In conversation, each one learns what the other thinks about him. Conversation is a valuable help, if he resolves in advance to be faithful; at the same time, it counteracts the danger that he may become stuck in a voluntary or involuntary isolation, thus becoming gradually a victim of his own loneliness. It is not only the individual who lives in various worlds with their divergent expectations and demands, which never attract and fulfill more than a part of the ego; this increases exponentially in partnerships, whether in marriage or outside it. Conversation cannot remove these boundaries, but it has the task of toning them down and reducing sources of friction. At the same time, it bestows a wholesome distance. The spoken word gives protection against the superior power of physical closeness, that is, in marriage. The person who wants to understand his life partner needs this balance too.

Once again we are directed to the world of the thoughts. Mutual responsibility begins in the way in which each thinks of the other. This is how the ground is prepared for reciprocal considerate attention. The person learns what demands he can make of the other and what he can reasonably expect of her only if he spends time with her lovingly in his thoughts. A prophylactic ethics of this kind determines in advance the outcome of the conflicts that are often kindled by peripheral everyday things. It goes without saying that this style of speaking and dealing with one's partner helps avoid a deadly fixation upon him. Of its nature, conversation widens boundaries and ensures that new encounters will open up further rooms of the human spirit. The person who engages in conversation need not fear succumbing to self-sufficiency: he is impelled to draw other partners into the conversation while at the same time seeing that human beings are always linked by tasks that they have recognized and accepted in common. Such tasks immensely increase his moral strength, precisely in situations of vacillation when he loses faith in the meaningfulness of his past efforts. Marital sexuality must be integrated into a high culture of conversation if it is not to degenerate into banality or aggressiveness—for then it can become a nightmare. It is obvious that such a style of conduct must be practiced in the time of preparation for marriage. It then becomes spontaneously clear what demands a person can make of a partner.

Experience shows that there are unmastered forms both of marriage and of celibacy, thanks to a wide range of omissions. The moral theologian must ponder the question how he is to meet these persons in a constructive manner; once again, self-respect plays a decisive role. It erects a protective wall against everything that closes in upon a person. Celibacy cannot be lived without a high intellectual culture; it is precisely the celibate who needs to face lofty demands because this helps him to weather the crises that arise. Through all the activity of his everyday life, he must attempt to create free spaces for leisure; this will only improve the quality of his professional work. Since his choice of life is an expressive action of the purest kind, his life is not compelled to be efficient. What is expected of him is contemplation, reflection, and wisdom—the success of his life is measured in terms of his capacity for this. This is why he must have the courage to be silent. This is possible only for the person who feels comfortable within his own four walls, the person who deals lovingly with his own thoughts and feelings, the person who is not gradually exhausted by his total absorption in the tensions of his professional work.

One final point: the celibate does not play any fixed social role. He expresses an existential that is common to all human beings. He lives in the manner of a sign something that accompanies the life of every person to a greater or lesser degree. This obliges him first to think with complete authenticity; he cannot afford to seek the protection of empty phrases and catchwords, and this is one of the greatest challenges to his wholly personal truthfulness. He is always at risk of evading this claim and slipping into a ready-made role pattern that excuses him from the burden of standing up to be counted. To deny oneself in this way eventually leads to hypocrisy. The ego and the role part company, and his life degenerates into an artificial construct to which a borrowed self-consciousness at second hand corresponds only too well. Such developments need not always be his own fault since general attitudes and expectations also help promote them, and the person who is exposed to the pressure of exaggerated expectations will seek salvation in flight. But this is not a genuine life.

A pretense of flawlessness generates nightmares. No one has the answers to everything—neither the Church as an institution nor the individual who serves it. Elitist categories simply fail to do justice to the reality of life, and it is very hard to go on fighting rearguard battles all the time. So it is no wonder that a pseudo-world is constructed where the immense effort expended on legitimation causes a person to forget the utter lack of spontaneous self-affirmation. And this often leads to a pathological hypersensitivity, the fear of conflicts, a defective ability to make sense of one's experiences, and the lack of an honest confrontation with one's own self. Friendship with married couples can have a healing effect here. It helps to relativize one's own problems, which may perhaps have been blown up to bizarre proportions, by showing that spheres of the fragmentary remain even in the happiest and (in the usual sense of the word) most successful of marriages. There is more celibacy in most people's lives than they themselves realize. This experience can make the celibate's own feelings more secure. The crises that arise now do not cause panic but are accepted with a healthy sense of reality and as something that is perfectly natural.[43]

The Structure of the Individual Decision

The fundamental decision and the decision about one's life are like centers of gravity around which all the other individual decisions fall into place. I mention only in passing that the intellectual and ethical virtues have a linking function here and that they lend support to the ethical profile by communicating constancy, easiness, and spontaneity to the action as well as joy at the action itself. These virtues develop a comprehensive framework of orientation with a high degree of subjective certainty, and they locate within this framework the numerous modes of acting and reacting that are often born of one particular moment and that always contain an element of the mastery of conflicts.

Viewed in this light, the correctness of the individual decisions is not simply derived from the goodness of the person; that would not do justice to the complexity

of the mediations. Rather, the virtues already contain substantial preliminary decisions that are antecedent to the individual action. They require further
differentiation to grasp the reality of the situations of decision rather than evaporat-
ing into insubstantiality. Naturally, virtues too are subject to developments in the
course of a life story. The various phases of life generate specific ethical challenges
that can be met only on the level of attitudes that are capable of development. In
this process, the intellectual virtues play a key role. They strengthen the power of
judgment in times of turmoil, when it is necessary to practice self-correction and
to acquire existential attitudes that will help in the life that lies ahead. In one's
youth, a person is perhaps only dimly aware of things that become increasingly
solid when she is older: gratitude, tolerance, willingness to understand others, self-
limitation, and the composed acceptance of something that her own decisions no
longer have the power to change. In this context, norm-ethical reflections have
much less significance since they do not reach as far as these deep levels of the
ethical personality. Rather, she discovers that truthfulness in relation to her own
self is the all-decisive theme of her life. This is where we must start when we seek
to locate the structures of the individual decision in the metaphysics of action that
has been sketched up to this point.

The truthfulness that is required in relation to one's own self begins in the *finis
operantis* of which I have spoken in connection with the fundamental decision.
The philosophical influences that were mentioned there must be consistently
transposed to the individual decision since there is a relationship of mutual compenetration between the two; indeed, it does not seem mistaken to give the
fundamental decision the status of an *analogatum princeps* and the individual decisions the status of *analogata secundaria*. This sheds light on the *finis operantis* in the
new context: it presents to the acting person the specific object of his action,
which moral theology calls the *objectum morale*.[44]

This observation immediately calls for further differentiation. What does the
verb "present" mean here? Looking back to the fundamental decision, we must
emphasize that the specific object of action is never understood in isolation: the
concept of objectivity is not identical to that of empirical knowledge. The moral
theologian operates with a relational objectivity in which the specific object of
action is thought of a priori in its relationship to the final goal; in other words, it
is seen in a teleological perspective. The perspective opened up by the fundamental
decision communicates itself to the individual decision via the *finis operantis*, and
the individual object of action is desirable because (and to the extent that) it can
be integrated into this perspective. It is thus already interpreted and evaluated; the
totality of the preliminary anthropological decisions flows into it and constitutes
its moral relevance.

But more remains to be said. The *finis operantis* is characterized by its immanent
complexity: it consists of motivation and intention. Both concepts must be understood in terms of the metaphysics of action since they are based on the
presuppositions in the metaphysics of knowledge that have been set out earlier.

Accordingly, the motivation turns to the ethical truth qua goodness and stores up ideas about value that the ethically good has already analyzed in terms of their substance and their relevance to the various spheres of life. The primary function of the motivation is to guarantee the goodness of the action, but, as I have indicated, it is not entirely devoid of content: its content remains unthematized. In the intention, conversely, which is directly oriented to the guiding anthropological ideas and translates these into the appropriate concrete form which they are to take, the accent lies on the correctness of the action. The intention projects goals for action that correspond to the guiding anthropological ideas that have been accepted while at the same time taking into consideration the demands of the specific situation.

This requires a complex intellectual activity, which remains exposed to a high risk. The best description of it is a hermeneutical mediation that must include a full analysis of the concrete situation. At any rate, the non-thematic consciousness of the fundamental decision is thematized via the unambiguous reference to the object. It is in this way that responsibility for the individual decision is assumed reflexively. This does not in the least mean that the object of action in its pure givenness is devoid of significance, or that it would at best take on the rank of a raw material that can be formed arbitrarily—for such an assumption would not accord with all the presuppositions that I have adduced up to this point. The critical realism that I assume presupposes that the empirical givenness supplies indications that are taken up intellectually by the *finis operantis* in which motivation and intention collaborate, and that these indications are given a new form in the process of interpretation and evaluation.

The *finis operantis* thus finds its logical continuation in the *finis operis*. There is an undivided collaboration between the two.[45] This refers to the external performance of the action, which brings its own dynamic into the total action. This should make it obvious that one cannot simply attribute to the *finis operis* the significance of a *finis naturalis* since the nature that the *finis operis* gathers in itself is understood, interpreted, and formed. This must be explicitly underlined in today's intellectual context, for otherwise one will easily expose oneself to the charge of a concealed anthropological dualism.[46] Rather, an *ordinatio rationis* is at work: the subject matter discussed with reference to normative nature returns here in the perspective of the metaphysics of action. By bringing a project to the *finis operis*, the *finis operantis* establishes it in its own specific moral status. And what the *finis operis* contributes to the morality of an action it owes to the *finis operantis*, which takes the initiative and prepares the ground for this.

Here we see an immensely dramatic turning point. Its counterpart is represented by the intellectual tradition in the manuals of moral theology, which insisted on elaborating its metaphysics of action with a starting point in the *finis operis*. When this theology affirms that the morality of an action is defined *primo et per se* by the *finis operis*, this shows a form of thought that was influenced by a reductionist epistemological realism and appealed to a *moralitas ex objecto* that had nothing to do with a naturalistic fallacy but succumbed to an essentialistic objectivism and thus totally failed to do justice to the reality of personal actions. Closely pursuing scholarly ideals that corresponded to the natural sciences and to jurisprudence, moral theologians endeavored to ensure intellectual certainty for action and to buttress this with metaphysical arguments. This appears understandable if one bears in mind the intellectual climate of the past. Nevertheless, it represents a remarkable decline from the speculative heights of Saint Thomas' thinking.

More is required here than a simple recourse to Thomas. The indispensable elements that he contributes must prove their worth again and again in fresh conversations with the philosophical currents of the modern period. The theorem of inherently evil actions is an excellent paradigm here since it can illustrate all the points of view that have been presented up to this point.

The Intrinsically Evil Actions

The problem of intrinsically evil actions is so complex that we must avoid presenting it in a way that gives the impression of smoothing out the rough edges.[47] Usually, three different positions are presented, and each time the word "intrinsically" (per se) takes on a different meaning. First, moral theologians refer to the specific character of ethical truth: the claim it makes is "intrinsically" obligatory, that is, irrespective of any positing or confirmation on the part of a human authority. A human legislator can define moral claims more precisely, but this does not in any way alter their antecedent fundamental validity. This is a commonplace of moral theology and has therefore no specific contribution to make to this particular debate.

A second modality opens the door to much more serious conflicts. It is immediately connected to the metaphysics of action that has been elaborated here, and it concerns specifically the relationship between the inner and the outer action, between the *finis operantis* and the *finis operis*. The intellectual interest is the definition of the morality of an action based on the external performance, which contains in itself all the criteria necessary to undertake a moral evaluation of the total action. No matter what the condition of the inner action may be (which constitutes itself through the collaboration between motivation and intention), it is incapable of specifically altering the morality of the totality; all it can do is diminish or increase the guilt. It remains a purely subjective factor and plays no role in the objective evaluation. It is obvious that this construct depends on clear epistemological presuppositions. The realistic option that is chosen here limits the metaphysics of action to the external performance while the inner action is assigned to the realm of psychology. The close link between the metaphysical and the moral categories shows itself in a reductionist—more precisely, an essentialistic and objectivistic—manner. It is tacitly presupposed that the external performance of an action allows us to grasp its essence completely.

It is obvious that behind this lies an epistemology that understands every act of knowing as a passive assimilation to its specific object: the human intelligence is receptive and forms a faithful copy of its object by means of the imagination. This epistemological option has repercussions on the level of the theory of action: the collaboration between motivation and intention remains passive and receptive vis-à-vis the execution of the action. This option fails to see that an actively interpretative influence proceeds from the inner action, and that the phenomenon on its own does give offer sufficient information about its significance. If, however, we wish to speak of a moral evaluation, we must know what an action signifies.

This does not mean that the external action is meaningless, mere raw material in the hand of the inner action. It supplies essential indications that must not be overlooked. Nevertheless, the external action remains open to interpretations that derive from transcendental criteria. Above all, the distinction between effective and expressive actions draws attention to this point. In individual cases, therefore, one must ask: What type of action is this? What modes of human goods does the work of understanding and interpreting center on? Are the phenomena of action susceptible to the evaluation to which this understanding and interpreting lead? Clearly, there is no doubt about the justification of the "intrinsically." The questions concern the differentiated use of this category.

We must also look closely at the third position, where the interest is transposed to the problems concerning the relationship between the individual action and the historical circumstances. An ethical action is described as "intrinsically" bad when its morality is certain antecedently to all imaginable historical circumstances and independently of them. This theorem presupposes that this is in fact possible; obviously, this is in direct opposition to the threat posed by historicism and relativism. It is indeed understandable and justified since, ultimately, the human person must remain the lord of the history of his freedom. Nevertheless, questions about the underlying understanding of history persist.

History is tacitly reduced to the temporal sequence of events, in view of which absoluteness in the form of immutability must be safeguarded. This is done by means of the metaphysics of action since ethical action would disintegrate into insubstantiality if there were no unquestionably accepted point of reference on that level. However, we must ask whether such a way of thinking does full justice to the understanding of history as an anthropological category; one is inclined to suspect that it simply ignores important contributions by the history of philosophy in the modern period. If history is understood as the progressive grasping of the absolute, one can safely operate with an inner reservation vis-à-vis overhasty attempts at absolutization. It is of course true that a formal language covers up these problems, and the use of language is not always consistent.[48] A murder or a lie is forbidden under every imaginable circumstance, but such concepts still need to be interpreted. One can indeed define approximately what they mean, and this is sufficient for normal cases. It would be unrealistic to demand a higher degree of certainty, and this is in fact unnecessary. The other sciences too operate with reservations, and every normative statement contains an element of the hypothetical.

At this point, moral theology must ask whether and to what extent its understanding of metaphysics borrows without reflection obsolete ideas about the laws of nature. Is self-correction necessary? Can moral theology learn something from contemporary discussions in the philosophy of science? With regard to the theorem of intrinsically evil actions, at any rate, one must ask whether the concrete circumstances of an action can contribute perspectives that have not been sufficiently taken into account in the past, and whether further differentiation of valid positions is needed, if the claim made by reality is to be met. This does not lead to a relativization of the absolute: the only intention is to grasp this absolute in a more appropriate manner, and this is done via the interrelationship between individual decisions and historical circumstances.[49]

The Hard Task of Weighing Things Up

To discuss the theorem of "intrinsically" evil actions, as we have just done, means bringing into play a number of current presuppositions at which we shall now look briefly. For example, proportionalism attempts to prevent excessive demands from being made of metaphysical categories. The complexity of normative human nature continues on the level of the theory of action, and the strategic weighing up of goods and damages is inescapable, above all when one bears in mind that action takes place within boundaries that are determined both by creatureliness and by the history of human guilt.[50] What is possible here and now, and what demands can be made here and now—not least with a view to the long term? No one has ever denied that such an evaluation indicates the presence of antecedent categories, but these categories remain embedded in the inevitable hermeneutical circle between norm and situation, a circle that must be dissolved into a spiral again and again. This has nothing to do with a lapse of ethical thinking into the categories of pragmatism, and still less, of technicism. Such a suspicion can occur only to one who has misunderstood the necessity of the contribution made by hermeneutics; it may be prompted by the sort of reflection on ethical norms that is not aware of this necessity, or at least does not explicitly thematize this awareness. The moral theologian knows that all evaluations of goods remain tied to the fundamental good of a comprehensively successful good life; he does not in any way doubt the principle of *pars pro toto*. The rights that are linked to the individual goods also have their place in this process in which fundamentality, strength, and indispensability are the leading aspects.

At first sight, this could give the impression that these considerations will lead to a lesser degree of certainty than is provided by the thinking that we find in the manuals of moral theology. This impression is incorrect: all we are doing is attempting to integrate coherently into the theory of action intellectual elements (e.g., that of the lesser evil) that are present in our own tradition by establishing a more sophisticated metaphysical basis. It is therefore easy to dispel all the reservations that have been expressed with regard to the justifications of norms in teleological terms (since these always point to theories of action). Essentially, all we are doing is bringing the evaluation of goods into the dimension of time, with the principal aim of making an exact analysis of the object of the action, as this is embedded in time. It is obvious that the scientific ideals of analytical philosophy have provided inspiration here.

There is no action without consequences—to assume the opposite would be utopian. This means that it is only logical to speak of a responsibility for the consequences on condition that these are foreseeable, calculable, and capable of being influenced. This statement requires further clarification.[51] The following criticism has been voiced in the course of scholarly discussion: a universal teleology must end in an excessive, boundless intellectual demand since no one can envisage all the imaginable consequences and direct his conduct in accordance with them. All that he ever sees is segments of reality. This may be granted, but he must bear in mind that norms already contain in themselves an experiential potential that has grown in the course of history and that has consequences (even if this is not immediately obvious, thanks to the formulation of these norms in propositions). The acting person is aware of this. He adopts as a matter of course models of action in which this experience has found expression. Naturally, this does not have the status of a universal teleology. But the burden of evaluating the consequences is lightened or even lifted altogether.

More needs to be said, however. When teleological reflections attempt to lend greater precision to the idea of the object of action and resist any simplifying use of the axiom *actus specificatur ab objecto*, we must distinguish more exactly the various types of consequence. For example, there could be consequences that present no intellectual challenge to the previous understanding of the object of action since they too were presupposed when the action was performed. But things may turn out differently since there could be consequences that one had not envisaged. This forces critical reflection on whether one's earlier normative reflections suffice, or whether additional criteria are needed. In every instance, only consequences that one has understood and evaluated will be included in the normative discourse and will guide this.

Finally, we must add that the consequences always have the last word, either as a confirmation or as a question. This insight has important implications for the present discussion. Once the object of action has been appropriately recognized, it must be implemented in view of the consequences that have likewise been appropriately recognized, and one must not take account of any consequences that might relativize the object of action. The same applies to another distinction that is frequently mentioned by scholars, namely, the distinction between necessary and free consequences. Necessary consequences stem from the nature of the act, while free consequences have their origin in the freedom of another person. This distinction does not invalidate the ideas presented up to this point. At most, only the specific manner of evaluation is affected since the strategy of action may entail a change in the demands made of the underlying list of criteria. The conclusion that this suggests is that the conflict between deontology and teleology is due to differing forms of thought. In other words, it is a pseudo-conflict.

The Tension between the Goal and the Means

It is only logical to extend the same line of thought to the relationship between the goal and the means. It is a commonplace in moral theology that this is a relationship of appropriateness; that the immanent logic of the complex structure of the action must not be broken open; and that the end does not justify the means. All that interests us here is the exact definition of this relationship, which depends ultimately on the necessity of the goal.[52] In other words, the good that is the goal must be assessed with regard to its loftiness and its urgency. If the means will cause damage of some kind, we must ask where the stronger rights lie, on the level of the goal or on the level of the means.

An acceptable balance must be achieved between these two levels without excluding the dimension of the future. It is understood that basic ideas about a successful life influence the way in which this balance is understood. But one must also bear in mind strategies of action: the acting person looks at the same time for alternative possibilities of action that cause less damage, or perhaps even no damage at all. If such possibilities present themselves, one must grasp them. In short, the *finis operantis* not only ensures the formal morality of an action by projecting it in view of the goal. It also regulates, in the light of this goal, the steps that must be taken to attain it. Accordingly, an evident *ordinatio rationis* is at work, ensuring the correspondence between the *finis operantis* and the *finis operis* and thus the relationship between matter and form. It is the *ordinatio rationis* that generates the definitive morality of an action.

This proposition shows us how to deal correctly with the other auxiliary structures of moral theology, such as the principle concerning actions with a double effect and the distinction between direct and indirect action.[53] Once again, the ultimately decisive point of reference lies in the *finis operantis*, which serves as a hermeneutical key to dealing with the phenomenon of the performative action, which does not always present itself in a completely unambiguous way but must be accompanied by interpretation. On its own, the analysis of phenomena yields only approximate values, and one cannot expect too much of it; it is the interpretation that brings precision. This is completely obvious in the case of defining what is direct and what is indirect, and this has nothing to do with a devaluation of the phenomenon—all I wish to underline is that the epistemological realism must not be overdone. Instead, one should draw a distinction between a primary and a secondary criterion. The former is established through the evaluation of goods, together with the underlying hierarchy of goods while the latter derives from the "functionality" of the structures of action. These two criteria must be adjusted to each other, and this requires a further process of evaluation. The same problem was discussed earlier by analogy in the context of the principle concerning actions with a double effect. Here it concerns the third condition, namely, the equal causality of the consequences of the action. The phenomenon of the action presents itself here under the aspect of its immanent temporality. The temporal sequence of individual steps does not abolish the unifying bond of the intention. Once again, we see that a naïve epistemological realism is not capable of offering convincing solutions to cases of conflict.

The Dilemma of the Incommensurable Goods

The dilemma of the incommensurable goods may seem obvious, but it is only one step on the path toward an inherently consistent theory of action. All we have done is to expose reductionisms; the positive task is linked to the process of evaluation, to the way in which one deals with goods in the medium of time in a manner that is legitimated by preliminary decisions of an anthropological character. It is here that we encounter the term "incommensurable goods," which designates the key problem. It refers to goods that cannot be directly compared with one another. Evaluations come to a natural stop here, and to pursue them any further would court the risk of meaninglessness.

However, this is true only at first sight. In reality, there are subterranean passages linking the various levels of the human goods, and these links guarantee their unity in distinction. Incommensurable goods are always located on a lofty level of abstraction—for example, freedom, progress, friendship, or life. What these mean in concrete terms is determined by a continuous process of creating links.[54] It is indeed true that one cannot directly set off freedom and life, or friendship and progress against one another, and one is not entitled to sacrifice the one in order to gain the other. One is left with the hard work of interpretation, guided by the endeavor to maintain the distinctions and to ward off every risk that they may be leveled down. But even if the exact distinction between "direct" and "indirect" is questionable, it remains to be decided to what extent an indirect act of sacrifice may be demanded against the background of the idea of a comprehensively successful life, that is, a synthesis of ethical and anthropological truth that preserves the autonomy of each. What is true of every evaluation of goods is even truer in this case: it is the more fundamental goods that deserve the strategic preference since they perform an indispensable service of the higher goods. Similarly, the goods that are more certain deserve the strategic preference over those that are less certain. When a conflict arises between fundamentality and certainty, between an objective and a subjective category, the decision goes in favor of the latter, at least in the form of a methodological presupposition. However, when one must choose among various prospects of success, all other things being equal, the decision must go in favor of the greater success, which is understood as the assurance that the goods in question will be realized.

The life story too is a component that must not be forgotten here. The ideals and the preferential options that the individual brings into his ethical conduct determine the outcome of this evaluation. It is here that the final decision is taken about the goals that seem to him to be necessary and about what loss is acceptable. In the course of his life, each person acquires a measure of freedom to bear this burden, which he cannot unload onto the shoulders of anyone else. The concreteness of a life story is fulfilled in the concreteness of this decision, which requires an extremely fine discernment of spirits. In such crises, the extent to which the individual has grown into an ethical personality and the consistency with which he pursues his life project are revealed—unintentionally and, hence, with the character of a testimony. Ethical norms of conduct are indeed indispensable, but their grasp of the fullness and intensity of this reality is never more than approximate. Just as grasping is more than the concept and thinking more than the word, so too the person is more than the norm. The "surplus" of the person generates spontaneity in conduct that can no longer operate in terms of norm ethics but only in terms of virtue ethics.

At this point, it seems appropriate to return once more to temporality as an existential, and to link it to freedom. A person's freedom is displayed in the way in which he deals with his time. One who lives based on ideals that encompass a large span of time is so free that he need not make the fulfillment of his life dependent on attaining particular goals. He can confidently postpone the fulfillment of his expectations without despairing of the meaningfulness of his life since he is profoundly convinced that the success of his life is linked to the purity of his disposition. He is free from the compulsion to examine his success. The individual goals that he chooses, the things he desires to achieve, have their origin in that serenity of spirit that is bestowed only on the one who hopes. The justification of his own life is entrusted to the judgment of God. It is impossible to achieve a higher measure of truthfulness than this.

The Word as a Path to the Deed

The coercions of life in society continue to exist for the ethical personality too, but now they are subject to a new dynamic. The spoken word bears the most original witness to this. As people speak with one another, so they act with one another. One who savors the time of his life leads a life without distractions. He is wholly at home in himself and acquires the superiority that is necessary if his neighbor is to be treated as a person with full rights. Here, we can no longer speak of any "life-lie"—it is no wonder that his word is true. The infallible knowledge of his own frailty makes him shrink back spontaneously from the humiliation of another person that goes hand in hand with every lie. For the root of all inequality lies in the abuse of language. When distrust is sown, the germ of the dissolution of human ties is already in the ground. Fellowship can succeed only where there is a climate of spontaneous trust. This does not dispense one from the necessity of making differentiations against the background of all the presuppositions in the metaphysics of action that I have set out up to this point, for ultimately, the word is the full form of the deed. All the individual decisions participate in the word and are decided in advance by the word.[55]

First of all, then, we can say that the word is the most spontaneous self-interpretation of the speaker. All information about facts and circumstances is necessarily located within this relational framework. This does not in any way impair the necessary objectivity since ultimately it is always persons who speak to one another, not facts and circumstances. The overcoming of an uncritical realism on the level of the metaphysics of knowledge is complemented here by a variant in the theory of communication. What does this "self-interpretation" mean? First, we must bear in mind that the spoken word, as a deed, penetrates into the deep dimension of ethical action. The existential testimony of the speaker is concentrated in the word. The word reveals the dynamic of the fundamental decision and the decision about one's life, which are held together by the bond of the virtues—this gives the word its vitality. The information about facts and circumstances always contains a self-communication on the part of the speaker, either in a deliberate selection and shaping of the contents of what he says or in the highest possible impartiality. I said earlier that one must not only draw a distinction between effective actions and expressive actions since there is always also a blending between them; the same is true of speech, where the effect and the expression almost perfectly merge. It is therefore only logical to affirm that calculation is utterly out of place in speech. Speech is a privileged free space for spontaneity, and this must be protected.

This is connected to the personal intimate sphere that everyone needs—irrespective of all the specific variants due to a person's age or culture—if he is to lead a life of self-respect. It is not for nothing that speech is characterized by the dialectic between revealing and concealing. A bashfulness of the mind employs the word to protect itself; sometimes this is done by observing silence. The more pronounced this bashfulness is, the less distortion there will be in communication. Truth presupposes freedom as a condition of its possibility. Where freedom prevails, a whole spectrum of expression succeeds as it were automatically, and this reveals the riches, indeed the "surplus" of the speaker. No external coercion dictates what can and cannot be said; this is up to the free and liberating choice of the partners in communication, who enjoy the basic trust that sees even in silence a gesture of closeness. But a rigorous examination of conscience is necessary: Why do I speak, and why do I keep silent? All of a person's wrong attitudes to her neighbor can conceal themselves in inappropriate speaking and silence, but they find the decisive response in this examination of conscience.

It takes time to gain a foothold in truthfulness. Each person grows cautiously into the truth, and often crises prompt a growth spurt. The person who lives attentively will be conscious of the limitations on her ability to bear burdens. These limitations change only slowly. She must grow into further spaces of the spirit and thus acquire mastery over her life. At all times, she is tempted to run away, either into the inner dimension of thinking or into the external dimension of action, but mastery over her life makes her master of all the relevant circumstances in her life. The person who is moved and touched by the virtue of truthfulness attempts to create situations in which a maximum revelation of the truth is possible. He knows that he is responsible for the presuppositions of successful communication, and in keeping with a prudent preventative ethics, he clears away obstacles from the path, even if only by indicating which gestures are inclined to promote confidence. This gives him a sure instinct for the right moment—and the other person too has his own time to accept and to cope with the truth.

The virtue of truthfulness reveals itself as a virtue that accompanies others on the path. One must be willing to go a part of the way with one's dialogue partner, sharing the high points and the low points with him, if one wishes to learn this art. Sustainable relationships take time, and nothing so distorts human beings' dealings with each other as isolated contacts that are tied to particular moments. These bear in themselves the germ of untruthfulness precisely because they necessarily remain noncommittal. They lack the dimension of time and are shrunk down to one single point. They do not permit the emergence of a consciousness of mutual responsibility. But where time is spent together, people become so well acquainted with each other that even admissions of guilt (should these be needed) become possible. In moments of doubt in relationships, therefore, one's questions are guided not by a presumed right to the truth but by trust, the spontaneously bestowed good that provides the criterion for interpreting the words or the silence of the other person.

These questions will be more easily answered if one is willing to make it easier for the other person to bear the burden of the truth. If the truth is not to kill, it demands closeness devoid of calculation—and this can be bestowed only by the person whose life project gives him existential security. He gives his neighbor too security, thereby showing that every fellowship of communication is likewise a community in solidarity. What should be done in individual questions of legal, societal, or political life cannot be separated from this basic insight; one could easily multiply examples, but it suffices here to think of the admission of guilt, of the obligation to supply information in order to prevent losses, or of keeping silence because of loyalty. It is the interpretation of one's relationship to one's neighbor that ultimately decides what, and how much, one says or does not say; and this also tells one how much right to the truth the other person has. It is obvious that the concerns of society too have their place in this process. But the greater the anonymity of the structures, and the less one is confronted with the consequences of one's own speaking or silence, the fewer checks there will be on power interests, on manipulation, and on the open pleasure in making an outward impression. The result is that although people claim to be communicating, they are in fact divided.

The Coercions Involved in Cooperation in Evil

Action in common has its origin in speaking with one another. Once the culture of dialogue has been acquired, it applies to every situation where people cooperate and is the best guarantee that even if coercions and entanglements are not overcome, they will at any rate be mitigated. It is important to state this because the task of evaluation is particularly hard in such situations thanks to the grey areas that are shaped, in an act of free judgment, by one's completely personal style and by the measure of self-respect that one has attained.[56] Ultimately, it is not a question only of assessing the good and the damage, nor only of the most precise description possible of what one regards as the lesser evil: there are also subjective factors that are mostly incalculable and have their origin in freedom's power to escape from existing coercions or to offer a better alternative to these coercions. This is always linked to the courage to take a stand and to suffer disadvantages. This puts one's truthfulness to the test, and this is why the rank of an ethical personality makes itself known above all in such situations that require an "oath of disclosure." Accordingly, the all-important question is whether one exerts oneself to the full, or whether double standards are revealed by an acceptance of existing or putative coercions. The person who is entangled in situational coercions knows perfectly well that every solution—even if he reflects on it with all the honesty that is required—leaves behind a consciousness of a stigma, indeed of embarrassment and humiliation. He experiences himself as a victim, and the more distinctive his personality, the more painful will this be. He has allowed the reins to be taken out of his hands, he has fallen into line—and this leaves an open wound, no matter how convincing the reasons he presented for doing so. But the self-love that he ought to have demands that he have the courage to put up resistance early on and nip these tendencies in the bud so that he is not crushed by the growing weight of the cooperation with evil. It is important to look ahead prudently so that he is armed in advance for moments of high stress and is not caught unawares by the force of circumstances. Only then can he submit to the evaluation of goods and losses, see the validity of rights that may have been infringed, reflect on long-term effects, and perhaps assess the offense that he has given.

Other factors that are involved concern the customary distinction between necessary and contingent cooperation. It is certainly relevant whether the cooperation in the occurrence of culpable individual actions or structures is necessary, or whether these events would have occurred anyway. This affects reflections on the strategy of action. A person's responsibility grows in keeping with his possibilities of influencing events, and more exacting demands are made of the reasons he puts forward to justify his actions. Similarly, the degree of entanglement in such a situation is an important factor. The closer the association, the more is he compromised—and this in turn has repercussions on the criteria of legitimation, not least because he understands that it lies in his interest to escape such assaults on his freedom as soon as possible. Naturally, it is not only a question of reducing his participation as much as possible since that too could end in hypocrisy. This impression is particularly unpleasant when people indulge in hair-splitting reflections on the distinctions between direct and indirect action or between doing something and merely allowing something to happen. Here it should be recalled that the structures of an action never offer more than a secondary criterion and that this is fully functional only in union with the primary criterion, that is, the intentionality that governs the action. In situations of cooperation, the intentionality of the principal acting person is the matter at issue: is he incurring guilt or merely acting in error? The more fundamental the contrast between the participants, the more difficult it is to justify a cooperation, no matter how well intentioned it may be, and no matter how minimal the damage that is done. All this must be borne in mind in the evaluation. And this explains the principle that one should first prevent damage before one does good. The validity of this principle as a fundamental framework of orientation is undisputed although it cannot dispense one from drawing a comparison between the damage that is avoided and the goods that one thereby fails to realize. The varied situations of entanglement in public and in private life—here I have in mind above all the spheres of politics and commerce—must pass through the critical filter of these reflections.

Notes

1. Furger, *Gewissen und Klugheit*; and Furger, *Einführung in die Moraltheologie*, 66–71.
2. Jüngel, *Tod*, 148–54.
3. Kutz, "Gedanken zur Tugend der Wahrhaftigkeit"; and Hörmann, *Wahrheit und Lüge*.
4. Wolbert, *Der Mensch als Mittel und Zweck*.
5. Thomas Aquinas, *Quaestiones Disputatae De Veritate* I.9.
6. Hilpert, ed., *Selbstverwirklichung*.
7. Ginters, *Die Ausdruckshandlung*.
8. Müller, *Die Wahrhaftigkeitspflicht*; and Deneke, *Wahrhaftigkeit, eine evangelische Kasuistik*.
9. Schavan and Welte, eds., *Person und Verantwortung*.
10. Ziermann, *Die menschlichen Leidenschaften*.
11. Hofmann, "Vorurteil."
12. The manuals of moral theology discuss this subject under the heading of the mental reservation and the right to the truth.
13. Augustine's classic definitions of lying must be put in a transcendental-philosophical and hermeneutical context. Augustine, *Contra mendacium* 12.6 (PL 40, 537); *Enarrationes in Ps.* 7 (PL 36, 85); and *Enchiridion* 22.7 (PL 40, 243).
14. Self-justification signals the convergence of the theological and the anthropological dimensions.
15. The present section presents a brief typology of untruthfulness without any claim to completeness.
16. Elsässer, "Kommunikation," 158.
17. Demmer, "Mitwirkung."
18. Furger, "Wahrhaftigkeit."

19. Behind an intellectual malfunctioning of this kind lies an unrealistic view of the human person.

20. Here it suffices to recall the dramatic story of the freedom of religion. Chappin, "Die Kirche und die Werte"; and Utz, "Die Religionsfreiheit."

21. Overcoming the remnants of a scientific ideal that takes geometrism as its criterion is as yet an unfinished task.

22. See Demmer, *Die Lebensentscheidung*, 248–58.

23. Häring, *Ausweglos?*

24. The tiresome subject of dispensations needs to be thought through afresh, starting from first principles. For some relevant indications, see Demmer, "Die Dispens von der Lebenswahl."

25. Despite all the monographs about poverty, and the slogans about the preferential option for the poorest of the poor as the very embodiment of what the religious life means, in reality this theme tends to be taboo.

26. Demmer, "Kann der Zölibat heute gelebt warden?"; and Demmer, *Zumutung aus dem Ewigen*.

27. See K. Golser, "Das Gewissen als verborgenste."

28. Thomas Aquinas, *Summa theologica*, I q. 79 a. 11 ad 2.

29. Ebeling, "Theologische Erwägungen."

30. Honnefelder, "Praktische Vernunft und Gewissen."

31. Werner, "Das Gewissen im Spiegel."

32. Kleber, *Glück als Lebensziel*; and Biser, "Weg zum geglückten Leben."

33. Reiners, *Grundintention und sittliches Tun*; and Fuchs, "Personale Grundfreiheit und Moral."

34. For a critique of this thinking, see Höver, *Sittlich handeln im Medium der Zeit*, 9–49.

35. Rahner, *Geist in Welt*. This thesis needs to be translated into the terms of the theory of action.

36. Coreth, *Vom Sinn der Freiheit*, 46–50.

37. The reflection on the foundations of moral theology lacks a confrontation on a deeper level with modern theories about truth against the background of the Scholastic tradition; see, however, Kissling, "Die Theorie des kommunikativen."

38. Pesch, "Die Theologie der Tugenden."

39. Demmer, *Deuten und handeln*, 224f.

40. Coreth, *Vom Sinn der Freiheit*, 7.

41. The distinction between the *finis operantis* ("the goal of the one who acts") and the *finis operis* ("the goal of the action") goes back to Scholz, *Wege, Umwege und Auswege der Moraltheologie*, 67 and passim.

42. Kramer, *Unwiderrufliche Entscheidungen*; and Hartmann, "Person und Treue."

43. Thome, "Lebens- und Glaubenskrisen."

44. Stanke, *Die Lehre von den "Quellen der Sittlichkeit,"* 30–36.

45. On this, see Hörmann, "Die Prägung des sittlichen." One must not overlook the fact that key concepts undergo a change in meaning, with differentiations in keeping with changes in the history of ideas.

46. As is done by Rhönheimer, *Natur als Grundlage der Moral*, 18, 86f.

47. Fuchs, "'Intrinsice malum'"; and Demmer, "Erwägungen zum 'intrinsice malum.'"

48. A formal language operates with concepts that bear a value or a disvalue. It needs to be interpreted before it can be applied to phenomena of action.

49. This accusation is found, inter alia, in Pinckaers, *Ce qu'on ne peut jamais faire,* 85f.

50. The concept of the evaluation of goods is associated with Schüller, "Zum Pluralismus in der Ethik." For English-language literature, see Hoose, *Proportionalism.* See also Hürth, "Güterabwägungstheorie."

51. Spaemann, "Über die Unmöglichkeit."

52. Schüller, "Die Quellen der Moralität."

53. Kol, *Theologia Moralis,* 662, notes that on its own, the analysis of the phenomena of an action does not always give sufficiently unambiguous information. In that case, it is enough to have recourse to the intention of the acting person.

54. Demmer, "Erwägungen zum 'intrinsice malum.'"

55. Furger, *Ethik der Lebensbereiche,* 146f.

56. Demmer, "Der Anspruch der Toleranz."

CONCLUSION

THE PATH THAT WE HAVE SKETCHED is long and winding, and the reader may be left with the question whether it lacks concrete vividness. This reaction is understandable since decisions must be concrete: they do not permit one to escape into generalities. And everyone needs visual aids that show him how he should act in confusing situations. He automatically compares the suggested solutions with his own experiences, and no one is so autonomous that he could be content to do without suggestions of this kind.

Nevertheless, such a reaction has its limitations, thanks to the uniqueness of every situation of decision. No one is spared the burden of decision. There is never more than an approximation to reality in all the casuistry that is offered to a person, and if he looked for nothing more than this, his action would inevitably be distorted. This is why we had to look at the deep dimension of the ethical personality and elaborate a metaphysics of action in personalistic categories. Ethical action is born of underlying attitudes that are built up and that increasingly take shape in the course of a life story. This, therefore, is where our thinking must begin if action is to succeed; the casuistry that offers an immediate guidance for action is then of less significance. And no matter what help is offered for correct action, he must never forget that what is at stake is the comprehensive success of his own life story. The decisive perspective is the process whereby he becomes an ethical personality, and it is on this level that preliminary decisions are taken.

In today's intellectual climate, a person may be tempted to flee into the past and to appeal to classical models of a theory of action. In this way, she makes herself invulnerable, and she has the opportunity to display her scholarship. But this does not help! It is of course true that she must always include the contribution of her own tradition since this contains a treasure of earlier experience that cannot simply be discarded; but the history of ideas continues and brings new challenges that are rooted in a great variety of philosophical approaches. To fail to meet these challenges would be to ignore the requirement of the hour. This is why we sought to develop basic elements of a metaphysics of action that are suited to place the tradition of the discipline of moral theology on a more differentiated basis, without breaking the link to this discipline. It was necessary to reflect on epistemology since one can observe precisely at this point a malfunctioning in the reflections on the bases of moral theology, and this inevitably affects the underlying theory of truth. The understanding of ethical truth had to be made more precise. In addition to the conceptual distinction between goodness and rightness, which is indispensable for the norm-ethical discourse, it was necessary to define the real relationship between these two, which is a problem of the theory of action. We were thus thinking in terms of mediation, and the task was to establish a balance between the inner and the outer action, between the attitude and the deed.

Our interest in the theory of truth led us directly to study the virtue of truthfulness. A person is an ethical personality to the extent that he faces the challenge of truthfulness. By activating clear options with which he completely identifies, he checks the abiding tendency to lie and to flee. He attempts to become a completely rounded human being, no matter how arduous this may appear, but he never forgets that this is a lifelong task that demands every ounce of his strength. The price of turning back from this task would be a "life-lie." At this point, we could have taken up the traditional moral-theological teaching about lies, but this did not seem very promising since it is not a suitable instrument for bringing hitherto unknown material to light. It seemed, therefore, more fruitful to tackle the teaching about ethical actions directly and to develop this further since it is here that the basis is laid for dealing both sensitively and flexibly with this painful topic of life in society. In this way, since norm-ethical perspectives always remain embedded in borders that are laid down by virtue ethics, it was easy to counteract the suspicion that the path taken in this book amounted to a clandestine laxism. Our declared goal has been to make a higher truthfulness possible and to make the reader more sensitive to this. In order for this to succeed, we had to show that a free and spontaneous emotional commitment lies at the root of ethical imperatives: the empowerment precedes the task, even if this sometimes demands that a person employ all his strength, and he spontaneously shrinks back. And this is why truthfulness cannot do without courage. Both are bestowed on the person who knows that his life is kept safe in the kindly hand of God.

BIBLIOGRAPHY

Anzenbacher, A. *Was ist Ethik? Eine fundamentalethische Skizze*, Düsseldorf, 1987.

Apel, K. O. *Diskurs und Verantwortung. Das Problem des Übergangs zur postkonventionellen Moral.* Frankfurt a.M., 1988.

Arens, E. "Zur Struktur theologischer Wahrheit. Überlegungen aus wahrheitstheoretischer, biblischer und fundamentaltheologischer Sicht," *Zeitschrift für katholische Theologie* 112 (1990): 1–17.

Bender, W. *Ethische Urteilsbildung.* Stuttgart, 1988.

Biser, E. "Weg zum geglückten Leben. Ein kleines Kapitel zum Verhältnis von Glaube und Lebensglück," in *Glück und geglücktes Leben. Philosophische und theologische Untersuchungen zur Bestimmung des Lebensziels,* ed. P. Engelhardt, 184–200. Mainz, 1985.

Bucher, A. J. *Ethik—eine Hinführung.* Bonn, 1988.

Bujo, B. *Die Begründung des Sittlichen. Zur Frage des Eudaimonismus bei Thomas von Aquin.* Paderborn, Munich, Vienna, and Zurich, 1984.

Cassirer, E. *Freiheit und Form. Studien zur deutschen Geistesgeschichte,* 3rd ed. Darmstadt, 1961.

———. *Philosophie der symbolischen Formen,* 4th ed. Darmstadt, 1960.

Chappin, M. "Die Kirche und die Werte der Französischen Revolution," *Internationale katholische Zeitschrift Communio* 18 (1989): 477–90.

Coreth, E. *Vom Sinn der Freiheit.* Innsbruck, 1985.

Dell'Oro, Roberto. *Shaping the Moral Life: An Approach to Moral Theology.* Washington, D.C., 2000.

Demmer, K. "Der Anspruch der Toleranz. Zum Thema 'Mitwirkung' in der pluralistischen Gesellschaft," *Gregorianum* 63 (1982): 701–20.

———. *Deuten und handeln. Grundlagen und Grundfragen der Fundamentalmoral.* Freiburg i.Br., 1985.

———. "Die Dispens von der Lebenswahl. Rechtstheologische und moraltheologische Erwägungen," *Gregorianum* 61 (1980): 207–51.

———. *Die Lebensentscheidung. Ihre moraltheologischen Grundlagen.* Munich, Paderborn, and Vienna, 1974.

———. "Erwägungen zum 'intrinsice malum,'" *Gregorianum* 68 (1987): 627–31.

———. "Kann der Zölibat heute gelebt werden?" *Herder Korrespondenz* 44 (1990): 473–78.

———. "Mitwirkung," in *Neues Lexikon der christlichen Moral*, ed. H. Rotter and G. Virt, 507–11. Innsbruck, 1990.

———. *Moraltheologische Methodenlehre.* Freiburg i.Ue., 1989.

———. "Natur und Person," in *Natur im ethischen Argument*, ed. B. Fraling, 55–86. Freiburg i.Ue., 1990.

———. *Sittlich handeln aus Verstehen. Strukturen hermeneutisch orientierter Fundamentalmoral.* Düsseldorf, 1979.

———. *Zumutung aus dem Ewigen. Gedanken zum priesterlichen Zölibat.* Freiburg i.Br., 1991.

Deneke, A. *Wahrhaftigkeit, eine evangelische Kasuistik.* Göttingen, 1972.

Dunkel, A. *Christlicher Glaube und historische Vernunft. Eine interdisziplinäre Untersuchung über die Notwendigkeit eines theologischen Geschichtsverständnisses.* Göttingen, 1989.

Ebeling, G. "Theologische Erwägungen über das Gewissen," in *Wort und Glaube*, 3rd ed., 429–46. Tübingen, 1960.

Elsässer, A. "Kommunikation," in *Wörterbuch christlicher Ethik*, 3rd ed., ed. B. Stoeckla. Freiburg i.Br., 1983.

Engelhardt, P., ed. *Glück und geglücktes Leben. Philosophische und theologische Untersuchungen zur Bestimmung des Lebensziels.* Mainz, 1985.

Feil, E. "Autonomie und Heteronomie nach Kant," *Freiburger Zeitschrift für Philosophie und Theologie* 29 (1982): 389–441.

Fuchs, J. "'Intrinsice malum.' Überlegungen zu einem umstrittenen Begriff," in *Für eine menschliche Moral*, vol. 1, *Grundfragen der theologischen Ethik*, 313–31. Freiburg i.Ue., 1988. (Eng. trans. "An Ongoing Discussion in Christian Ethics: 'Intrinsically Evil Acts,'" in *Christian Ethics in a Secular Arena*, 71–90. Washington, D.C., and Dublin, 1984.)

———. "Personale Grundfreiheit und Moral," in *Für eine menschliche Moral*, vol. 1, *Grundfragen der theologischen Ethik*, 35–51. Freiburg i.Ue., 1988.

Furger, F. *Einführung in die Moraltheologie.* Darmstadt, 1985.

———. *Ethik der Lebensbereiche. Entscheidungshilfen.* Freiburg i.Br., 1988.

———. *Gewissen und Klugheit.* Lucerne and Stuttgart, 1965.

———. "Wahrhaftigkeit," in *Neues Lexikon der christlichen Moral*, ed. H. Rotter and G. Virt, 846–52. Innsbruck, 1990.

———. *Was Ethik bedeutet. Deontologie oder Teleologie—Hintergrund und Tragweite einer moraltheologischen Auseinandersetzung.* Einsiedeln, 1984.

Genilo, Eric Marcelo. *John Cuthbert Ford, SJ: Moral Theologian at the End of the Manualist Era.* Washington, D.C., 2007.

Gillen, E., *Wie Christen ethisch handeln und denken. Zur Debatte um die Autonomie der Sittlichkeit im Kontext katholischer Theologie.* Würzburg, 1989.

Ginters, R. *Die Ausdruckshandlung.* Düsseldorf, 1976.

Golser, K. "Das Gewissen als verborgenste Mitte im Menschen," in *Grundlagen und Probleme der heutigen Moraltheologie*, ed. W. Ernst, 113–37. Würzburg, 1989.

Graham, Mark. *Josef Fuchs on Natural Law.* Washington, D.C., 2002.

Habermas, J. *Theorien des kommunikativen Handelns*. Frankfurt a.M., 1981. (Eng. trans. *The Theory of Communicative Action*. Boston, 1985.)

Häring, B. *Ausweglos?* Freiburg i.Br., 1989.

Hartmann, N. "Person und Treue," *Wissenschaft und Weisheit* 50 (1987): 55–72.

Hedwig, K. "Die philosophischen Voraussetzungen der Postmoderne," *International katholische Zeitschrift Communio* 19 (1990): 307–18.

Hilpert, K., ed. *Selbstverwirklichung. Chancen—Grenzen—Wege*. Mainz, 1987.

Hofmann, R. "Vorurteil," in *Wörterbuch christlicher Ethik*, 3rd ed., ed. B. Stoeckle, 259f. Freiburg i.Br., 1983.

Höhn, H. J. "Vernunft—Kommunikation—Diskurs. Zu Anspruch und Grenze der Transzendentalpragmatik als Basistheorie der Philosophie," *Freiburger Zeitschrift für Philosophie und Theologie* 36 (1989): 93–128.

Honnefelder, L. "Praktische Vernunft und Gewissen," in *Handbuch der christlichen Ethik*, vol. 3, ed. A. Hertz, W. Korff, and T. Rendtorff von Herder, 22–25. Freiburg i.Br. and Gütersloh, 1982.

Hoose, B. *Proportionalism. The American Debate and Its European Roots*. Washington, D.C., 1987.

Hörmann, K. "Die Prägung des sittlichen Wollens durch das Objekt nach Thomas von Aquin," in *Moral zwischen Anspruch und Verantwortung*, ed. F. Böckle and F. Groner, 233–51. Düsseldorf, 1964.

———. *Wahrheit und Lüge*. Vienna, 1953.

Höver, G. *Sittlich handeln im Medium der Zeit. Ansätze zur handlungstheoretischen Neuorientierung der Moraltheologie*. Würzburg, 1988.

Hünermann, P., and Schaeffler, R., eds. *Theorie der Sprachhandlungen und heutige Ekklesiologie*. Freiburg i.Br., 1987.

Hürth, F. "Güterabwägungstheorie," *Stimmen der Zeit* 116 (1929): 128–40.

Jüngel, E., *Tod*, Stuttgart and Berlin 3rd ed., 1973 (Eng. trans. *Death: The Riddle and the Mystery*. Edinburgh, 1975).

Keenan, James F., and Thomas Kopfensteiner, "Moral Theology out of Western Europe," *Theological Studies* 59 (1998): 107–35.

Kissling, C. "Die Theorie des kommunikativen Handelns in Diskussion," *Freiburger Zeitschrift für Theologie und Philosophie* 37 (1990): 233–52.

Kleber, H. *Glück als Lebensziel*. Münster, 1988.

Kol, A. van. *Theologia Moralis*, vol. 1. Barcelona, 1968.

Kramer, H. *Unwiderrufliche Entscheidungen im Leben des Christen*. Munich, Paderborn, and Vienna, 1974.

Kutz, S. "Gedanken zur Tugend der Wahrhaftigkeit," *Concilium* 3 (1967): 388–91.

Lotz, J. B. *Transzendentale Erfahrung*. Freiburg i.Br., 1978.

———. "Zur Thomas-Rezeption der Maréchal-Schule," *Theologie und Philosophie* 49 (1974): 375–94.

Mieth, D. *Die neuen Tugenden*. Düsseldorf, 1984.

———. *Moraltheologie und Erfahrung*. Freiburg i.Ue, 1977.

Müller, G. *Die Wahrhaftigkeitspflicht und die Problematik der Lüge*. Freiburg i.Br., 1962.

Müller, G. L. "Was ist kirchlicher Gehorsam? Zur Ausübung von Autorität in der Kirche," *Catholica* 44 (1990): 26–48.

Muschalek, G. *Gott als Gott erfahren. Glaube und Theologie im säkularen Denken.* Frankfurt a.M., 1974.

Pesch, O. H. "Die Theologie der Tugenden und die theologischen Tugenden," *Concilium* 23 (1987): 233–45.

Pinckaers, S. T. *Ce qu'on ne peut jamais faire.* Fribourg and Paris, 1986.

Puntel, L. B. *Wahrheitstheorien in der neueren Philosophie. Eine kritisch-systematische Darstellung.* Darmstadt, 1978.

Rahner, K. *Geist in Welt,* 2nd ed. Munich, 1957. (Eng. trans. *Spirit in the World.* London, 1994.)

Reiners, H. *Grundintention und sittliches Tun.* Freiburg i.Br., 1960.

Rhönheimer, M. *Natur als Grundlage der Moral. Eine Auseinandersetzung mit autonomer und teleologischer Ethik.* Innsbruck, 1987.

Riesenhuber, K. *Die Transzendenz der Freiheit zum Guten. Der Wille in der Anthropologie und Metaphysik des Thomas von Aquin* (Pullacher Philosophische Studien). Munich, 1971.

Römelt, J. "Glaubende Kirche und Ethik," *Theologie der Gegenwart* 31 (1988): 144–54.

———. *Personales Gottesverständnis in heutiger Moraltheologie vor dem Hintergrund der Theologien von Karl Rahner und Hans Urs von Balthasar.* Innsbruck, 1988.

Sala, J. B. "Immanuel Kants Kritik der praktischen Vernunft," *Stimmen der Zeit* 113 (1988): 841–54.

Schaeffler, R. *Die Welchselbeziehungen zwischen Philosophie und katholischer Theologie.* Darmstadt, 1980.

———. "Wahrheitssuche und Reinigung des Herzens. Zur Frage nach dem Zusammenhang von Erkenntnisfortschritt und Moralität," *Internationale katholische Zeitschrift Communio* 17 (1988): 412–22.

———. "Zur Anthropologie und Ethik der Hoffnung," *Münchener Theologische Zeitschrift* 33 (1982): 1–24.

Schavan, A., and B. Welte, eds. *Person und Verantwortung. Zu Bedeutung und Begründung von Personalität.* Düsseldorf, 1980.

Schnackenburg, R. *Die sittliche Botschaft des Neuen Testaments,* v. 1, *Von Jesus zur Urkirche.* Freiburg, 1986.

Schockenhoff, E. *Bonum hominis. Die anthropologischen und theologischen Grundlagen der Tugendethik des Thomas von Aquin.* Mainz, 1987.

———. *Das umstrittene Gewissen. Eine theologische Grundlegung,* Mainz 1990.

Scholz, F. *Wege, Umwege und Auswege der Moraltheologie. Ein Plädoyer für begründete Ausnahmen.* Munich, 1976.

Schüller, B. *Die Begründung sittlicher Urteile,* 3rd ed. Düsseldorf, 1988.

———. "Die Quellen der Moralität. Zur systematischen Ortung eines alten Lehrstücks der Moraltheologie," *Theologie und Philosophie* 59 (1984): 535–59.

———. *Wholly Human: Essay on the Theory and Language of Morality.* Washington, D.C., 1986.

————. "Zum Pluralismus in der Ethik," in *Pluralismus in der Ethik. Zum Stil wissenschaftlicher Kontroversen*, 27–44. Münster, 1988.

Schulte, R. "Wie ist Gottes Wirken in Welt und Geschichte theologisch zu verstehen?" in *Vorsehung und Handeln Gottes*, ed. T. Schneider and L. Ullrich, 116–67. Freiburg i.Br., 1988.

Schuster, J. *Ethos und kirchliches Lehramt. Zur Kompetenz des Lehramtes in Fragen der natürlichen Sittlichkeit*. Frankfurt a.M., 1984.

Schwemmer, O. "Die Bildung der Vernunft aus der Erfahrung. Zur Grundlegung einer philosophischen Anthropologie," *Zeitschrift für evangelische Ethik* 26 (1982): 40–61.

Simon, J. *Wahrheit als Freiheit. Zur Entwicklung der Wahrheitsfrage in der neueren Philosophie*. Berlin, 1978.

Spaemann, R. "Über die Unmöglichkeit einer universalteologischen Ethik," *Philosophisches Jahrbuch* 88 (1981): 70–89.

Stanke, G. *Die Lehre von den "Quellen der Sittlichkeit." Darstellung und Diskussion der neuscholastischen Aussagen und neuerer Ansätze*. Regensburg, 1984.

Thome, A. "Lebens- und Glaubenskrisen als Chancen personalen Reifens," *Trierer Theologische Zeitschrift* 81 (1972): 84–101.

Thönissen, W. *Das Geschenk der Freiheit. Untersuchungen zum Verhältnis von Dogmatik und Ethik*. Mainz, 1988.

Türk, H. G. "Gottesglaube und autonome Vernunft. Fundamentaltheologische Überlegungen zur Diskussion um die autonome Moral," *Theologie und Philosophie* 58 (1983): 395.

Utz, A. F. "Die Religionsfreiheit aus katholischer Sicht," *Internationale katholische Zeitschrift Communio* 19 (1990): 155–75.

Virt, G. *Epikie—verantwortlicher Umgang mit Normen. Eine historisch-systematische Untersuchung*. Mainz, 1983.

Weber, H. ed. *Der ethische Kompromiss*. Freiburg i.Ue., 1984.

Werner, H. J. "Das Gewissen im Spiegel der philosophischen Literatur von 1945–1976," *Philosophisches Jahrbuch* 90 (1983): 168–84.

Wolbert, W. *Der Mensch als Mittel und Zweck*. Münster, 1987.

————. "Naturalismus in der Ethik. Zum Vorwurf des 'naturalistischen Fehlschlusses,'" *Theologie und Glaube* 79 (1989): 243–67.

————. "Wozu eine Tugendethik?" *Theologie und Glaube* 77 (1987): 249–54.

Wolkinger, A. *Moraltheologie und Josephinische Aufklärung. Anton Luby (1749–1802) und sein Verhältnis zum Naturrecht, zur mathematischen Methode und zum ethischen Rigorismus (Jansenismus)*. Graz, 1985.

Ziermann, B. *Die menschlichen Leidenschaften* (Kommentar zur deutschen Thomas-Ausgabe 10). Graz, Vienna, and Cologne, 1955.

INDEX

action, theory of. *See* theory of action
actus primus, 119, 122
actus secundi, 122
actus specificatur ab objecto, 139
analogatum princeps and *analogata secundaria*, 134
analogy of the truth, 41–42
Anzenbacher, A., 24n4
Apel, K., 83n24
Aquinas. *See* Thomas Aquinas
Arens, E., 25n12
Aristotle, 46
ars vivendi, 37
Augustine of Hippo, viii, ix, 25n8, 128, 146n13
autonomy, 28, 94

being and knowing, tension between, 54–57
Bender, W., 82n21
biography. *See* life stories
Birth Control Commission (Pontifical Commission on Population, Family, and Birth), vii
Biser, E., 147n32
body, theology of, 26–27
Bucher, A., 83n24
Bujo, B., 82n9

Cassirer, E., 24n1
celibacy, 115–18, 131, 132–33
Chappin, M., 147n20

Christian humanism, 57–60
Christian revelation
    action theory and, 69–73
    conscience shaped by faith, 29
    dependence of ethical norms on, 3–4
    explicit faith ethic, weaknesses of, 59–60
    God's action and human action, 3–4, 17–24
    intellectual demands of, 22–24
    mercy and truth, relationship between, 111
    natural law and law of Christ, 23–24, 56–57, 111
    nature of God, thinking about, 11–12
    negative theology and, 17
    providence and the Jesus event, 20–22
    reason and faith, relationship between, 12–13, 14, 30, 57, 70, 73
    spiritual happiness, courage to seize, 31
    truth of faith and, 42
Church. *See also* magisterium
    moral theology, ecclesial dimensions of, 79–82
    solidarity in, 114–15
    states of life in, 115–18
    truthfulness of, 109–12
communication and ethical personality, 92–98
community of consensus, 45–46, 47
conflict
    ability to engage in, 35–36

157